Es Cuba

LIFE AND LOVE

on an

ILLEGAL ISLAND

Lea Aschkenas

SEAL PRESS

Es Cuba
Life and Love on an Illegal Island

Published by
Seal Press
A member of the Perseus Books Group
1700 4th Street
Berkeley, CA 94710

ISBN-10: 1-58005-179-0
ISBN-13: 978-1-58005-179-8

9 8 7 6 5 4 3

        Library of Congress Cataloging-in-Publication Data
Aschkenas, Lea.
Es Cuba : life and love on an illegal island / by Lea Aschkenas.
p. cm.
ISBN-13: 978-1-58005-179-8 (pbk.)
ISBN-10: 1-58005-179-0 (pbk.)
1. Cuba--Description and travel. 2. Aschkenas, Lea. I. Title.
F1765.3.A83 2006
917.291--dc22
2005023858

Cover design by Gia Giasullo
Interior design by Amber Pirker
Printed in the United States of America by Worzalla
Distributed by Publishers Group West

Con mucho amor, para
Alfredo Sánchez, Sherry Gooltz,
Bernie Aschkenas, and Ruth Gooltz.

contents

Prologue   VII

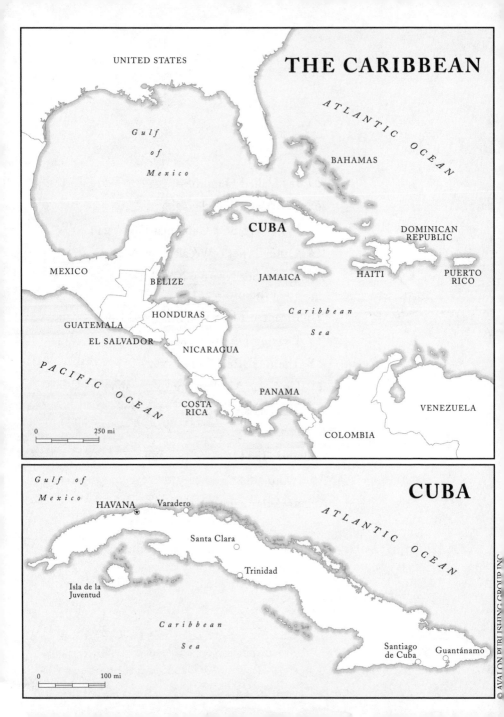

I went to Cuba because a volcano erupted in Ecuador.

I had recently left a reporting job with a newspaper in the United States, and I wanted to take some time off to travel. A friend had just returned from Ecuador with rave reports about a small town in the south. I arranged to study Spanish at a language school there, and I set up a home stay with a local family.

This was in November of 1999, and soon after I made my plans, two volcanoes in Ecuador began spewing lava and molten ash, causing the closure of the Quito airport and the evacuation of several towns located near the volcanoes.

Several countries and a few islands away from Ecuador, something else significant happened that November—something that caught my attention and gave me a new idea for my travels.

I didn't exactly go to Cuba because of Elián González, the little boy who was found off the coast of Miami like a modern-day pilgrim on Thanksgiving Day. But what this whole overblown crisis did for me, as it did for many Americans, was to bring Cuba to the forefront of my national consciousness. It reminded me that, just ninety miles from the southern tip of Florida, there was a country that was both politically and philosophically a world away from the United States. It was an island more foreign than any place I'd been before; an island that was the only communist country in the Western Hemisphere and one of the few remaining in the world at large; an island whose president, following the 1999 death of Jordan's King Hussein, had become the longest-ruling leader alive.

Yet, in truth, that's about all I knew of Cuba in November of 1999. I was born in 1973, the year that Fulgencio Batista, who represented prerevolutionary Cuba in all its capitalist glory, died in exile in Spain with the three hundred million dollars he had embezzled from his native land. I was born thirteen years after the U.S. travel and trade embargo on Cuba, a dozen years after the Bay of Pigs Invasion, and more than a decade after the Cuban Missile Crisis.

In 1980, when more than one hundred thousand Cubans immigrated to the U.S. via the Mariel Boatlift, I was too young to be interested in world events. In 1996, when the Helms-Burton Bill was passed, further tightening the strings on trade with and aid to Cuba, I was working at a newsmagazine in Central America, immersed in the political trauma of that region. The Elián González crisis was the first major Cuban news event I'd heard about in my twenty-six years of life. Until then, Cuba had been for me a sparse collection of unrelated images. Cuba was five words—"Castro" and "Bay of Pigs Invasion" —in the 1980s Billy Joel song "We Didn't Start the Fire." Cuba was a sweet, syrupy drink, a mixture of rum and Coke called a "Cuba libre." Cuba was a group of older black men with top hats and suits who played saxophones and sang love songs. Cuba was a forbidden land, although I didn't know exactly why.

Unfortunately, I wasn't alone in my ignorance. When I went to an international travel clinic for a gamma globulin vaccination before my first trip, one of the lab technicians asked me, "Cuba, that's in South America, right?"

One friend requested a photo of Fidel and me. "Or if you can't manage that," he said, laughing, "at least get a photo of you by one of his statues."

But unlike Stalinist Russia, Cuba has no monuments of its leader. Where, I would later wonder, had my friend gotten the idea that it did? Certainly not from any actual photos, since even the most intrepid of photographers would be hard-pressed to find a statue of Fidel or a building or town named after him in Cuba.

This general lack of knowledge about Cuba extends even to the venerable *New Yorker* magazine, where the January 26, 1998, cover of a special issue on the island featured a self-satisfied Fidel smoking a fat cigar. Sitting on a white sand beach beneath a gently swaying palm and surrounded by the immensity of the Caribbean, Fidel and his backdrop seemed to comprise the quintessential Cuba. Except that, as all Cubans know, Fidel quit smoking in the early 1980s, commemorating the event by creating a national nonsmoking day.

The U.S. people and media are misinformed about Cuba because of the embargo, which is not only a blockade of food and medicine but also essentially a stranglehold on the transmission of information.

While I hope to break this imposed silence with my story, it is not my intention to present an exhaustive book on the island's politics. Yet it would be a lie to say that this is not a political book. As an American, it is impossible to talk about Cuba, let alone to make the choice to travel there, with all the red tape and implied illegalities, and say that it is not political.

My book is the story of a changing Cuba, caught between communism and capitalism. It is the story of a romance with a country and with one of its *compañeros*. Ultimately, it is a story about the personal legacy of politics, the staying power of history.

In Spanish, *revolución* is a feminine word; people refer to it as a "she." Among the Revolution's many promises was a better life for *cubanas*. As a woman in Cuba, I was privy to the guarded stories of other women. Many opened up to me about what they saw as the successes and failures of the Revolution, and I could trace the history in the life trajectories of the three generations of Cuban women I shared a house with in Havana. There was the grandmother, who had lived more than half her life before the Revolution; the mother, who had entered adolescence with the Revolution; and the granddaughter, age twenty-four, who had come of age during the dissolution of the Soviet bloc, when Cuba's economy nearly collapsed.

And then, of course, there is my own story of being a woman in Cuba, an American woman involved with a Cuban man, who is now my husband. I met him my first week in Havana, and I traveled with him throughout the island. I saw Cuba through my eyes and through his. As travelers, we were in a sense both foreigners. In his twenty-six years, Alfredo had never left Havana, and the difficulties we encountered traveling as an American–Cuban couple underscore both the disadvantages of the country's tourism industry and the strange, almost surrealistic situation of current-day Cuba.

My book takes place over the course of ten months, during two extended stays on the island. From February to November of 2000, my life revolved around Cuba. During my first trip, with no access to the Internet and only the most rudimentary of mail systems that often took up to three months to deliver a letter to the U.S., I soon lost touch with most of my friends back home. Because I kept prolonging my departure date, I missed my five-year college reunion, and one friend who attended later told me that she had started a joke regarding my whereabouts.

"When people asked about you," she said, "I told them, 'When the U.S. returns Elián, Fidel will return Lea.'"

Both times I returned to the U.S., I felt as if part of me was still in Cuba. I was always talking about it, clipping out articles on it, or writing about it. I was helping friends and strangers with their travel plans to go there, giving them letters and gifts for my Cuban friends, or making plans for my own return once I could earn enough money for a plane ticket back. In the U.S., people often asked why I didn't just get a job in Cuba, but finding work as a foreigner in a socialist country with an average monthly salary of twelve dollars is not exactly easy.

Like the island of Cuba itself, I lived in a floating world those ten months, dividing my life between two countries that appeared to so enjoy antagonizing each other that it often seemed each one existed solely as a paradigm for what the other was not.

Both times I returned to the U.S., people asked me about salsa clubs and Santería, cigars, old American cars, and Elián González. They solicited my opinions on poverty, the pending death of Fidel, and the music of the Buena Vista Social Club.

And, both times, they asked why I had gone to Cuba in the first place. Some people weren't satisfied with my Ecuador volcano story. But life truly is random, and besides, I believe that the more interesting questions are why I stayed on so long my first trip, and why I returned. This is the story I tell in these pages.

Part 1

1

Es Cuba

The first new word I learned in Cuba was *sobornar,* to bribe.

It was a Sunday evening in February, at the start of my second week on the island, and I was waiting to enter the Coppelia ice cream park, Havana's hot-spot hangout populated by teenagers and grandmothers alike. Regardless of the weather or the time of day, the line wrapped around two city blocks and then snaked back in on itself, winding around the corner of L and 23rd Streets.

I stood on 23rd, smushed between a stoplight and a giant billboard of Elián González. With a bewildered expression on his face, the coveted little boy peered out from behind a mesh wire fence with the words, DEVUELVAN NUESTRO NIÑO, Return Our Child, branded in red beneath him. The air was heavy with humidity and the slow burn of patience being pushed to its utmost limit.

I had come here with my friend Alfredo more than an hour ago, and now he was off making the rounds of Coppelia, searching for a way to bypass the wait. Fifteen minutes after he left me to ponder the predicament of Elián, Alfredo returned to the line, a furtive glimmer in his eyes.

"Do you have a dollar?" he asked in a soft voice, almost a whisper. *"Fula,"* he added to clarify. *Fula,* which in street slang means "stupid," also means "U.S. money."

In Cuba, I had quickly become fluent in three types of currency. There were Cuban pesos and U.S. dollars and something else called convertible pesos, which were essentially dollar equivalents. Supposedly, you could use convertible pesos in both dollar and peso stores. But for bribery, the dollar was the currency of choice.

Alfredo grabbed my hand, and we rushed past the crowds of Cubans fanning themselves with the thin paper cones that the *maniseros,* or peanut vendors, used to package their goods. We stopped when we reached a police officer guarding the front of the line. He was decked out in the traditional beret and hyphen-short mustache, and when Alfredo nodded at me, I handed over my dollar. The officer moved aside for a moment, allowing us to pass into the esteemed two-story ice cream parlor with its sweet odor of coconut and chocolate, of rich, cold cream.

I could tell it was a bittersweet triumph for Alfredo. For a few more dollars, we could have each gotten our ice cream instantly at Coppelia's dollar kiosk, where the foreigners and fortunate Cuban *fula*-holders lined up, ordered, and ate their ice cream in a matter of minutes, the envy of everyone else.

Even though I'd only been in Cuba for a week, this scene already had a sort of déjà vu quality. It reminded me of the time I was riding through Havana in a tourist bus, and at a red light, we pulled up next to a *camello,* one of Cuba's humongous humpbacked buses, where people pushed up against each other and sweat like waterfalls. As the tour guide on my bus spoke into his microphone, pointing out this hospital and that elementary school, I saw the smudged faces of the Cubans staring out of the dirty *camello* windows into the spacious luxury of my bus.

I had never planned to travel Cuba in a tour bus. I'd come here on a monthlong language program with Global Exchange, a San Francisco–based social justice organization. The participants I'd spoken to from previous trips told me about riding *camellos* and living with Cuban families. But when the director met my program in Havana's José Martí International Airport, named after the nineteenth-century poet who died fighting for his country's freedom from Spain, we learned that Global Exchange was now working directly with Cuba's tourist agency. We were promptly whisked off in a tour bus to an exclusive hotel in a wealthy neighborhood on the outskirts of the city.

I met Alfredo my third night in Cuba. I was still reeling from the culture shock of my lavish accommodations and of Cuba itself—its crumbling buildings and vibrant street life, its lingering sense of hope. It was a rare cool Havana evening, and Alfredo was wearing a too-big white sweatshirt and gray pants, frayed at his ankles where he had attempted to alter them. His hair hung in tidy, Tracy Chapman–style spiral dreadlocks. He was kicking something around on the sidewalk and looked up nervously, startling me with his unassuming and almost self-conscious beauty and his doelike eyes, as I approached with my friend Heather and Alfredo's friend Gerardo.

Heather was part of my program, and she had met Gerardo at a salsa club our first night. This evening she had invited me to go out with them, but when Gerardo met us outside Hotel El Bosque, where we were staying, he told us he'd brought a friend.

"He's waiting at the bus stop," Gerardo said. I remember thinking at the time that it seemed strange, but soon I would realize that it made perfect sense from Alfredo's perspective. He was proud to be Cuban and angry with what had been termed Cuba's "tourist apartheid," whereby Cubans were restricted from tourist hotels and foreigners often had more rights than Cubans. If he couldn't fully participate in the social life of his country, he would not stand on the outskirts and watch. Alfredo just wouldn't take part.

That night, as Alfredo and I and Heather and Gerardo were walking down the cobblestone streets in the touristy neighborhood of Old Havana, Habana Vieja, we were stopped by a police officer, who requested Alfredo and Gerardo's ID cards.

The officer, a *mulato* with the uniform navy beret, walked over to the street corner with the cards and started making calls on his walkie-talkie. The night was silent except for the faint notes of a salsa band that we had passed in Plaza de Armas.

Before the police officer arrived, we had bought a bottle of Guayabita del Pinar rum and were planning to sit on the Malecón, Havana's seafront wall, to drink and talk. Alfredo had opened the bottle and spilled a few drops on a street corner.

"That's to appease Eleggua, a god of the Afro-Cuban religion," Gerardo told us.

Now, while we waited for the policeman to complete his conversation, I watched a drop of the sticky rum slide down Alfredo's right thumb, and I admired his long black fingers, so thin and almost delicate.

When the police officer returned, he handed Alfredo and Gerardo their ID cards and turned to face Heather and me.

"I just want to let you know that most of our young men are up to no good," he said. "They use foreign women for their bodies and their money. They're *jineteros.*"

Jinetero, or hustler, was a word I heard nearly daily in Cuba, but it didn't exist before the legalization of the U.S. dollar in 1993. I expected Alfredo or Gerardo to say something in response to the policeman's accusation, but they stood motionless, staring at the ground. Heather rolled her eyes at me.

"It's just a power play," Alfredo told me afterward as we sat along the Malecón. "They don't usually do anything to you."

We sat looking down at the Caribbean, where the waves swirled in little tide pools around the coral and discarded Cristal beer cans. While Heather and Gerardo drew shapes in the air, trying to communicate with each other without a language in common, Alfredo told me about his job as a light and sound technician with Cuba's National Symphony Orchestra. He invited me to a concert the coming Sunday.

At the theater, Alfredo proudly showed me his name on the front page of the program. After the concert, he gave me a tour of the building, with its two theaters and top-story bar overlooking the city. Outside of Hotel El Bosque, this was the first place I'd been to in Havana that had air-conditioning. While Fidel had not wasted any energy maintaining the houses of Havana, he went all out to preserve the country's art and cultural centers. Alfredo told me that a month ago Fidel had visited the symphony and had given everyone a raise.

"So now I make the peso equivalent of $15 a month," Alfredo said. "That's the only good thing Fidel's done in a while."

Prior to my visit to Cuba, I had heard that Cubans rarely referred to Fidel by name, except if they were praising him. Yet despite stories about hand gestures representing Fidel's trademark beard, strangers openly approached me on the street to complain about their leader or Cuba's current economic crisis. Before I could pursue this any further with Alfredo, he changed the topic.

"Are you hungry?" he asked. "I can take you somewhere that's an important place in Havana." Smiling, he added, "It's my treat. It's in Cuban money."

Once we got inside Coppelia, where waitresses rushed about in red plaid miniskirts, Alfredo was able to pay in pesos. There were a few free tables, but Alfredo sat down next to a father and son who were so immersed in their ice cream that they barely noticed our presence. They leaned over their stainless-steel saucers, hungrily gulping up spoonfuls of their *ensaladas*, which consisted of several heaping balls of ice cream piled one on top of the other.

When the waitress came over, I asked for a mix of chocolate and coconut, but she turned to Alfredo, shaking her head and speaking so quickly I couldn't understand. Then Alfredo started arguing with the waitress—that much I could make out—and he was losing. After several minutes of this heated yet cryptic back-and-forth, the waitress put her hands on her hips and stood her ground, refusing to discuss the issue any further.

Alfredo turned to me and, speaking slower, said, "She says you can't mix the flavors. It has to be all coconut or all chocolate."

"Okay," I said. "I can just have chocolate, but why is it like that?"

"Es Cuba," he told me, shrugging his shoulders. That's Cuba.

I laughed, and after a moment, the irritation on Alfredo's face faded, along with the wrinkles in his scrunched forehead.

"Such a fight just to get some ice cream, and in the end it's the same difference anyway," he said after the waitress left. "I told her I'd have whatever flavor you didn't get, so we can just share."

We waited anxiously for our ice cream, biding our hunger. Or maybe I just projected my hunger onto Alfredo. It seemed to me that Cubans didn't eat a lot. I passed through my first week in Cuba in a constant, almost airy state of mind-numbing hunger, not quite filled by the tomato and cucumber salads offered at the hotel with breakfast, lunch, and dinner. But the Cubans I met seemed to eat just as little or less and not really mind. They had coffee and a piece of toast with guava paste for breakfast, got a free Spam sandwich for lunch at work if they were lucky, and then for dinner had their first full meal of the day—salad, rice and beans, and chicken or pork. As a vegetarian, my meals were all the more basic, and tonight I hadn't eaten at all. I doubted Alfredo had either, since he'd met me at four o'clock to walk from my hotel to his theater, Teatro Amadeo Roldán. I met him outside the hotel, and as I saw him walking toward me, I noticed what looked like a tiny white package in his hands. *Oh no,* I thought, *not another present.*

We had gone out earlier in the week and, because I had told him I was a writer, Alfredo brought me a book. Its title, *La Pesadilla de la Realidad,* The Nightmare of Reality, was scribbled across the black cover in neon-yellow, drippy, horrific letters reminiscent of those from a supermarket science-fiction book.

"I haven't read it," Alfredo said shyly. "But I saw it in the store, and I thought you might enjoy it."

"Thank you," I said, trying my best to feign excitement. "It looks great."

Before going to bed, when I took a closer look at the book, I was pleasantly surprised to discover that it was actually a collection of essays on the writing life. But as sweet and innocent as it was, the gift somehow unsettled me. I didn't want gifts. I wasn't looking for romance in Cuba. Even just a week into my stay, the economic inequality between Cubans and foreigners was making me uncomfortable.

After college I lived in Central America, so I was familiar with poverty. But that sort of overt poverty, as well as the variety I saw daily back home on the streets of San Francisco, was different. I somehow felt separated from it. Often the poor I'd seen outside of Cuba were uneducated. Their clothes were too big or too small, ripped or stained. Their hair was often knotted or unwashed. Many of them were homeless, holding up signs describing their varying levels of destitution.

Unlike the poor I'd encountered outside of Cuba, Alfredo had a professional job. He'd studied Italian and Portuguese. His clothes were clean and neatly pressed. Intellectually we communicated on the same level, yet Alfredo's existence challenged all my assumptions about poverty and the way the world functioned.

Although I knew his $15-a-month salary was more than most Cubans earned, I'd been in Cuba long enough to know that it didn't buy much in the new, post-U.S.S.R. economy. When I looked at the book he'd bought me, I could just make out the smeared peso price written in pencil inside the front cover and, with a few quick calculations, realized it was nearly a full day's salary.

I knew I couldn't measure this situation by capitalist standards, because most people in Cuba owned their own homes, and everyone had free health care and education. So a day's salary did not need to be divided in as many ways as it did in the U.S.

I had friends back home in that twenty-something, struggling-artist phase who, like Alfredo, also lived paycheck to paycheck. Maybe they were worse off, because most of them went without health insurance. But Alfredo was not going through a phase. He was settled in a way that none of these friends were, yet he still couldn't afford the $1 bribe to get into Coppelia. Did this make him poor in my eyes? In his? Was poverty poverty if you couldn't see it on the surface? Did poverty exist if everyone around you was in the same situation? But was everyone really equally poor if the dollar kiosk at Coppelia had quite a few Cubans lined up?

Before I came to Cuba, I had read somewhere that surrealism was the final stage of socialism, and I was seeing the truth in this aphorism daily. Something was going on in Cuba that I didn't yet have the words to explain, something not unlike the quiet, sudden flash of lightning that signals a thunderstorm.

On the evening of our Coppelia visit, I was relieved to discover that the white package I'd imagined to be another present from Alfredo was actually just a *pañuelo*. People carried *pañuelos* around to wipe the sweat off their faces and to wipe the food off their mouths in restaurants that had no napkins and that served drinks in plastic cups replete with hot-pink lipstick and bite marks.

As he got closer, Alfredo waved at me with the *pañuelo* still in his hand.

It unfolded and flapped in the heavy air, its white cutting through the clear blue sky like the peace flag of a ship coming ashore in an unknown land.

When I waved back and started walking toward him, Alfredo lowered his hand and, in one smooth horizontal motion, wiped the *pañuelo* across his forehead to sop up his sweat.

Cuba was hotter than any place I'd ever been—stickier and more humid than its Caribbean neighbor, Costa Rica. The sweat started up the minute I stepped out of the shower in the morning, and it didn't stop until I stepped back into the shower in the evening, at which point there was enough of it to mix with the soap and create suds on its own.

But inside Coppelia, it was refreshingly cool. Alfredo and I placed our bowls side by side so we could combine the coconut and chocolate. Unfortunately, after all the struggle it had taken to get inside Coppelia, it became obvious that its ice cream had seen better days. It was melty on the surface, but then I'd crunch down on a chip of ice. Still, I shoveled spoonfuls into my mouth, hoping to appease the rumblings of my nearly empty stomach, silently berating myself for not having stopped at the *chopping,* dollar store, to pick up some snacks earlier. But then what would I have bought? Tomato paste? Oval-shaped saltines without the salt? Mayonnaise? The pickings were slim—if there were any at all. The previous week I had noticed that the *chopping* near Hotel El Bosque was running low on its floor-to-ceiling supply of sunflower oil, a staple in Cuban cooking. The next day all the oil was gone—and the next, and the next. There just weren't reserves in Cuba. Things came when they came and disappeared just as frequently. Even produce, despite Cuba's fertile terrain, could not be counted on to make it to the market with any sort of regularity.

During the Pope's visit in 1998, a joke circulated around Cuba, a play on the word *papa,* which means both "pope" and "potato." "What do Cuba and the Vatican have in common?" the joke went. "They've both only had four *papas* in forty years."

But beyond shortages was the old peso–dollar predicament. Although it may not have been the tastiest or most varied of meals, we could have found something for dinner if we had paid in dollars. Alfredo, though, didn't have dollars.

That first night I met him, Heather and I had paid for everything, not because (as the police officer suggested) Alfredo or Gerardo ever asked us to do so. We paid because, that early on in our trip, we knew only the tourist trail, which was paved in dollars. We didn't know that instead of taking a fancy, air-conditioned, state-run taxi, you could simply stick out your thumb and *coger una botella*. For about ten percent of the price of a state taxi, you could just hitch a ride in one of the many beat up but still functioning cherry-red '59 Chevys that chugged down Havana's narrow side streets.

As I would later learn, Alfredo and Gerardo chose to sit quietly that first night, sucking up their pride and looking the other way as we paid for the *fula* taxi rides. After seeing our ritzy hotel and the plush tour buses parked out front, they had mistakenly, albeit understandably, assumed that this was the type of travelers we were. They worried that we might be uncomfortable in the messy and rumpled reality that was their Cuba.

After Coppelia, Alfredo insisted on accompanying me on the hour-long trek back to Hotel El Bosque. We walked through the tree-lined streets of Vedado, a neighborhood of old mansions, which were somehow still elegant despite their crumbling exteriors. After my third near-fall along the dark, bumpy streets, Alfredo offered his hand, and I accepted. His skin was dry but still soft, smooth like a worn stone.

The nighttime street life in Havana was more active than in most Latin American cities I'd been to. Old Cuban men crowded around rickety card tables, playing dominoes well into the early morning hours, and little girls danced salsa beneath balconies with boom boxes. But when Alfredo and I cut through a park near UNEAC, the National Union of Cuban Writers and Artists, the action abruptly stopped.

With a gazebo, a bed of grass, and some tall palms, the park near UNEAC was the prettiest I'd seen in Havana. Generally, the parks here consisted of a city block–sized slab of cement, some skeletal benches with more than a few slats missing, and a statue of José Martí or another fallen revolutionary. But pretty or not, all the parks seemed devoid of people after sunset.

Since my first night in Cuba, I had been baffled by this phenomenon in a country that otherwise appeared awake twenty-four hours a day. Tonight, though, I realized the reason behind this seeming emptiness. As dim as the streets of Havana were, at least there was the glow of house lights and the occasional streetlight to give people some sense of location. But in the parks, there were no lights, and it was pitch black.

As Alfredo and I approached the gazebo, I heard a rustling, and I jumped. Although I was physically in Cuba, I still sometimes reverted to U.S. thinking, where a noise in an unlit city park could only be interpreted as impending danger—a mugging, or something worse. But here in Havana, my startled reaction was followed by Alfredo's laughter. As my eyes adjusted to the darkness, I saw why. Slowly, the outline of not one but several couples in various stages of passionate entanglement came into focus.

"This doesn't happen in your country?" Alfredo asked, still laughing as we continued on.

"Well, maybe," I said. "But . . . not like that. Not in the park."

"We Cubans, we are like . . ." Alfredo paused, searching for the words to translate his culture. "We are like . . ." he repeated and, in this precise moment, two small, mating dogs stepped out from the dark, jerking around on the sidewalk in front of us.

"Like that?" I asked.

"Well, maybe," he said. "But . . . not like that. Not in the street." Now we both laughed.

We walked up a few blocks to 23rd Street, the main thoroughfare of Havana, which eventually, on its northeastern end, dead-ends into the sea. Tonight we were heading in the opposite direction. We passed the famous street corner of 23rd and 12th, where everything, including a cinema and a cafeteria, is named for its location. This is where, after the Bay of Pigs Invasion, Fidel stood and declared Cuba a socialist country, announcing its allegiance with the U.S.S.R. Today the spot is memorialized with a plaque proclaiming WHAT THE IMPERIALISTS CAN'T FORGIVE IS THAT WE HAD A SOCIALIST REVOLUTION IN FRONT OF THEIR VERY NOSES.

"I wish I had my camera," I told Alfredo.

"It's just propaganda," he said. "You could use up all your film just photographing the political signs of Cuba. It doesn't mean anything. It's just shit." He said the word "shit" in English.

"You don't believe in the Revolution?" I asked him as we crossed the street and walked along the yellow wall of the enormous Cementario Cristóbal Colón, where revolutionary heroes were buried alongside poets and firefighters in elaborate marble tombs. On a tour of the cemetery earlier in the week, a guide had told me that there was no more room for people to be buried here. Now those who had relatives in the Cementario Cristóbal Colón were called back two years after having buried their loved ones. The coffin would be opened so the family could retrieve the bones, making room for new bodies.

"It's difficult to believe in the Revolution when you've come of age during the Special Period," Alfredo said, referring to the euphemistically named years following the collapse of the Soviet bloc, when Cuba's economy took a nose-dive and the tropical island began experimenting with tourism to recover.

"This is what I know," Alfredo said. "I've grown up with shortages and the inequalities of tourism. Can you tell me why I can't enter a hotel and why tourists have more rights in my country than I do?"

I shook my head, understanding, but still taken aback by his question.

"I don't like to talk about politics, because it makes me sad and angry," he said. "And I don't want to be that way around you."

"Okay," I said. "We don't have to talk about politics now."

"There is so much more to life," he said. "I would like to know more about your writing. What is it like to be a writer in your country? How do you know when you're ready to tell a story? How do you start?"

In Cuba, people who studied writing or art or music, regardless of their postuniversity success, received a regular salary from the government along with their diploma. Whether or not Alfredo believed in the Revolution, his questions reminded me of one of its successes—its educated people and their fascination with learning. In Cuba, unlike in Guatemala or Spain or so many other countries I'd been to, no one asked me if I knew Michael Jackson or Madonna. People asked me about universities and medical care in the U.S. And my writing. Everyone seemed to have a high opinion of writers. "¡Qué lindo!" How beautiful! they would say.

I told Alfredo about my writing process and how, although I'd been too overwhelmed to get anything down on paper yet, I did want to write some articles about Cuba.

"You need to write it while it happens," he said, "because otherwise you won't remember. I can tell writing is important to you and you've come here with certain goals, so if I'm bothering you at all, you can just tell me, 'Listen, I need to write today,' or 'I need to spend time alone,' and I'll understand."

I was happy to hear this, because Alfredo had called me nearly every night since we first met and, as much as I did like him, I was feeling crowded.

"Are your parents writers too?" Alfredo asked.

"No, but they've always encouraged me."

"My grandmother's the one who's encouraged me the most," Alfredo said. "I live with her, and my sister lives with my mother. My parents are divorced, and my father lives near the airport with his new wife and daughter. Of all of them, I think that I love my grandmother the most. She was just more caring with me than my mother or father. And she's older and wiser."

A tall black man who had been walking toward us while we were talking smiled as he approached. When he was almost directly in front of us, he raised his hand and swung it forward to high-five Alfredo.

"*Socio,*" he said. "*¿Qué bola?*" Probably unrecognizable in any other Spanish-speaking country, in Cuban street slang this roughly translated to, "Friend, what's going on?"

"*Americano,*" Alfredo exclaimed in response. *Americano?* This guy he was talking to sounded like a certified Cuban to me. Or maybe Alfredo was trying to introduce me, although his friend just smiled, nodded his head, and continued on his way.

"What did you say to him?" I asked Alfredo.

"*Americano,*" Alfredo repeated and then, laughing, added, "I think you know that word."

"But why did you use it with him?"

"Oh, it's just something we say to people we like, to our friends."

Now I was really confused. American money was called *fula,* or stupid, but people who were respected were called *americanos.*

"Hmm," Alfredo said when I pointed this out. "I never thought about it like that."

"So does that mean people here like Americans?" I asked.

"We know the difference between your government and your people," Alfredo said, reiterating a phrase I'd heard many times since my arrival in Cuba. "I complain about Cuba," he continued, "but that doesn't mean I want the U.S. to intervene. If they did, I would fight to protect Cuba."

We were now coming up to the Almendares Bridge, which crossed the river of the same name and would drop us off in front of Hotel El Bosque. This was the beginning of Miramar, a wealthy Havana neighborhood where many diplomats lived and whose entrance was marked by a rooftop billboard of, as Alfredo might call it, "shit." The famous, solemn face of Che Guevara in his red-starred beret stared out at us next to the words Your Example Lives. Your Ideas Endure.

An almost full moon cast a spotlight on the cyclists chugging past us on their clunky Chinese bikes. There was not a car on the bridge, and the river swished slowly, softly beneath us.

"Do you have a bike?" I asked Alfredo.

"No," he said. "I did, but we were short on money so my mother had to sell it." He was silent for a moment and then, changing the subject, asked, "So what is your dream as a writer?"

"I'd like to be able to earn a living as a freelancer," I said. "What are your dreams?"

"I want to teach music," Alfredo said. "I'm taking drumming classes now. I want to always live in the world of culture. And I have one more dream."

"What?" I asked. We were now standing outside Hotel El Bosque and I'd noticed that Alfredo kept glancing up at the sky. "What are you looking at?"

"I'm looking at my lucky star." he said, "I have a dream that maybe it will give me permission to kiss you."

Uhhh. . . . Latino cheesiness at its best. I laughed.

"What do you think?" Alfredo asked.

I thought about how I didn't want to get romantically involved. And then I looked at the almost childlike earnestness in Alfredo's dark eyes, his smooth skin, just a shade lighter than the mysterious night sky. I looked at the smile that lingered hesitantly at the edge of his lips, not yet sure whether to unfurl. I leaned forward.

"You don't have to ask the stars," I said.

2

⁓⁓⁓⁓⁓

Only the Moment

Amaury, a fair-skinned, green-eyed bellboy who worked the night shift, was waiting for me when I walked into Hotel El Bosque.

"Lea," he called out, "I have some important news for you."

But then, as I approached, Amaury put his hand up as if to stop me, rolling his eyes in the direction of one of the overhead lights.

"The camera," he whispered.

"What?" I asked and then threw in my most commonly used Spanish phrase, *"No entiendo."*

Instead of explaining, Amaury took a step backward and continued to do so each time I stepped forward, as if he were dancing a slow-motion salsa. We stopped only once we arrived in a shaded area of the lobby, with Amaury backed up against the wall.

"I couldn't tell you my news over there," he said, "because there's a hidden camera in that light."

"How do you know?" I asked, wondering why no one else was retreating to dark corners to converse.

"When you're Cuban, you know these things," Amaury said cryptically. "But it's okay now. We're out of range."

I glanced up at the offending light, but it seemed the same to me as all the others. I looked skeptically at Amaury, but he didn't seem to notice. He was a man on a mission, and he'd arrived at his destination.

"I heard you were looking for a bike," he said, lowering his voice so that the word "bike" came out like a whisper, a bad word disguised in hushed tones, the name of a disease. A criminal act. In fact, if Amaury was suggesting what I suspected—renting me a bike from the black market—then it was indeed an illicit act.

After a week of being toted back and forth in a tour bus to Spanish classes at the José Martí Language Institute, I had started searching for a bike so I could get around on my own. Cuba had no bike rental shops, but still I made an attempt to go through the official channels. When my program went on an afternoon cycling tour coordinated by the University of Havana Bike Club, I asked our guide if I could rent one of the twenty-plus bikes that they had brought for us.

"This is the last day we have them," she said. "Tomorrow they go to the province of Pinar del Río for a three-week trip." The bikes would not be back in Havana until March 2—the day before my program ended, the day before my flight back to the States.

Next I asked Alvaro, our Cuban tour guide. Although I saw him every day for a month, I never really knew Alvaro. Unlike the inquisitive Cubans I met everywhere else, Alvaro never asked anyone in my program anything—not why we chose Cuba, not what we thought of his country, not how long we planned to stay or whether we might travel. Alvaro was, quite literally, just our tour guide, a nicely dressed man who picked us up at our hotel every morning and, during the drive to school, highlighted the successes of Cuba's Revolution. With the same monotone voice, as if reading down a list, he detailed the history of every building we passed on every ride we took through the city.

Only once, when we passed by Coppelia—with its endless peso line for

Cubans and its short, speedy, dollar line for tourists—did Alvaro stray from his official script, letting slip an understandably snide aside.

"Cubans will wait hours for their ice cream," he said, then added with a pained smile, "but the dollar line is quick because we know you don't have the time."

I chalked up Alvaro's lack of charisma to his precarious position as a tour guide for a group of Americans. Historically, in pre-Revolution times, the planeloads of wealthy Americans who flocked to Cuba came for several of the same self-serving reasons—climate, casinos, cigars, and cheap prostitutes.

But after the Revolution or, specifically, after the U.S. blockaded Cuba, the character of the island's U.S. tourists changed completely: The few Americans who came to Cuba came with a common leftist political conscience and a shared disdain for the behavior of their predecessors.

The people in my Global Exchange program—tourists who preferred to be called by any other name—were not the type to sign up for formal tours like those Alvaro led. And I think that, in leading us around his country, Alvaro was as out of his element as we were.

Unlike solidarity sojourners from other countries who flew to and traveled through Cuba on their own, U.S. travelers were denied this luxury by their government. The U.S. Treasury Department only granted visas to those with specific professional affiliations, such as journalists, doctors, musicians, or artists. Anyone else who wanted to visit Cuba legally had to do so on an established package tour whose every detail could be scrutinized and manipulated by both the U.S. and Cuban governments.

One morning on the way to school, as Alvaro was telling us about the character of Havana's various neighborhoods, I asked which one Fidel called home.

"Where does Fidel *live?*" Alvaro repeated incredulously, as though I had just asked what size underwear the president wore. "That's confidential," he said. "No one knows where Fidel lives. And it's necessary that it stay this way for security purposes."

During the Revolution, Fidel didn't have a home. His young son and wife lived in a house in the Vedado neighborhood, but Fidel moved between any number of abodes offered to him by friends, relatives, and fellow revo-lutionaries. In one such home on 25th Street, Fidel would enter and exit through a back window to keep a low profile from Batista and his cohorts.

I wondered what it must have been like to live such a clandestine ex-istence. And I wondered if Fidel could ever have imagined that even forty years after he came to power in 1959, he would still be on the run—this time from a foreign government that made no secret of its desire to see him dead.

I had not spoken with Alvaro since our conversation about Fidel's where-abouts. And when, several days later, I told him about my discussion with the bike guide and asked how else I might rent a bicycle, he looked at me with a similar expression of disbelief.

"Well, that's it. The bike club is authorized to rent bikes," he said, shrug-ging his shoulders in defeat, slightly lifting his arms while he did so, his palms facing upward, open and empty. "There is no other way," he repeated.

But I knew there was more to the story. From hearing how Alfredo earned dollars by scalping tickets for sold-out symphony shows and from my own re-cent Coppelia *sobornar,* I had learned that in Cuba there was always another way. And so, apparently, had Amaury. Through the grapevine, Amaury had learned that I was looking for a bicycle, and he'd lost no time in procuring one.

"I have a bike that you can rent for a week," he said, leaning forward so that his back was no longer against the wall, although his face remained in shadow. "Only three dollars a day."

"Is it your bike?" I asked. "How do I get it?"

"It's a friend's bike," Amaury said. "It's here now, outside, if you want to see it."

I nodded, and Amaury motioned for me to follow him as he emerged from the dark. I walked behind him and past the reception desk, where one of his coworkers smiled knowingly at me. We stepped outside into the warm night and crossed the street to the hotel's parking lot. Virgilio, an older man who guarded the cars, waved to us as we came close.

"La bicicleta," Amaury said to Virgilio and, turning to me with a proud smile, added, "He's guarding your bike."

Virgilio unlocked a fence at the back of the parking lot and then disappeared behind a corner. He surfaced again a few minutes later, wheeling out my prize—a beat-up, maroon, single-gear Flying Pigeon, one of the many fifty-pound clunkers donated by China in the early 1960s. The upholstery stuffing in the back seat sprouted out through several long, diagonal cracks like weeds in a city sidewalk.

"Test it out," Amaury said. "Give it a spin around the block."

The bell didn't work, and the brakes worked just infrequently enough to trick me into believing maybe I just hadn't squeezed them hard enough the previous time. A dangerous assumption, which nearly caused me to collide with Amaury as I finished up my test drive and skidded down the steep slope, which led to the hotel.

"Probably it's best to walk it down the hills," Amaury suggested, patting the handlebars like an overprotective parent. "It's not a new bike, but it should get you wherever you need to go."

I didn't disagree with Amaury. I'd seen the bikes people shuffled around on in Havana, and my Flying Pigeon, although it rode more like a grounded refrigerator on wheels, was nothing to scoff at.

From the seat of my Flying Pigeon, I saw a different Havana than the one I'd experienced my first week. Without Alvaro's narration, the city opened up to me on its own. No one shouted out statistics about infant mortality rates or recited the history of the UJC, the Union of Communist Youth. I chugged along past newsstands, elementary schools, and peeling, nearly empty but still open pharmacies. I stopped whenever I wanted, to buy a guava or mandarin orange at the farmers' market or to detour down less-trafficked side streets. I was happy, free, sweaty, and anonymous—or as anonymous as you can be in such a communal city as Havana.

Biking in Havana, I soon discovered, was a social event where two, three, and sometimes even four people piled onto a single bike. One morning on my three-mile ride to school, I passed a family of four—a mother and daughter squeezed onto a rear seat extension and a baby in the father's lap up front. Soon I got to know the bikers along my route, not necessarily by name, but by face, and we'd wave to each other as we passed.

If, that was, we passed each other at all. These were not fast bikes, and soon I gave in to the lethargy of my Flying Pigeon, completely losing track of time in the surreal 1950s land of twenty-first-century Havana.

In the afternoons, as panels of experts on everything from architecture to agriculture paraded through Hotel El Bosque to talk to my program, I searched for clues as to why Cuba, despite its gains in health care and education, had physically remained so grounded in the past. Before I came to Cuba, I would have said it was the fault of the embargo, but early on in my stay, I was surprised to discover how few Cubans shared my viewpoint.

"The embargo is a terrible, cruel thing," a history teacher I met on the street told me one day. "But its dissolution will not be our salvation. Maybe Fidel would like everyone to believe that, but there are problems here that are ours alone."

Although the evening speakers were interesting and helped fill the gaps in my knowledge of Cuban history, I soon realized that I could learn more about real life in Cuba from unofficial sources on the street. I also grew tired of doing everything with a group. So, just as I had earlier abandoned the tour bus for the bicycle, I began ditching the afternoon lectures and the planned evening activities in favor of exploring Havana on my own or spending time with Alfredo.

Alfredo and I went to more shows at the symphony—a jazz quintet and a guitar concert where the musicians not only plucked the strings of their instruments but also banged on the bodies of their guitars like drums. We went to Cine Yara, across the street from Coppelia, to see a Cuban film about Tropicana, a ritzy cabaret in the Marianao neighborhood. We wandered the streets, looking for events that were supposed to be taking place—Carnaval or a *peña*, a musical gathering, on someone's rooftop in Habana Vieja—but they never materialized.

"*Es Cuba*," Alfredo would say, shrugging his shoulders sheepishly by way of apology.

One evening we ate at a peso restaurant. Alfredo ordered dessert with his dinner and, when I asked him why, he told me that the supply could run out at any time.

"Here, when you find something you like, you have to go for it, because you never know when it might disappear," he told me. "In Cuba, there is only the moment."

Later that evening, as I was telling Alfredo about my life in California, the solitude of being a freelance writer, my vegetarianism, and my morning runs through the mountains and the Zen center near my house, he said, "I think I'm falling in love with you."

"That's impossible," I said. "You've just met me, and do you know how many times I've heard that line in foreign countries?"

"No, I don't," he said. "I don't know because Cubans aren't allowed to travel. You need an invitation and then special permission, and if you're young and single, it's usually denied anyway, because you're considered a possible immigrant. This island is like a prison."

And then, in a perfect, seamless switch, Alfredo told me why he was proud to be Cuban. "We don't have violence," he said. "Health care's free. Education's free. We're masters in music."

As we talked that evening, I recognized something in Alfredo's words, in his body language and flourishing hand gestures. It was that odd, seemingly contradictory mix of melancholy and optimism that I had come to recognize as the character of his country. I saw something in Alfredo, as I did in Cuba itself, that both saddened and inspired me. I saw signs of hope in places where, on the surface, it appeared that there should be only despair. I experienced kindness from him that, despite the police officer's premature warning that first night, demanded nothing in return. I felt something that I could only identify as the arrival of a long-awaited happiness when I woke early every morning, refreshed after just five hours of sleep, excited for the new day.

3

꧁꧂

Revolution Lessons

On my final morning with my Flying Pigeon, excited about the opportunity to cycle the streets like a Cuban, I offered a ride to Kate, a woman from my program, as she had missed the bus to class. All the Cubans I'd seen biking coupled up, or tripled or quadrupled up, had made the communal ride look, if not effortless, at least entertaining, kind of like a party on wheels where those pedaling were distracted from their toil by the pleasant chatter of their passengers.

Yet from the start, my passenger and I were a mess, nearly toppling the bike as I pedaled out of the parking lot. We persevered, though, and when we finally arrived at the José Martí Language Institute half an hour late and with sweat streaming down our faces, the director rushed over to tell us that our teacher couldn't make it that morning.

Lisset was always late or absent. Yet after just my first week in Cuba, I knew better than to hold this against her. I knew now that to attribute Lisset's lateness to her being irresponsible would be like saying that Cuba didn't have medicine because health care wasn't a priority of the government.

In Cuba, the obvious assumption was almost always the wrong one. Here the reality, the truth of a situation, lay behind an intricate web of other explanations as complex and twisted as history itself. Cuba did not have many medicines because of the U.S. embargo, which also prevented so many of the other material goods the island needed from arrivng.

Lisset's reasons for not being on time were also political. Like most Cubans I met, she had a heightened sense of responsibility, both personal and communal. From the frantic expression on her face, I could tell it pained and embarrassed her to be late, but there was little she could do about the situation. She lived several bus rides away from the institute, and at least once a week her route was blocked or diverted by a Free Elián rally held in front of the U.S. Interests Section. Since relations with Cuba had been formally cut off in 1960, the name of the former U.S. Embassy had been adjusted to reflect the current status of noncommunication between the two nations.

Lisset didn't try any mediating on the part of Cuba or the U.S. From the start of class, she spelled things out as she saw them. As a Revolution baby, born in 1959 when Fidel came to power, Lisset was caught between the optimism of her birth year and the less romantic reality of her current life.

"When I was little and I thought about being a professional, I thought I might have a very different future," Lisset told our class one day. She talked about the way that education was emphasized after the Revolution, especially for women, who now had easier access to professional jobs. "After the Revolution, sexism in the workplace was outlawed," she said.

A billboard I saw everywhere in Havana read HOY COMO SIEMPRE, MUJER ES REVOLUCIÓN. Today, As Always, Woman Is Revolution.

And I had noticed, during my short time in Cuba, that there was less machismo here than in other Latino cultures. Here men still approached me on the street, but it was not to whistle or make lewd comments. True, there was a sound, a sort of *psst, psst,* that I often heard walking down the streets of Havana. And I did meet several foreign women who spent a short time in Cuba and mistook this harmless hiss for some sort of catcall. At first, I did the same, refusing to turn around whenever I heard *psst, psst.* But then one day the *psst psst*-ing seemed particularly persistent— and the sun especially hot and the stench emanating from an open trash container unusually foul—and I decided I just couldn't take it anymore. At the next *psst, psst* I heard, I whirled around to confront the scoundrel face to face.

"What do you want?" I demanded of an elderly man sitting on a wobbly footstool beside a bucket of flowers for sale.

"Finally you stop," the man said, contorting his wrinkly face into a smile, apparently unaffected by my outburst. I wondered if maybe he was hard of hearing. "I've called to you every day you walk by here," he continued. "But you never seem to notice."

"I'm not used to answering to every person who hisses at me on the street," I said.

"Oh, yes," the man said, still calm. "Many people want to know a foreign woman like yourself. But I have a question for you."

"What?" I asked, still defiant.

"Does every person who hisses at you do this?" The old man reached into his bucket and pulled out a tall, full sunflower and handed it to me. "That's all I wanted," he said. "To give you a flower and say, 'Welcome to the neighborhood.'"

I closed my hand around the sunflower, its stem rough like the scaly kiss of a cat.

After this encounter, I began paying more attention to the *psst, psst* sounds I heard on the street. And I noticed something that, in my previous look-straight-ahead state, I had missed entirely. It was not just men *psst, psst*-ing at women. Men *psst, psst*-ed at men. Women *psst, psst*-ed at men. One day an older woman *psst, psst*-ed to ask if I would hold her arm and help her cross the street.

Of course, there were still some hisses I chose to ignore, but for the most part I was pleasantly surprised when I responded, even to the *psst, psst*-ing men. They often asked about my impressions of their country or whether I'd like to go on a date to the Revolutionary Museum or to an Afro-Cuban dance performance. The come-ons were not only more cultured than those I'd encountered elsewhere in my travels, but they were also more human. In Cuba I was not an object to be ogled but an actual person with whom men wanted to converse.

It was this sense of respect and genuine interest that had originally attracted me to Alfredo. I appreciated how, from the start, he had always asked me intelligent questions, about my family, about my writing, about my life in the U.S. But then, as we spent more time together, I began to notice a not-so-subtle shift in his end of the conversations, a rush toward intimacy that unsettled me.

Ever since Alfredo announced that he was falling in love with me, he had begun inviting me out every night and kept asking if he could introduce me to everyone as his girlfriend. He embarrassed me with his *piropos,* a word that my dictionary translated simply as "compliments," but which in Latin America was more akin to an exalted oral art form.

A compliment, in my experience, was "You look nice tonight." A *piropo* was Alfredo dropping to his knees, crossing himself (although he often did it backward, since he had no Catholic training), and saying in English, "Oh my God," when he saw me.

Still, I couldn't force myself to end things with Alfredo, because I so enjoyed my time with him—our visits to Havana's different cultural events, our long talks as we walked back to Miramar, our extended goodbyes outside Hotel El Bosque.

Like Cuba, with its 1950s cars and ongoing struggle for sovereignty, my relationship with Alfredo also seemed frozen in time. At the end of each night, we played out the same scenario, kissing in a shaded spot off to the side of Hotel El Bosque like young, infatuated lovers who were tragically being forced to part. But we were not lovers. There was no possibility of inviting Alfredo into Hotel El Bosque, and he did not have his own place to invite me to either. And somehow I was relieved by this.

Even though each time I saw Alfredo I felt that sort of excited, choking sensation I always associated with first attraction, I wasn't yet comfortable calling myself his girlfriend, or him my boyfriend. I was slower, more guarded with my emotions, and these differences, combined with the financial inequalities that plagued our relationship from the start, made me fear that we would never be on an equal footing.

I wondered sometimes whether Alfredo would have behaved the same way if I were a *cubana* or whether, with more time for things to develop, he would have been content taking things slower. I wondered whether a *cubana* would have returned the *piropos* or blown them off.

With these and other related questions looming in my mind, I asked Lisset if she would talk to me about her role as a woman in Cuba. She agreed, and after class one afternoon, we sat in the empty room, with the sun pouring in through the louvered blinds, accentuating the dust that had accumulated on the window ledge.

"You remember when I told you that sexism was outlawed after the Revolution," Lisset said. I nodded. "Well, that doesn't mean machismo doesn't exist today," she said. "All that means is that its presence is illegal. Cuba is still a very *machista* country. I work, but when I come home, I still have to do everything. And it's not like in the U.S., because Cuba is an underdeveloped country. We don't have prepared foods. We don't have washing machines. We have to make our meals from scratch, wash our clothes by hand. Once in a while my husband makes dinner, and I say, 'Thanks,' but most nights I make it, and no one says, 'Thanks.'"

Lisset had a daughter from a previous marriage, and she told me she had no intention of having any more children. "Not now," she said. "Life is too difficult. It wouldn't be wise to have a bigger family when it is such a struggle for just three people."

I thought about my travels elsewhere in Latin America—in the Guatemalan highlands and the capital of Nicaragua, in a group of islands off the coast of Panama and in the rainforests of Costa Rica, where women much poorer than Lisset had baby after baby, digging themselves deeper into destitution. Why hadn't they taken Lisset's practical approach?

Religion, I decided, was probably the difference. While much of the rest of Latin America was still awash in Catholicism, Cuba was refreshingly free of any moral dictums regulating birth control or abortion. Despite the taboo against religion in the early years of the Revolution, religious people were now allowed to join the Communist party, and Christmas had been an official holiday for several years. There were churches throughout Havana, and even a synagogue, yet from what I saw, no one seemed to be rushing to join an organized religion.

I asked Lisset what wishes she had for her daughter's life. "I want her to study a lot, to be a cultured person," she told me. "I don't want her to be materialistic, although I know that you need some material things in life. Sometimes, as a present, I'll pick a flower for her, so she'll know there are more important things than the material."

Lisset told me she wanted her daughter to believe in dreams, even though many of her own had not panned out. "I don't regret being a teacher, because education is important, but it's just that I never thought I'd live like this as a teacher," she said.

"What do you mean?" I asked. I knew Lisset didn't earn dollars and maybe didn't have many luxuries, but she was doing a job she believed in, and she seemed to be in good health, always full of energy when she was teaching. "I don't understand," I said. "How is it that you live?"

"Oh, Lea," she said, sighing and brushing back her dark, feathered hair. "There are things that I can't say because of my pride. I don't want people to know all I don't have, but for people who don't have private jobs where they earn dollars, or who don't have relatives in the U.S. sending them money, life is very, very difficult. And it's the worst for women. An example is that right now I don't have a broom. My husband says, 'So what? Who cares?' But that's because he never cleans anyway. But for me it matters. I have to use an old T-shirt, and it's an embarrassment that I'm a professional and can't even afford a broom because they're sold in dollars. What would've taken one hour to clean now takes three with my T-shirt."

Lisset looked at me awkwardly, as if afraid that she had revealed too much.

"Listen," she said suddenly. "I am proud to be a Cuban. I don't want to live anywhere else. I just want things to get better here."

4

We Were Promised Socialism

I met my first *fidelista* friend in a nursery in Miramar, beside a fragrant *mariposa*, Cuba's national flower. She seemed to be taking notes about the flowers and looked up, startled, as I approached her with my friend Amy.

Amy, a women's studies major, was in my program and was taking a year off from college to travel. In just two weeks, we had become close friends and had discussed staying on after the program to study for another two weeks and then travel for two more. When I told Amy about my interview with Lisset, she invited me to go with her to the Federación de Mujeres Cubanas. After the Revolution, Federation of Cuban Women buildings were set up as women's resource and support centers in each municipality in Cuba.

When we finished class one afternoon, Amy and I set off to find the FMC in Miramar. A teacher at the language institute told us to head south, but we walked in that direction for a good twenty minutes without encountering any sign markers along the way. Finally, when we approached a nursery with its entrance gate swung wide open, we went in to ask for directions.

After her initial surprise at seeing us, the woman standing near the *mariposa* put down her notes and smiled.

"How can I help you?" she asked with a sort of professionalism I had yet to see in any service sector job in Havana—other than, of course, those geared toward tourists. But there were no other tourists to be found in the nursery, only a few Cubans walking around, prodding at the plants.

"Excuse me if I looked shocked when you came in, but it's just that you look a lot like an old friend of mine who's moved away," the *mariposa* woman said, pointing at Amy.

In Cuba, the phrase "moved away" didn't just mean someone had relocated to a new city. In a country where people generally were born, grew up, and died in the same neighborhood, to "move away" implied something much bigger, more permanent and desperate. The seriousness in this woman's voice told me that her friend had probably moved to the U.S., that great land of opportunity and no return. *La Coca Cola del olvido,* the Coca Cola of forgetting, is how people in Cuba referred to the U.S. when talking about those relatives in Miami who made the ninety-mile move and then lost touch with everyone in Cuba.

Amy and I introduced ourselves, and the woman leaned forward to kiss each of us on the cheek in greeting. She told us her name was Liudmila and then laughed as we struggled to pronounce it.

"It's a Russian name," she said proudly. "You know the Russians were very supportive of the Cuban Revolution and our people."

I nodded, but Amy looked a little confused. She had only studied Spanish for a semester and had never been to a Spanish-speaking country before.

"I can speak English if you like," Liudmila said in English, without even a trace of a Cuban accent.

"Where did you learn to speak like that?" I asked.

"I used to work in tourism," she said.

"And now you're a . . ." Amy paused, searching for the word. "A botanist?"

"Well," Liudmila said. "I like nature and plants, but this is just my after-school job. Actually, I'm an accounting student at the University of Havana."

"A dilettante," I said. "You're like a Renaissance woman."

"Yes, but . . ." Liudmila paused. "It's complicated."

I waited for her to continue, but instead she looked away, over at the *mariposa,* as if it might have something to add.

"Did you come here for a plant?" Liudmila asked.

We told her we were looking for the FMC, and Liudmila smiled once again.

"You know, I have never been there before," she said, cupping a hand over her mouth as if embarrassed. "Let me see if someone knows where it is."

Liudmila walked toward a green wooden shed in the center of the nursery. After a few steps, she turned around and waved at us.

"Come," she said. "I'll introduce you to everyone."

We walked into the shed, where an antiquated, rusting cash register sat atop a counter in an empty front room. In a windowless back room, two women and a man sat in rickety chairs, carrying on a conversation in the dim quarters. A thin mongrel dog lay on the floor panting.

"These are my friends, Amy and Lea," Liudmila said. We did the obligatory round of kisses, and then Liudmila asked, "Can anyone direct them to the FMC?"

"It's around here," one woman offered.

"I think it's on this street," the man said.

"Keep going straight," the second woman suggested.

Liudmila shrugged her shoulders at us. "Sorry we can't be of more help," she said. And then, as an afterthought, she added, "I could call my aunt. She's a member of the Communist Party. She knows where every organization is."

I thought it best not to get the government involved in the search, so I thanked Liudmila but assured her that we'd find our way. She led us out to the street.

"Come by again if you ever want to talk," she said as she waved goodbye.

We continued straight past the garden, following the final suggestion of Liudmila's coworkers, until we found another person to ask. But just two blocks from the nursery, I heard a voice calling out our names, and I turned around to see Liudmila's small, thin form running after us. She had changed her clothes, replacing a pair of faded green shorts and a gray tank top with midnight blue jeans and a white halter top, which contrasted with her dark black skin.

"Wait," she called out. "I want to come."

"Don't you have to work?" Amy asked when Liudmila reached us.

"No, it's okay," she said. "I'd be getting off soon anyway."

"You don't work a full day?" I asked. It was only three o'clock.

"Well, it's complicated," Liudmila said once more. Lowering her voice, she added, "You'll see. Everyone's off in the afternoons. *Para resolver sus problemas.*"

"What problems?" I asked.

Liudmila rubbed her fingers together to indicate money. "They are doing their other jobs," she said. "*Negocios.*"

This was another word I had learned from Alfredo early on. *Negocios* were under-the-table jobs—private businesses ranging from selling cigars to teaching Spanish to earning commissions for directing tourists to clubs or restaurants. *Negocios* were a way to earn dollars, or at least more pesos, to supplement minimally paid government day jobs.

Alfredo first told me about his *negocios* when I'd asked about a pair of worn Timberland docksiders that he always wore. Timberland products were not available in Cuba because of the embargo, and even if someone had managed to transport a pair to Cuba to sell, most Cubans would not have been able to afford them. When I asked how he obtained his shoes, Alfredo laughed.

"Just like you might," he said. "I bought them."

"But . . . " I paused, not sure how to word my question. "Weren't they expensive?"

"They were fifty-five dollars," Alfredo said. This was the equivalent of nearly four months' salary. "But Lea," he continued, slowing the rhythm of his words. "To you, it might sound like a lot of money for a Cuban and, well, it is, but what many foreigners don't understand is that we have no other option. When I was a teenager, it was illegal to possess U.S. dollars. Just for having one dollar, you could go to jail. Then one day they became legal, and today you can't live without them. So we do whatever we have to to acquire them."

"What did you do?" I asked.

"Everything," Alfredo said. "There was a girl in my neighborhood who was going to visit her father in the U.S. She asked if I wanted anything, and I said, 'a good pair of shoes.' I knew they would be expensive, so I started thinking about *negocios*. This was during the Special Period, and everyone was scrambling. For a while I bred doves on my father's roof because people use them in religious ceremonies. Then I had an uncle who worked in a *panadería,* so each day he'd bring home a little dough, and someone else would know someone who could get tomato sauce or cheese. Every day after work, I'd bike to my uncle's house, and we'd make pizzas to sell. It was almost all profit."

I wanted to ask Liudmila if she too had *negocios,* but she had so many questions herself that it was difficult to get a word in edgewise. She asked Amy and me about our program, about our impressions of Cuba, about our families. And then, with little prompting, she told us about her life. She told us that she lived with her mother, grandmother, and younger brother, who was eighteen and the complete opposite of her.

"He's from another generation," Liudmila said wearily.

"How old are you?" I asked.

"Twenty-four," she said and, when I had difficulty stifling my laugh, added, "I know what you are thinking. It doesn't seem like such a big age difference. But when I talk about age I don't mean just numbers. I don't mean *his* age so much as *the* age, the time he is coming of age in. It is very different from when I was a teenager. All my brother wants is to be out in the streets and to go to clubs, to meet foreigners. And that is what his classmates want too. That's how they all are."

"And how are you?" Amy asked.

"I'm calmer," Liudmila said. "I study and spend time at home with my mother and grandmother. When I was eighteen, the U.S. dollar was just being legalized. There were not so many *jineteros.* People were content to just get by instead of always thinking about getting ahead or getting out." Liudmila lowered her voice an octave. "I think my brother wants to get out."

"To the U.S.?" I asked.

She nodded. Once again, I wanted to ask more, but once again, Liudmila started in with her own questions, conveniently changing the subject to our search for the FMC.

A few blocks down the street we finally found the building, an elegant white colonial house with large columns, guarded by a statue of a nude woman who looked more like a Roman mermaid than a *cubana.*

Inside a nearly deserted lobby, the receptionist told us that the director and most of the staff were in a meeting.

"But I can give you a tour if you like," she added, looking eager to abandon her desolate post. She walked us through the 1950s-style building, with its avocado green walls and faded photos of Fidel and Celia Sánchez, a *guerrillera* who aided Fidel in the Sierra Maestra during the final years of the Revolution. In 1980, Celia lost her own battle against breast cancer, and her premature death transformed her into a sort of female Che.

"This used to be a mansion, but its owners fled after the Revolution," the receptionist told us as we entered a converted dining room, which now served as a multipurpose room. A few children's books were scattered across a wooden table, and the receptionist told us that some day the FMC hoped to have a computer here.

"Basically this is just a place where women can come to talk about their issues and get help with their lives," she said.

I stopped by a framed black-and-white photo of Fidel hanging on the wall, remembering how a friend back home had requested a photo of me and Fidel. I stood beneath the photo, Fidel's head a good foot or so above mine, as it would probably be in real life, and I pulled my camera out from my backpack. But when I asked the receptionist to take my picture, she took one look at Fidel and me and shook her head before rushing out of the room.

Amy looked confused and Liudmila a little worried. Before I could say anything though, the receptionist ran back in, dragging a chair behind her. She placed it to the side of Fidel and extended her hand to take the camera.

"Now," she said proudly, motioning for me to step onto the chair, "you can be on the same level."

After the tour, Liudmila, Amy, and I sat down to talk in a sunny spot on a threadbare couch.

I asked Liudmila about the HOY COMO SIEMPRE, MUJER ES REVOLUCIÓN billboard.

"It's true," she said. "I have heard stories from my mother and grandmother about life before the Revolution, about how difficult it was for women to go to school. After the Revolution, everything changed for the better. Women are represented in all parts of society now. Look, the other week there was the Women's March for Elián."

"I heard that the women had to go," Amy said, retelling a story that had been circulating among travelers in Cuba. "I heard that the buses to the march left from people's offices, and each woman's name was checked off as she went."

"I didn't go," Liudmila said. "I couldn't make it, and I don't think anyone was made to go. But this is just my story. If you want to know the truth about life here, you need to talk to many, many people."

As I nodded thoughtfully, a smile flashed across Liudmila's face.

"Maybe you could start with my family," she suggested. "You could come back to my house with me now and interview my mother and my grandmother. I know they'd enjoy meeting both of you."

"I'd love to," Amy said. "But I promised a friend I'd meet him back at the hotel in an hour."

"Well," Liudmila said, looking hopefully at me. "You can still come, right?"

When Liudmila told me that she lived in the renowned Buena Vista barrio, I envisioned elegant old men tooting their trombones on every street corner. But while we were walking for nearly an hour through deteriorating neighborhoods, I mentioned the movie to Liudmila. She told me she'd never heard of it, and I realized that the Buena Vista Social Club had perhaps enjoyed more fame in the U.S. than in Cuba. Although Buena Vista was in Playa, the same municipality as Miramar, it was quite different—a side of Havana I hadn't seen yet. There were none of the tree-lined streets of Vedado here, nor any of the elegantly crumbling mansions of Miramar. Buena Vista looked like a shantytown on the hillside, with tiny houses clustered one on top of the other. Still, there was something beautiful about it, especially as we arrived, at the hour of sunset, and the streets seemed silent and still, save for the faint rhythm of Lou Bega's popular song, "Mambo #5," floating out of some nearby window.

We climbed three flights of steps to reach Liudmila's house. Before we entered, she turned to me and said apologetically, "It might be a little dark for you. Light bulbs are very expensive these days."

Liudmila opened the door to a tiny but tidy house. A blue refrigerator separated the kitchenette from the dining/living room, where an older woman wearing an apron stood up from an armchair whose springs protruded in her wake.

"Grandma, this is my friend Lea," Liudmila said. "She wants to learn about Cuban women."

"Well, you've come to the right house," the grandmother said. "Please, have a seat."

I sat in a second armchair, and Liudmila pulled up a chair from the dining-room table for herself. Above us was a six-bulb chandelier that had only one bulb. From the darkness of the kitchenette, another woman appeared, ladle in hand.

"Is your friend staying for dinner, Liudmila?" she asked.

"This is my mother," Liudmila said. With a worried expression on her face, she turned toward her and asked, "But we don't have any meat, do we?"

"That's fine," I said. "I'm a vegetarian."

Liudmila's mother smiled. Like Liudmila and the grandmother, she was a small, thin woman with a calm, dignified air about her.

"*Vegetariana,*" she repeated, drawing out the last letter like in an Italian word. "We don't have many of those here," she said. "Cubans like their meat."

"But now we *are* like vegetarians," Liudmila said. "We eat eggs, but never meat. It's just too expensive."

"Times are difficult, Lea," the grandmother said. "Although, of course, they were more difficult for our people before the Revolution." She pinched her skin as she spoke, a common gesture to denote skin color.

"My mother cut sugarcane all her life, and I worked as a maid when I was younger," the grandmother said. "I worked for people who had a lot of money and were very demanding. I lived in their house, and I was only allowed to leave once a week. I would have liked to try out another profession, to go to school, but that just wasn't a possibility. Back in those days, you had to pay for education."

"You had to pay for everything," Liudmila's mother chimed in from the kitchenette.

As the grandmother nodded her head, another woman, petite but still sturdy-looking like the rest of them, walked in through the front door. Her short hair was windblown, and she exhaled deeply as she pulled up a chair to join our growing circle.

"What a day," she said. "I had to walk nearly two hours to get here from work. All the buses were off to the countryside to pick up people for the Elián rally tomorrow."

"Another one?" I asked.

"Yes, another," she said wearily, looking at me as though she had just noticed my presence. "Who are you?"

"This is a new friend of mine from the United States," Liudmila said.

"Well, welcome. I'm her sister," the woman said, pointing to Liudmila's mother.

"Do you live here too?" I asked.

"No," she said. "I just stop by every once in a while."

"She's the one who's a member of the Communist Party," Liudmila told me. Liudmila's aunt was the first person with such an affiliation to be formally introduced to me, and I looked closely at her for any telltale signs. Of what, I wasn't exactly sure. A red flag tucked into her purse? A desire to dominate other people? I realized that, by virtue of living in a capitalist country with a history of persecuting communists, I had been taught a sense of disdain for communism, but I had never been told precisely why. And here in front of me was an actual, admitted communist. She was a woman like any other, worn out by the situation, yet still hanging on, however tenuously. And, in this moment, she preferred to talk pop culture rather than politics. She was the first Cuban to ask if I lived close to Hollywood.

"I love movies," she told me. "Chinese kung fu ones are my favorite."

"I like dramas—*Fried Green Tomatoes* and *The Piano*," Liudmila said.

A teenage boy in shorts and an oversized T-shirt walked in, presumably Liudmila's brother, and he was immediately questioned.

"Sci-fi," he answered, without even pausing to think about it.

"It's love stories for me," the grandmother said.

As the mother brought out a bowl of steaming white rice and another of garlicky black beans, she announced, "It's always been my dream to attend the Oscars."

"What about you, Lea?" Liudmila asked.

"I like dramas too," I said, and Liudmila smiled, as though my choice cemented the certainty of our friendship.

"Do you want to wash your hands before dinner?" Liudmila asked.

She walked with me into a bedroom with two sets of bunk beds.

"We all sleep here," she told me. "My mother and grandmother in one and me and my brother in the other."

To the side of the bedroom was the bathroom. Liudmila pulled out a small bar of pink soap from under the sink. There was one bottle of shampoo in the curtainless shower, and a pair of frayed, doily-esque underwear hung over a back window.

When I returned to the main room, the grandmother was ushering everyone around the table. The mother brought out the third and final plate— cabbage sautéed with tomato sauce and onions. Everything smelled delicious, but I wondered how there would be enough for all six of us.

"I should probably be heading home," the aunt said. "At least it looks like the buses are running in this part of town."

She kissed us all goodbye and made a quick exit. The brother sat in her chair, and the grandmother pushed the black beans toward me.

"*Somos pobrecitos,* Lea," she said. We're poor. "But you are our guest."

I took a small portion from each of the plates and somehow everyone managed to get a few spoonfuls too. After the mother took her serving, there was still about half a spoonful of black beans left over. She looked into the bowl for a moment and then dumped the remaining morsels on my plate.

"All right," she said, the great feat accomplished. "*Buen provecho.*"

During dinner she told me about a computer class she had just started taking. In my two-and-a-half weeks in Cuba, I had seen only one computer— a yellowing old Macintosh that retrieved emails for the fifty or so students at the José Martí Language Institute.

"Where are you taking the classes?" I asked Liudmila's mother.

"Oh, there's a computer center in downtown Havana," she said. "There are donated computers, and the foreigners teach you how to use them. But it is so difficult, Lea. I'm afraid I'll never learn it."

"You will." *Tú verás.* You'll see, I said, throwing in a Cuban phrase I had learned recently. *"Tú verás"* was the countersentiment to *"Es Cuba,"* and I'd heard Alfredo use it with as much frequency. Instead of implying that this was how things were and that was that, *"Tú verás"* suggested that perhaps they might change. How, exactly, was never addressed. But most Cubans, with their sort of enduring optimism-against-all-odds attitude, didn't seem fazed by this.

And, sure enough, *"Tú verás"* comforted Liudmila's mother. She patted my hand and thanked me for my advice.

I looked around the house, wondering what we would do now, wondering what the family did in the evenings. There was no telephone, but a small TV rested on a dresser in the corner of the living room.

"Would you like to see photographs?" Liudmila asked me. I nodded and she retreated into the bedroom, returning with a tiny photo album filled with black-and-white shots of Liudmila and her brother. In one photo, Liudmila wore a long, frilly dress.

"That was my *quinceañera,*" she told me. The elaborate stories my Latina friends in the U.S. had told me about their fifteenth-birthday celebrations always made me think of the sweet-sixteen ceremonies of my mother's generation.

Liudmila would have turned fifteen in 1990, the last year of the U.S.S.R., the year before Cuba itself began to collapse. Liudmila was smiling in her *quinceañera* photo. There was no hint of future unhappiness here, nor of the struggles that would soon befall her family and her country. Shortly after the *quinceañera,* the photos stopped. There was still one page left empty in the album.

"They're very nice pictures," I told Liudmila. I wondered, though, where the father was. There was no extra space in the slumber-party bedroom, and no one had made any mention of him. Liudmila looked around the main room. For a moment I thought she might pull out another photo album that would solve this mystery, but instead she asked if I'd seen a *libreta.* When I told her I hadn't, her mother pulled a ration book out of her wallet.

"You have to see this, Lea, if you want to understand the Cuban situation," she said.

The *libreta* was a tiny book about the size of a checkbook, but wider. Inside were the family's address and names. And then there were the rations—eggs and bread, chicken and ham, salt, potatoes, rice, soap, beans, and toilet paper. The listing itself was scarce, but then Liudmila told me that often many of the items weren't even available.

"Before the Special Period, it was different," she said. "There was enough of everything. And now, even when there is availability, we're rationed so little, it can never last."

"Imagine," her grandmother said. "We only have one bar of soap left for all of us for the next two weeks."

"*No es fácil.*" It's not easy, said the mother. "Have you seen a *bodega?*" Once again I shook my head. I had heard much about the ration stores but had never actually been to one.

"I'll show you," Liudmila said. "You have to pass it to catch the bus to your hotel anyway."

I said my goodbyes to Liudmila's family and wished her mother luck with her computer classes.

The sun had set while we ate dinner, and all the details I had noticed on the way here were now obscured. Liudmila and I walked a few blocks and then stopped beneath a darkened balcony.

"That house," Liudmila said quietly, "is the house of a *babalawo,* a high priest of the Afro-Cuban religion." We both stared up silently. "He's probably working now," Liudmila said. "This is his *negocio* too. Foreigners come to him, and they pay lots of money to have their fortunes told. Once I helped out because these women only spoke English, so I translated their fortunes."

"Did the *babalawo* pay you?" I asked.

"No," Liudmila said. "But I'm not interested in *negocios.* I just want to study and take care of my family."

"And what about your father?" I asked.

"Oh, my parents are divorced," Liudmila said nonchalantly. "Or really, I don't know if they ever got married. But when I was sixteen, my father left. He lives an hour away. Sometimes I visit him on school vacations, but we're not very close."

By now I realized that Liudmila was good at changing the subject when we approached one she didn't want to discuss.

"The *bodega* is just around the corner," she said. "I hope it's still open."

But it wasn't. There was only an empty counter behind a set of bars.

"Well, it doesn't look that much different when it's open," Liudmila said. "I'll catch the bus back with you so you don't get lost."

I told her it wasn't necessary, but she insisted on coming, as well as buying my passage. On the bus she told me, "I like Hotel El Bosque. I enjoy going there. When I was in tourism school, I wanted to work there."

"And why didn't you continue with that?"

"Really, I wanted to be a lawyer," Liudmila said. "But here you have to take a test in your field before you go to the university, and I didn't pass the one to study law."

The same thing had happened with Alfredo and music. But with him, instead of choosing another subject, he'd abandoned college and gone through a series of odd jobs, from construction worker to guard. Finally he had made his way into the music world, although as a technician with the symphony, he was on the opposite side of where he would've liked to have been.

"At first I didn't know what I'd do when I didn't pass the law test," Liudmila said. "But then everything here changed, and dollars became legal, and tourism started up, so I thought I'd try that. I thought maybe I could do it. I told myself I'd get to meet a lot of people from different places, and I would of course be earning a better salary than doing anything else. But in truth, you're only cleaning beds. You're just a maid, and I never wanted to be a maid."

I thought about Liudmila's grandmother's story about her maid job, followed by her declaration that everything had improved since the Revolution. And I remembered a joke I'd heard from an economist who'd come to talk to my program.

In the streets of Havana, a drunk man gets arrested for being a public nuisance, the joke goes. The police take him back to the station and call his wife to come pick him up.

"We think he's gone crazy," they tell her.

"Why do you say that?" she asks.

"Well, on his ID card, it says he's a doctor, but he keeps telling us he's the doorman at the Habana Libre," a ritzy hotel in the Vedado neighborhood.

"Oh," the wife says, laughing. "Now I understand. When he drinks too much, he gets these delusions of grandeur."

I remembered, too, talking about salaries one night with Alfredo on one of those long walks back to Hotel El Bosque. Alfredo had been complaining that policemen made nearly forty dollars each month, compared with the twelve dollars earned by professionals, such as teachers or doctors.

Even in the darkness, I could imagine the expression on Alfredo's face. His brow would be furrowed, his dark eyes big and angry. He would be ready to jump into one of his complaining tangents; on the first night, he'd informed me he didn't want to go into one of them when he was with me. Yet like everyone else in Cuba, he still did.

Despite what I'd heard in the U.S. about Cubans being afraid to complain about the government, I found Cubans unbelievably candid and critical, more critical than many Americans are of their government. Cubans demanded more of their collective reality than people in any other country I'd visited. And they seemed to complain about everything—the trash in the streets, the overcrowding on the *camellos,* the salary disparities.

On this particular night with Alfredo, I finally got tired of it.

"I don't know why you complain so much," I told him. "It's like that everywhere, but worse in most places. When I worked at a newspaper, all of us reporters had studied for many years. No one in advertising had gone to college, but they all earned well over twice our salaries. People who pollute and use sweatshop labor and don't pay their workers minimum wage earn exorbitant salaries. And . . ." As I was trying to come up with another shocking example of economic injustice, Alfredo put his hand on my shoulder, forcing me to stop walking and face him.

"But Lea," he said softly, countering my own budding rage and, in just three succinct sentences, explaining what I had so far failed to understand. "You live in a capitalist world," he said. "But in Cuba, we were promised something better. We were promised socialism."

When the bus dropped Liudmila and me off at Hotel El Bosque, not being able to invite her in, I offered to walk with her to the bus stop for Buena Vista.

"Oh, no, I think I'll walk," Liudmila said, quickly adding, "I like walking."

It occurred to me suddenly that maybe she didn't have the money to catch a bus home. Maybe she had used it up on our fares over.

It seemed late to walk all the way back to Buena Vista, especially in Liudmila's wobbly clogs, which made her walk at the pace of an eighty-year-old woman.

"What time is it?" I asked, glancing at Liudmila's watch. But there was no time on the digital face. It was as blank as the night itself.

"Oh, the battery's broken. But I like the watch just for decoration," she said. She kissed me goodbye but, after a few steps in the other direction, her clog clunks came to a stop and she turned around. She tapped at her watch, an odd expression on her face as if she'd forgotten what she was going to say. She waved goodbye and, before turning back and disappearing into the darkness, said in a voice so low I wasn't sure if she was talking to me or to herself, "I'll be fine."

5

The Poolside Affairs

The following day, not too far from where I'd first met Liudmila at her nursery in Miramar, I made another new friend, this time a precocious nine-year-old girl who wasted no time in attaching herself to me.

"What are you doing?" she asked as she sidled up to me at a curbside pizza stand. She was wearing her school uniform, colored like the Cuban flag, with a red jumper, a white blouse, and a blue kerchief tied loosely around her neck.

I was getting my afternoon street pizza, as Amy and I referred to the greasy concoction of undercooked dough, watered-down tomato sauce, and synthetic cheese that people sold from their front windows—or from little cutouts that served as makeshift windows. The pizzerias, one of a handful of private businesses legalized in 1993, had infrequent hours. Some days they opened at 7 AM, some days at 11 PM, and some days not at all.

While I waited for my pizza, I would check out the surroundings of where my food was prepared. From my patient post at the window, I could see the clean, bare-bones kitchens and, beyond them, the dimly lit living rooms.

Here, framed black-and-white family photos sat on precariously balanced coffee tables next to the requisite collection of empty rum bottles, which Cubans displayed on their living room floors or TV tops as proudly as Americans displayed their rows of uncorked wine bottles in ornate mahogany racks.

When my pizza was handed to me on a pale brown paper towel, I would stand out in the stinky street with the other customers, folding our twenty-five-cent pizzas into half moons and squeezing their excess oil onto the sidewalk to make our meals a little more palatable.

Inevitably, someone would walk by while I was eating and call out, "¿España? ¿Francia? ¿Inglaterra? ¿Italia?" trying to guess my country of origin. Early on in my stay, I had learned that this was a rite of passage, one that all travelers to Cuba experienced at several points in their journeys.

I would shake my head "no" to all the Western European countries shouted out, and then there would be a barrage of Eastern European countries before everyone moved on to South America. But never once did they ask whether I was from the U.S. During my first few days, before I grew tired of this guessing game, I'd play it for all it was worth, waiting until the last minute, until the last confused call of "¿Argentina?" or "¿Uruguay?" before I would reveal my true identity.

"Oh!" the Cubans would exclaim. "American? Really?"

The little schoolgirl standing next to me at the street pizza stand somehow guessed my identity right away.

"Have you seen Elián?" she asked me.

"Elián?" I repeated.

"Some day I will go to the U.S. and bring him back," the girl informed me, her voice sturdy and determined. "What are you doing here?" she asked.

"I'm studying Spanish," I told her, wishing I had a mission as exciting as hers. "This is my last week of class, and afterward I'm probably going to travel around Cuba with a friend."

The girl nodded, unimpressed. "And now?" she asked, staring at me with the caramel moons of her eyes. She was beautiful in that quintessentially Cuban way—skin so many shades of humanity, hair that was part afro-kinky and part honey brown. "What will you do now, after you finish your pizza?"

"Well, I was just planning to go back to my hotel."

"Can I come? Maybe I could spend the afternoon with you."

"Don't you have to go back to school? It's only twelve thirty."

"Oh, that's okay," she said with a nonchalance reminiscent of Liudmila's when she deserted her job to go to the FMC with me and Amy. "All we do in the afternoon is have art classes."

I looked at her hesitantly.

"Oh, please," she begged, clasping her hands in front of her. Then she turned away from me and pointed down the street. "My mother's right there, talking to a friend. I'll go ask her if it's okay."

Before I could respond, the little girl was off and running toward two women standing in the middle of the sidewalk. She grabbed each one by the hand and led them over to me. They introduced themselves and told me the girl's name was Guelmis. And then, before I could respond with my own name, they were off again.

"Have fun!" the mother called out as she and her friend crossed the street. "Take good care of my daughter."

For the first few blocks of our taxi ride back to Hotel El Bosque, I sat stunned by what had just transpired. Then, as I tried to think of ways to entertain Guelmis, I remembered the swimming pool. For some reason, while Cubans were routinely questioned if they were seen dawdling in the lobby, no one blinked an eye when they walked through it to get to the pool.

"Do you have a bathing suit?" I asked Guelmis.

She nodded and, as if afraid that she might break the magic of this moment by inquiring why, simply ordered the taxi driver to stop.

"I live right near here," Guelmis told me as the taxi driver, pulled over, screeching on his brakes.

"I'm getting out here," Guelmis informed him as she opened the door. "But I'll be back in a minute, so don't go anywhere." She disappeared around the corner, and in what seemed like just a few seconds, she came running back toward the taxi with a frilly red bathing suit in hand.

I was hoping Amaury would be at the hotel, since I wanted to talk to him about renting the bike again, but there was another bellboy whom I'd never seen before. He wouldn't let Guelmis go up to my room, so she put her bathing suit on in the lobby bathroom while I went upstairs to change, irritated with this discrimination by Cubans against Cubans. Just a few days earlier, Alfredo told me that he used an Argentine accent when he called the reception desk to talk with me.

When I asked him why, he told me that otherwise people hung up on him.

"One time this woman told me that there was no one named 'Lea' in the hotel," he said. "But if they don't know I'm Cuban, they put me through right away."

"Why is it like this?" I asked Alfredo.

"Some people say it's the same reason why we can't travel," he said. "They say the government doesn't want us to talk to tourists because they're afraid that if we learn about life elsewhere, we'll become dissatisfied with the way things are here."

"Some people in the U.S. say that's why our government doesn't want us to see Cuba," I said.

"What do you mean?" Alfredo asked, perplexed. "What would you want that we have here?"

"People say our government's afraid that we'll start questioning the distribution of wealth; that we'll start asking, 'Why can't we have free health care? Why do we have to pay for education?'" I said. "But what do you think?"

"About where?" Alfredo asked. "About your country or mine?"

"About both," I said. "About either."

"I think," Alfredo responded, pausing as he stared into the distance. "I think that it makes no sense. I think that there is no reason why you shouldn't be able to come here legally; why we can't travel there. Why we can't enter our own hotels."

Despite Alfredo's dismissive response, I believed there had to be a reason, and I continued to survey people to discover what it might be. Some people told me Cubans were not allowed in hotels because the government was trying to protect the tourists and didn't want them to be bothered by *jineteros*. Others said this tourist apartheid was about protecting the Cubans themselves, upholding their dignity by preventing prostitution, which had been rampant in Cuba before the

Revolution, was outlawed afterward, and in recent years had been making a steady, albeit illegal, comeback.

I had seen little evidence of prostitution during my three weeks in Cuba. But then prostitution, like so much else in Cuba, lay in the unnamed spaces, in the subtleties of speech or movement. Every evening on various street corners in Havana, *cubanas* lined up outside touristy salsa clubs, where the covers were in dollars. These women waited for foreign men to invite them in. In exchange, they offered an evening of dance and libations, Cuban-style—a good story for the men to take home and then, depending on how grateful or attracted the *cubanas* were feeling when the club closed, perhaps something more.

There was too great a sense of obligation on the part of the women for this to be considered a simple, consensual, one-night stand, yet it wasn't exactly prostitution in the traditional sense either. Most of what I had seen of Cuban–foreigner relations lay in an even more nebulous category.

Today at the pool was a perfect example. At first glance, it looked like the typical resort scene of vacationing couples lounging in the sun, sipping tropical cocktails. But when I looked closer, I noticed that every other couple was composed of an attractive, slender Afro-Cuban girl in her late teens or early twenties with a hairy, beer-bellied foreign man old enough to be her father.

If these girls had been actual prostitutes, they undoubtedly would have been denied entrance into Hotel El Bosque, despite the open-door pool policy. But these girls weren't prostitutes, and without such defined labels, where both parties know exactly what they're getting into, it really wasn't very clear what was going on. Today at the pool, in addition to the slobbery older men speaking loudly to their Cuban Lolitas in languages neither the *cubanas* nor I could understand, I spotted two women from my program with their Latin lovers. Melanie was here with Vladimir, her boyfriend of the past two weeks. After their first week together, Melanie had moved in with Vladimir's family, who, she complained, was always asking for money. And then there was Emily, a nineteen-year-old Brit who had also met her Cuban boyfriend recently and, within a matter of weeks, moved in with his family. Armando wanted to leave Cuba, and he and Emily were planning to get married as soon as possible.

In the two-week session of my program, there had been several others who had always been at the pool with their Cuban mates. There were two women who had both fallen for their younger dance instructors, who, within a week of the women's departures, had found new girlfriends in the next class of foreigners. And then there was the married man who had frequented the Hotel El Bosque pool with his younger Cuban girlfriend.

In all the relationships, the Americans bought gifts of clothing and food and cosmetics for their Cuban partners and their families. They took them out to restaurants the Cubans never could have afforded on their own, and they rented cars and showed them parts of their country they'd never seen before. They promised to stay in touch when they said goodbye. And then they flew back home to their real lives.

Maybe the people on my program did think they'd return some day and reclaim their true loves. Maybe those overweight old men actually thought their young partners loved them for something deeper than their pants pockets. Maybe some of them did. In each relationship, I felt like someone was being taken advantage of, although it wasn't always so clear precisely who or in which way.

All I knew for sure was that these daily scenes that were played out at the Hotel El Bosque pool confirmed my feelings about the inherent inequalities in romantic relationships with Cubans. Even though my situation with Alfredo was nothing like these poolside affairs, they still reminded me of why I had been so hesitant to get involved. They served as a warning sign of how things could go wrong.

As I contemplated the complexities of Cuban–foreigner relationships, Guelmis dove into the pool, oblivious to the stories of heartbreak and deceit unfolding around her. She joined in on a game of water polo, and when a Cuban band that played behind Hotel El Bosque every evening started up, she danced a solo salsa on the pool steps.

As the clock that hung above the poolside bar struck five, I told Guelmis I should take her home.

"Home?" she asked, sounding upset by my suggestion. "I don't want to go home yet. I like being here."

"But you have to go," I said. "I don't want to make your mother worry."

"Worry? Why?" Guelmis asked. "She knows I'm with you."

I laughed at the matter-of-factness of Guelmis's reply, at the simplicity and sense of security that existed in Cuba. I thought about life in the U.S. and an article I'd read recently, which said that most children who lived too close to school to receive bus service now got rides with their parents instead of walking. Their parents were afraid that, somewhere along their children's three-block walk to school, they might be kidnapped.

I told Guelmis I had plans for the evening.

"Oh," she said, in a serious, surprisingly adult voice. "Are you going on a date?"

"Yeah, kind of," I said. I had plans to meet Alfredo for a concert at the symphony.

"Well, be careful," Guelmis said smiling coyly. "*Los cubanos son candela.*"

Candela. Another *cubanismo* I had learned from Alfredo. Depending upon its context, *candela* could mean any number of things—a dilemma, a difficult situation, danger. Loosely translated, the English equivalent of Guelmis's words of warning was "Cuban men are trouble."

6

*Los Cubanos
Son Candela*

On my way to meet up with Alfredo, I passed an older man selling *Granma*, the government newspaper of Cuba. It was named after the yacht Fidel used in 1956 for his second failed attempt to overthrow Batista. Rumor had it that the paper was no more successful than the turbulent sea voyage from Mexico City, where Fidel had been living in exile. The yacht was crammed to capacity with eighty-two inexperienced sailors with, as Tad Szulc quotes Che Guevara in the book *Fidel: A Critical Portrait*, "anguish reflected in their faces, grabbing their stomachs; some with their heads inside buckets . . . their clothes filthy from vomit."

Perhaps it was fitting then that today when people spoke about *Granma*, the newspaper, they said it worked best as toilet paper.

By nine every morning, a mere forty-five minutes after the *Granma* was delivered to the newsstands, the thin tabloids were all gone. Cuba had neither the paper nor the printing presses to produce more, and because of this, the government limited everyone to just one paper.

Before the *Granma* even arrived, Cubans started lining up, asking each other, "*¿El último?*" For me, asking who was last in line seemed like an obvious, almost ridiculous question. But in Cuba, where lines were more plentiful than whatever allegedly resided at the end of them—food, concert tickets, a newspaper—the concept of queuing up had been reshaped to allow people to carry on their daily activities while waiting in line. Of course, it was always a risk to go visit a friend down the street after asking for *el último,* but in theory, as long as you returned before your turn came, your space was good. Someone else might come asking for *el último* in your absence, but they'd quickly be told that *el último* had stepped away for a moment. So they would stand patiently behind *el penúltimo*, graciously stepping back to make space for you when you returned and identified yourself.

The majority of people waiting in line most mornings seemed to be older, retired Cubans who used the newspaper's scarcity to their advantage. In a socialist world, they had somehow managed to cultivate capitalist market skills. They got around the one-paper-per-person rule by rushing off to the end of the line to start over again as soon as they received their first paper. This way they could get a handful before the supply was exhausted. Then these elderly entrepreneurs took to the streets for the remainder of the day, selling the coveted, albeit little-esteemed, papers for one peso—five times what they'd just purchased them for.

As I turned off 23rd Street into the residential Vedado neighborhood where Alfredo worked, the *Granma* vendors disappeared, as did the taxis and congestion of Havana's thoroughfare. The relative silence of Vedado's shady, tree-lined side streets reminded me of my late-night strolls back to Hotel El Bosque with Alfredo. Yet as much as I enjoyed walking with Alfredo, when he asked what time he should meet me at the hotel tonight, as it had become our routine to walk together to the symphony, I said I would just meet him there.

Lately I'd felt that I was always either with a group of foreigners or with Alfredo. I missed the sensation of solitude, the heightened awareness of my surroundings that I achieved when I walked alone through the streets of a foreign city.

I arrived at the symphony half an hour early and scanned the faces in the crowd, looking for Alfredo's telltale dreadlocks. Rey Guerra, a popular Cuban guitarist, was playing tonight, and the ticket line extended from the box office inside the symphony out onto the sidewalk.

I had never been to the symphony in the U.S., where the high cost of tickets and the formal black attire of its attendees had scared me off, but I felt perfectly at home at the symphony in Cuba. While tourism was claiming Cuba's salsa clubs, raising the cover prices and changing the character of the clientele, the country's film and theater productions remained largely Cuban affairs. With symphony tickets costing only twenty-five cents, the shows were accessible to and attended by everyone, from bohemian jeans-clad university students to women in evening gowns and families with crying babies.

Alfredo received free tickets for every concert, so he had given me an open invitation to attend any show I wanted. On the phone the night before, he had sounded particularly excited about this performance.

"I have a surprise for you afterward," he said.

Now he called out to me from his lookout post atop the marble theater steps and off to the side of the crowd. Despite the heat, Alfredo was wearing a tweed blazer. Its sleeves were too wide for his slender figure and slid down to his elbow as he waved for me to come over. Up close, I could see the sweat dripping down his face, his neck, and onto the collar of his white button-down shirt. He gave me a salty kiss on the lips before we pushed past the crowds and entered the theater.

The air-conditioning turned my skin cold and clammy as we walked through the corridor leading to the elevator. Alfredo called out to his co-workers along the way, and the men responded with high fives as they passed. The women giggled or called out coyly, *"Hola, Alfredito."*

Although Alfredo was little—about five feet, six inches—and skinny, everyone in Cuba, regardless of their size, seemed to be referred to in the diminutive form of *"–ito."* Alfredo's towering friend, Abilio, whom he sometimes simply called El Grande, was also nicknamed Mamito. Once I asked Mamito the meaning of his name, but I couldn't make out his answer. I repeatedly tried to have conversations with Alfredo's coworkers, but often they spoke too fast, and other times they just seemed nervous around me, unsure of how to address me or of what to say. Once, one of them asked if I spoke Spanish, and I felt offended, wondering what type of relationship they imagined I had with Alfredo, who didn't speak English. Sometimes I wondered whether the women were giggling at me when we walked by or if there was some joke between Alfredo and his coworkers that I just didn't get. Or maybe our being together—yet another Cuban–American couple in this enemy's land, where Americans were forbidden to travel—was simply an amusing spectacle in and of itself.

Tonight, as Alfredo and I stepped onto the elevator, a bleached-blond usher gave the requisite giggle and then winked at Alfredo.

"Why did she do that?" I asked.

"Because she's happy that I have a girlfriend," he said, wrapping his arms around me as the elevator doors closed. During our brief rise to the second-floor theater, I caught a glimpse of us in the elevator's mirrored walls. Did we look comical together? We were both thin but otherwise we encompassed two different physical worlds. There was my long, narrow Jewish nose and Alfredo's short, wider one, slightly flared at the nostrils like Che Guevara's. I was pale, even in the most tropical of climates, and Alfredo's skin was a deep, rich black. My eyebrows were thick, and his were pencil-thin. My sometimes wavy brown hair looked blond and straight compared with Alfredo's kinky black hair, with its curls pushed up in untamed patches beneath his swirled dreadlocks. Alfredo saw me staring into the mirror, and he smiled out at my reflection, leaning his head in closer, as if we were posing for a photo.

Alfredo had to work during the concert, so after showing me to my seat, he kissed me goodbye and disappeared behind the curtain. Soon, though, I heard a tapping off to stage right. I looked up, and there was Alfredo, smiling and waving at me from behind the sound box. I smiled back, but every time I glanced in that direction, Alfredo was staring out at me, beaming. It made me feel a little self-conscious, so eventually I stopped looking. When the curtains opened and Rey Guerra stepped onto the stage, I let myself slouch back into my chair, take in the music, and daydream about the coming weeks.

My friend Amy and I had planned to sign up for a two-week session of Spanish classes at the University of Havana and then to spend the final two weeks of March traveling down to eastern Cuba, heading home to the U.S. in early April. I was ready to leave Havana. I wanted to see what life was like outside the capital—and so did most of the Cuban friends I'd made. Few had had the opportunity to leave the city, and several of them readily invited themselves to join Amy and me on our trip.

Liudmila wanted to visit the Che Guevara Memorial in Santa Clara, where the martyr's remains had been transplanted from his deathbed in Bolivia. Alfredo wanted to see Santiago, Cuba's second-largest city, where the Sierra Maestra hid the rebels during the Revolution.

I didn't really want to travel in a group, and neither did Amy. Additionally, we were low on funds, and getting money in Cuba as an American was no easy task. American credit cards and traveler's checks didn't work. The few ATMs inside the big tourist hotels didn't draw on American banks. And only a handful of wire services in the U.S. were authorized to send money to Cuba. The surest, quickest, and often cheapest way to receive money was through a personal courier. If Liudmila and Alfredo came along, we would need to pay for everything, since a Cuban salary covered only the most basic of items, if that.

The situation created a strange dynamic between me and my Cuban friends. Basically, I paid for whatever we did, while the Cubans averted their eyes, never saying "Thank you" afterward. Whenever I tried to thank Cubans for anything, they would brush off my gratitude and say, *"No hay de nada, mi amor."* It's nothing, my love. In Cuba, it was rude to thank someone, thus implying that her kindness was out of the ordinary.

Here, pride took precedence over both manners and machismo in a country that—despite all its progressive post-Revolution women's-lib talk— was still steeped in the tradition of the men paying for everything.

Amy and I had discussed just inviting Alfredo and splitting his accommodations, food, and transportation costs between the two of us. It would only run us about an extra one hundred and fifty dollars each, but my hesitancy to invite Alfredo was less about money than about my desire to see Cuba as a woman traveler, not always attached to a Cuban man.

Tonight, though, I worried that while I bumbled around, trying to come up with a way to tactfully explain why I only wanted to travel with Amy, maybe Alfredo had already requested his vacation. Maybe this was why he was so excited. Maybe this was the surprise he had for me after the concert.

As soon as the theater lights came on, Alfredo ran over to me. He took my hand and said, "I want to invite you to a drink in the bar upstairs. We got paid today."

I felt relieved to discover that the surprise was only this, and I relaxed as we rode up another elevator, which we shared with a few more smirking, giggling female coworkers of Alfredo's.

At the Opus Bar, I sat at a table near a window overlooking the city while Alfredo rushed off to order drinks. He returned a few minutes later with two mojitos—the Cuban national drink, made of rum, tonic water, lime, sugar, and the all-important *hierba buena,* or peppermint leaf, a delicacy that was impossible to encounter anywhere in the country outside of a bar.

"Do you like your mojito?" Alfredo asked as proudly as if he'd mixed it himself.

"Muy rico," I told him and took a long swig from my straw to refrain from saying "Thank you."

"So now," he said, putting his hands on the table, one on either side of his mojito, "I want to tell you my surprise."

"This isn't it?"

"No, well, yes it's part of it," he said smiling. "But what I really want to tell you is that I love you. I love you very much. I'm going to say it in English and Spanish. *Te amo.* I love you."

Startled by this sudden declaration, I sucked up a strong strawful of mojito.

"I started to fall in love with you that first night," Alfredo said. "And each day I've felt something more. I think you are a wonderful woman. I've never met anyone like you, and I want to be with you forever and . . ."

I held up my hand, interrupting Alfredo.

"This is very flattering," I said, searching for the right words. "But you know I'm going home in April, and I just don't feel as strongly about you right now."

"That's okay," Alfredo said, unfazed. "One person usually feels stronger at first. Things will change. *Tú verás."* He continued, "Lea, there's so much I want to say to you. I want to tell you how I love your eyes and the way your tongue pokes out between your teeth when you smile. I want to kiss every part of you down to your *dedo gordo."* "Fat toe" was what Cubans called the big toe, and usually this expression made me laugh, but tonight it just added to my irritation at not being able to get through to Alfredo. I cast him a skeptical glance.

"I know, I know," he said, and for a moment, I felt a flicker of hope. "I haven't seen your *dedo gordo* yet," he continued, "but I'm sure it's beautiful."

"Listen, I have to go back to the hotel now to call my parents," I said, standing up.

"I'll walk you back."

"No, I think I need to go alone."

"You shouldn't walk alone through the streets."

"I'll catch a taxi."

"Let me help you."

Now we were walking down the staircase, with me a few steps ahead of Alfredo. "When can we meet tomorrow?" he asked when we reached the lobby. He put his hand in his back pocket. "Let me get my schedule."

The giggling bleached-blond usher approached us. Maybe she could help, I thought. Maybe she could grab Alfredo's hand to hold him in place and save him from embarrassing himself any further, allowing me a quick getaway. But no such luck. Everyone, it seemed, was crazy tonight.

Instead of setting Alfredo straight, the usher called out to me, "Alfredo's a good boy. *Cásate con él.*" Marry him.

7

Who We Are
Without Names

At 9:00 every night, the sky over Havana explodes. A cannon erupts and then a procession of soldiers, dressed in royal red military garb, come marching in, their knees jutting up at right angles. They stand at attention on the rooftop of La Cabaña, a looming stone citadel built in the 1700s to protect Havana after an invasion by the English.

This reenactment of the nightly blast that signaled the closing of the city gates starts promptly at nine and is over by a quarter after, but its impact lingers as the boom of *el cañonazo* echoes throughout Havana.

Tonight I heard the explosion all the way from the Teatro Nacional, a good five miles away. I was waiting here for Alfredo and, as the cannon went off, I recalled how we had come here on one of our first dates.

Tonight's cannon blast, on the evening following Alfredo's overwrought confession of love, seemed less auspicious, a somehow darker and more foreboding pretext to a less enchanted evening, the thought of which had made me feel nauseous all day.

When I'd woken this morning, I had remembered, with a bittersweet sense of relief, that when Alfredo had asked about meeting up the next day, I'd given myself an out. Instead of just setting a place and time as we usually did, I said that I would call him.

I put off calling him for as long as possible. I wanted to be alone with my thoughts, so I skipped class and caught a bus to Habana Vieja to see the famed Revolutionary Museum, the former Presidential Palace of Batista, which now housed the original *Granma* yacht. The 1956 voyage from Mexico to Cuba was a failure, which left Fidel and his few surviving *compañeros* hiding out in a sugarcane field for days on end before retreating into the nearby Sierra Maestra for shelter. But it was also here, in these mountains, where the rebels found a home for their revolution, a place from which they could organize and plot for the next twenty-five months until they emerged from the shadows, worn out but triumphant on the dawn of January 1, 1959.

Yet the history of the Revolutionary Museum did not end here, nor did it begin with the Revolution's first battle, in 1953. Rather, the museum used the broadest meaning possible of the word "revolution," essentially defining it as Fidel's lifespan. There was a photo of Carlos Manuel de Céspedes, the namesake son of the founder of the first War of Independence but a rightwing politician nonetheless and one who looked strikingly like Hitler. There were pieces of Che Guevara's hair, scraps of his socks, and a blood-spotted sheet salvaged from his deathbed in Bolivia, where he was murdered by CIA operatives.

I wandered into the Special Period Salon, which, perhaps as a tribute to the difficult times that plagued Cuba after the collapse of the Soviet Union, was nearly devoid of light. Whenever someone entered the darkened room, they stirred up a cloud of dust, casting a murky haze over the exhibit. On a back wall, I squinted to make out the words on a plaque entitled "The Effects of the Collapse of the Soviet Union." Like so many of the other museum pieces, the English translations soon dropped off until there were no more, as if the translator had become frustrated with her work and abandoned the project midway.

The display was a list that read like an inventory of loss, the obituary of a country. In the early 1990s, Russia stopped subsidizing Cuba's sugar crop, which left the country with massive amounts of surplus sugar. Then Russia cut off its fuel and oil shipments, and Cuba's transportation system nearly came to a standstill. Gas was rationed for private cars, and it was not an uncommon sight to see buses come to a dead stop in the middle of the street. Then the raw materials needed to run Cuba's social programs stopped arriving.

It was difficult to believe that the loss of just one trade partner could nearly bring about the collapse of a country, but I knew that ever since the U.S. had enacted its embargo against Cuba, it had also been attempting to prevent other countries from trading with the island, so smaller-scale trade losses were constantly occurring.

In 1974, when flooding caused the worst famine in Bangladesh's history, the U.S. refused to aid the struggling Asian country because it had been trading with Cuba. Although Bangladesh quickly cut off its trade with Cuba, it was not soon enough, and one hundred thousand Bangladeshis died as a result.

More recently, the 1992 passage of the Torricelli Act legislated that any country with a ship that sailed to Cuba to trade could not use the same vessel to trade in the U.S.

Next to the Special Period Salon was the Corner of Cretins, which played satirical homage to those who would support such legislation. Life-size paintings of Fulgencio Batista, Ronald Reagan, and George Bush lined the cretin wall. The dedication beneath Batista read THANKS, CRETIN, FOR HELPING US MAKE THIS REVOLUTION. Reagan got THANKS, CRETIN, FOR HELPING US STRENGTHEN OUR REVOLUTION, and Bush's caption read THANKS, CRETIN, FOR HELPING US CONSOLIDATE OUR REVOLUTION.

I laughed at the display, but I wondered how true its claims really were. Sure, Cuba had survived forty-one years of this economic terrorism, its hospitals and schools intact despite the lack of medicine and books. And, true, this sort of adversity did seem to unite the country in a very socialist, we're-all-in-this-together sort of way. But I also saw that many people were getting tired of the struggle of daily Cuban life.

Unlike the U.S.'s many international wars, which could devastate the other country in a matter of months, the embargo was like an incurable virus, slowly eating away at Cuba's core, gradually starving its population so that they grew crazy with hunger. Over time, in the way of the truly desperate, they began to lose context, to think only of the moment, and to seek some-one close by to blame.

I left the Revolutionary Museum feeling no more cheerful than I had when I'd entered. I walked over to a pay phone outside the museum, figuring this was as good a time as any to call Alfredo.

After we got through the usual small talk of how we'd spent our days, Alfredo said, "Well, tell me where you are and I'll come meet you."

"No, I can't meet you this afternoon," I said. "I need to spend some time alone."

"Okay, I understand," he said. "All the space you want, it's yours. What about tomorrow?"

"No, not then either."

"And the next day?" he asked.

"I don't think this is right," I said. "I just think this relationship is too se-rious for me right now."

"No me digas," he said. Don't say that. *"Lea, no me digas eso."*

A jittery feeling rippled through my stomach. "I'm sorry, but I can't say another thing right now," I said.

"I don't understand," Alfredo said. "I don't know what happened. Can we at least meet up in person and you can explain?"

His voice sounded weak now, and I thought about how, as much as I didn't want to discuss this anymore and risk further hurting Alfredo's feel-ings, I did owe him more than a telephone dismissal.

"Okay," I said. "When?"

"Anytime. You tell me."

"We can meet tonight. Maybe around nine, but I don't know where."

"Teatro Nacional," he said. "It's near my house. I'll be waiting for you."

Not too long after *el cañonazo* exploded, Alfredo emerged from the dark, walking toward me from the other side of the theater. He walked with his hands clasped behind his back. He acknowledged my presence with a nod but averted his eyes and stared at the ground until he reached me. Up close I could see that his eyes were red and watery. He handed me a book, which he had been guarding behind his back. I handed him a piece of paper, smudgy and wilted from the night air and the humidity of my hands.

After our phone conversation, I had rushed back to the hotel to write down the things I wanted to tell Alfredo. Then I passed by Liudmila's nursery to get some grammatical help.

When she finished reading my letter, Liudmila patted my hand and said, "It's good; honest but not unkind."

I'd written that I had enjoyed my time with Alfredo and that getting to know him had been a highlight of my stay in Cuba, but that I felt there was an inequality that I couldn't get beyond in our relationship.

"I remember that first night when you said you were falling in love with me," I wrote. "But I've never felt like that with you, and I've always felt that you were waiting for the moment when that would change. It's not fair to either of us. You should be with someone who feels as passionately for you as you do for her. For me, this has all been too fast."

While Alfredo sat and read my letter, I looked at the book he had handed me with the disclaimer, "It's a little tattered, but I think it will help you a lot with your Spanish."

The book was as yellowed and worn as parchment. The spine had two layers of masking tape to hold it in place. A black-and-white photo of a hand with a pencil lay just above a deep diagonal crease in the cover. The title was *Lo Esencial de la Ortografía.* It was a high-school grammar book that Alfredo had told me about before. I opened it and saw the copyright date of 1977, a decade before Alfredo had entered high school. The pages were water-stained with blotches in varying shades of brown, and the bottom part of the first page had been ripped off.

On the portion of the second page that showed through, Alfredo had written, "This book, with all of my love, I give to my great friend Lea for having known how to win all of my affection and all of my heart."

As Alfredo read my letter, he began to sniffle, and then long, silent tears rolled down his cheeks. He made no attempt to wipe them away, and when I tried to comfort him by putting my arm around him, he sat there limply.

"I can accept that you don't love me yet," he said. "I know that you are different from other women. I know you didn't come here looking for a boy-friend, but just because I love you, why does that mean we can't be together?"

"Because," I said, trying to word my explanation as tactfully as possible, "I don't know if what I feel for you will become love."

"But why do we have to live so much in the future now?" Alfredo asked. "Why do you Americans always think like that? I'm happy being with you, and you're happy with me too, right?"

Alfredo looked at me with an expression of panic, as if afraid he'd spo-ken too soon.

"I am happy with you," I said, "except when you're pontificating about love. It makes me nervous."

I remembered that during an earlier conversation, Alfredo had told me that men in Cuba didn't have girl friends, only girlfriends. Friendship with someone of the opposite sex was a foreign concept. But that was what I wanted. Or even something more, but without declarations of everlasting love and "Oh-my-God" knee-dropping rituals.

"I can change," Alfredo said. "I'll stop talking so much about love. I don't even have to introduce you as my girlfriend anymore if it makes you uncomfortable. And we can be . . . how did you write it here? Who we are without names."

"Okay," I said, touched by the earnest hopefulness in Alfredo's eyes. "If you really are clear on how I feel, I'd still like to hang out, to be friends."

"¿Amigos?" he asked, confused. "¿Amigos? What does that mean? Can I ever kiss you again?"

I smiled. "I think so," I said. "I think friends can kiss."

Alfredo wiped away his tears and smiled back at me. He held a shaky hand out in front of him. "Look at me. I'm trembling," he said, and then the faintest hint of a smile began forming on the edge of his lips. "Look what you've done to me."

"Lo siento," I said. I'm sorry.

Alfredo withdrew his hand and shook his head as though my apology wasn't necessary.

"So, do you want to come meet my grandparents now?" he asked. "They're really close by."

It seemed an odd time to bring me home to meet the family.

"Maybe you can interview my grandmother," Alfredo suggested. "I told her how you want to interview women here. I told her you're a writer."

I smiled, and we walked behind the theater and through the streets, which were dark but alive with music and conversation.

"This is the Nuevo Vedado neighborhood," Alfredo announced when we arrived at a nondescript cinderblock complex.

The door of his grandparents' apartment had a We Believe in the Revolution sticker. I looked at Alfredo with surprise. With all of his complaining about Fidel, I never would have imagined that he came from a *fidelista* family.

"Oh, they're old," Alfredo said before I could even ask. "Every old person supports Fidel."

"Why?" I asked as he tapped the front door with the palm of his hand, and the door opened into his grandparents' living room. It had a color TV and was decorated with earth-colored tile and a white couch with a simple brown throw shawl lying on one of the pillows.

"Because they say things were worse before. *Imagínate eso.*" Imagine that.

I followed Alfredo through a sliding-glass door in the dining room and onto a back patio, where chickens scurried beneath banana palms and almond trees. Alfredo's grandparents—a tall, dark black man and a shorter woman with milky brown skin, her hair tied back in a yellow kerchief—stood next to a rusted shell of a car.

Alfredo introduced me, and told me his grandfather repaired cars.

"I don't do anything mechanical," his grandfather said. "I just fix up the outsides. I make them look good, but then to get them running . . . well, that's another story."

"Maybe Lea can ask grandma some questions." Alfredo said.

"Oh, of course," his grandmother said. "Let me make you some guava juice."

We went back into the house, and while Alfredo's grandmother chopped and blended the pink-bellied fruit, I asked her about her life.

"I was born in the countryside, in Camagüey," she said. "My parents separated before I was born, and my mother died before I was two, so I lived with my grandmother. She worked as a maid for a doctor. We lived in his house, and I started working there as a maid when I was just eight. My ten-year-old sister worked there too. We only got paid every other month. When I was fourteen, I met my boyfriend, and I left with him to come to Havana. Then I had a daughter, Alfredo's mother, and then I got a job as a cook. I always just lived in rooms in houses, but then the Revolution came, and I helped as much as I could. I volunteered to help the poor, and when Fidel asked what I wanted, I wrote that I wanted a house."

I had heard about this—that after the Revolution, those who volunteered to work for the new social programs were asked to write down a dream of theirs, be it to travel or to own a car or a house.

"So the Revolution gave me this house," Alfredo's grandmother continued. "And most people own their own houses now. They pay rent until it equals the price of their house, and then it's theirs."

"What did the Revolution do for you as a woman?" I asked.

"The Revolution listened to women's needs. It gave us medicine. Sometimes now I have aches in my bones, but I've never had to pay for my medicine. When Batista was president, blacks had no rights, and the *campesinos* didn't have any electricity in the countryside. Everything I have is thanks to her—*la Revolución*. Before, there was everything," she said, "but it was only for the rich."

I nodded but remained silent, waiting expectantly for Alfredo to interrupt and point out the class disparities in today's Cuba as he always did with me when I got caught up in Revolutionary righteousness. But tonight Alfredo just stared straight ahead at the TV. *El Rey del Ganado,* a Brazilian *telenovela* dubbed into Spanish, was playing, and I doubted that Alfredo was really caught up in its interminable story of romance and deceit, its plot the same every evening. Still, he didn't speak, and neither did his grandmother. She just folded her hands neatly in her lap and smiled at her story. Soon the *telenovela* ended, and Alfredo looked up and asked if I was ready to leave.

After we said our goodbyes to his family, we set off on our long, familiar trek back to Hotel El Bosque.

"Was the *telenovela* good?" I asked Alfredo.

"I wasn't really paying attention," he said. "It's just a way of zoning out when my grandmother gets started talking about the Revolution. It's just a space for me to think about other things."

"What were you thinking about tonight?"

"Us," Alfredo said smiling. "I was thinking about how that letter made me sad, but how it's good that you gave it to me, because now I know what you want, what you're looking for. Because of your writing, I understand you better. When are you going to write about me?"

"About you?"

"Yes, a story about this Cuban boy you met who fell in love too quickly."

I laughed and wrapped my arm around Alfredo's back, pulling him in close as we walked through the hot Havana night. The sun was long gone, but its warmth lingered in pockets of humidity that swirled around us like soft, plump raindrops, like lingering reminders of a recent storm narrowly avoided.

8

Una Vida Plastica

The next morning, I left the maid a tip beside the white bath towels she always twisted into two kissing swans' necks, arched so that the negative space between them formed a heart. I pulled a pair of stiff underwear and a few soap-streaked bras off the window ledge where I hung them to dry each night after a scrubbing in my bathroom sink. I stared out the window at the spot on the sidewalk where Alfredo and I always kissed goodnight, and I watched as my program's tour bus pulled away, heading off to the airport without me.

I put on my backpack, which was so full it extended above my head like someone on piggyback, and I walked down the three flights of stairs to the lobby, where Amy was waiting for me with her own stuffed backpack. Outside, we waved down a taxi, and Amy handed the driver a slip of paper with the address to our new home in Centro Habana. We had met two Americans who had stayed at this *casa particular,* or private house authorized to rent rooms to foreigners, and they'd told us it was one of the nicest places in Havana.

Two weeks earlier, when I first told Alfredo that I was going to stay for another month, he invited me to live with his family.

"It'll be free," he said. "And there's plenty of space. I even have my own bedroom."

I searched Alfredo's face for a clue, a lusty twinkle in his eye or a sensual smile that would allude to something more, revealing the true meaning behind his generous yet premature invitation, given that we'd never even spent the night together. But Alfredo smiled an ordinary, sincere smile as he awaited my answer, no undercurrents or hidden motives apparent in his offer. Was this because he truly had nothing else in mind or was it because, in a country where taboos revolved more around political indiscretions than sexual ones, sex was more casual and less scandalous than it was in the U.S.?

Either way, I still didn't want to live with Alfredo and his family. I wanted my own space, and his proposal reminded me a little too much of the shotgun relationships of the Hotel El Bosque poolside. So I thanked him and then quickly declined, mentioning something about independence and having already made plans to live with Amy.

"Okay, no problem," Alfredo said, averting my eyes, an edge of defensiveness in his voice. "I just thought it might make things easier for you."

As the taxi wove its way through the congestion of Centro Habana, Havana's poorest neighborhood before the Revolution, people scattered in all directions. Unlike the quiet, tidy streets that surrounded Hotel El Bosque in the Miramar neighborhood, Centro Habana was a blur of noise and chaos and filth. The houses were crowded together like the brownstones of New York City, and old women wearing polka-dotted cotton nightgowns stood on their balconies, dumping brown wastewater into the streets. Children played baseball using splintered scraps of plywood, salvaged from collapsed doorways, as bats. Walnut-sized chunks of white and pastel cement submerged the sidewalk in front of one crumbled house, whose still-standing frame looked like it might come down with the next gust of wind.

Centro Habana reminded me of the opening line to John Steinbeck's

Cannery Row minus the whorehouses and the industry. Even here, in the center of Havana, there were no stores and nothing that vaguely resembled an office. Some buildings still had the names of movie theaters or shops hanging above them, but the doors were nailed shut.

I wondered why the Americans had so highly recommended this place we were moving to. But then the taxi deposited us in front of a weathered cement apartment on Animas Street, and when Amy jumped out to ring the bell, which was embedded in a tall wood-panel French door, I was once again reminded of how little in Cuba is as it appears on the surface.

The second Amy removed her finger from the bell and before she even had a chance to step back from the door, it swung open, revealing a tall, narrow staircase of at least twenty polished white marble steps. A small, olive-skinned woman in a red sundress stood at the top, holding a rope, which extended downward along the wall and, at its tail end, was tied to the door to facilitate its opening from above. We climbed the staircase, which opened into a huge living room with an ornate glass chandelier and a mosaic of pink and green floor tiles. A high ceiling kept everything cool despite the sweltering, stagnant air outside. There was more furniture in here than I'd seen combined in all the houses I'd visited in Cuba. There were two glass coffee tables and two rocking chairs, three couches with lace doilies on the arm rests, two armchairs, a mahogany shelf set with a VCR, a stereo, and a large television, which was playing *A Clockwork Orange*. A small ceramic lion and a figurine of the Eiffel Tower rested atop the entertainment system.

On a balcony overlooking Animas Street, an elderly white-haired woman stood beaming at Amy and me. I smiled, and she waved her arms excitedly in front of her. She took a hesitant step forward before the other woman rushed over to her, calling out, "*Mimi, espera.*" The younger woman wrapped her arms around the older one and walked her to one of the armchairs, bending down delicately to deposit her into her seat.

"My mother gets excited when we have visitors," she announced with a sigh when she'd completed the task, taking a step back the way a sculptor might do to get some perspective on her work in progress. "She's eighty-nine, too old to be walking by herself," she continued. "But still, she always tries. *Pobrecita.*"

"*Mimi,* these girls are going to be staying upstairs for a few weeks." The woman tapped my shoulder. "What are your names?"

We introduced ourselves, and the woman told us her name was Dinora.

"You can just call her Abuela," grandmother, Dinora said as she motioned to her mother, who quickly waved us over to her.

"*Un beso,*" a kiss, she demanded, jutting her chin out in my direction. The skin on her cheek was soft and freckled with age spots.

When Amy approached to offer her kiss, Abuela became more animated and announced, "*¡Mira que gorda está ella!*" Look at how fat she is!

Amy stepped back for a moment, looking as if someone had just slapped her face. Amy was tall and big-boned, with wide swimmers' shoulders, but she was also overweight. I knew, from living in other Latin American countries, that *gorda* was not necessarily an insult. Excess weight on women was often considered a sign of strength and feminine, full-figured beauty, but still, I'd never heard someone so bluntly declare it. I felt sorry for Amy, but before I could say anything, Abuela turned the tables.

"You need to give her some of your weight," she said, laughing as she pointed at me. "She's like a stick."

I laughed too, and so did Dinora. And so did Amy. And then Abuela settled down in front of *A Clockwork Orange* while Dinora gave us a tour of the house.

"This is my daughter Nitza's bedroom," Dinora said as she opened a door behind the living room, revealing a tiny space filled to capacity. The bed was covered with clothing—black evening gowns and flowered sundresses— and a half-open closet revealed a shoe collection that could have rivaled that of Imelda Marcos. A rainbow of nail polishes were scattered beneath a large mirror in the front of the room.

"We need to chop down one of these walls and make the room bigger," Dinora said. "There's just no space for Nitza to put anything away. *Pobrecita.* Usually it's not this messy, but she was in a rush to leave this morning. She had to go to Argentina for a week. She's a very bright girl—only twenty-four and already she's a doctor and speaks five languages."

"What's she doing in Argentina?" I asked, remembering what Alfredo had told me earlier about how difficult it was for Cubans to travel.

"Oh, well," Dinora said, shutting the bedroom door. "She's working as a flight attendant at the moment. My husband works for the airlines, too, as an engineer, so that's nice for Nitza."

I thought this seemed like a strange explanation, but I also sensed, from the rushed manner in which Dinora continued down the hall, that she wasn't planning to elaborate now.

We walked through a tall set of French doors, like those leading to the balcony, and into a spacious but spartan bedroom with a double bed and a dresser, but little else.

"This is where I and my husband, Luis, sleep," Dinora said. "It needs remodeling too. My dream in life has always been to have a library, but look, here I am a university professor, and we can't even afford a bookshelf."

"What do you teach?" Amy asked.

"Russian," Dinora said, pausing. "But I'm on a little sabbatical now. I'm taking some time off to take care of my mother. If I didn't do it, no one else would."

I looked back through the open bedroom door and into the living room, where Abuela sat, still in front of the TV but now accompanied by an older black woman.

"Oh, that's her friend Rosa. They met years ago in the *círculo de abuelos*," Dinora said. *Círculos de abuelos*, formed after the Revolution, encourage community and exercise in the country's elderly population. It wasn't an uncommon sight in the mornings, before the afternoon heat set in, to see groups of older people doing jumping jacks in the parks of Havana, their weathered limbs flailing about in front of a bust of José Martí.

"Fortunately, Rosa comes over every day to visit," Dinora said, lowering her voice. "I sometimes think I might go crazy otherwise, especially when Luis and Nitza are at work and it's just me and Abuela alone all day. I need some fresh air, some young energy around the house, so I'm glad to have you two here."

I smiled. Within a matter of minutes, Dinora had revealed so much, while also bringing up so many new questions, that I didn't know how to respond. But Dinora didn't seem overly concerned with my silence. She continued on with the tour, pushing open a third set of French doors leading into a room that was nearly identical to the one we'd just left.

"This is Abuela's room," Dinora said. Here, atop the dresser, was a framed photograph of a heavily made-up girl who also adorned the living room wall. "That's Nitza," Dinora said proudly.

The final room in this long corridor was the dining room. An oval-shaped table took up most of the space, and an avocado green refrigerator sat in the corner next to a grocery store–sized icebox. We walked into the kitchen, where the contents of a pressure cooker bubbled and popped on the stove, and then we turned into an open-air hallway, narrowed by a wall separating the house from the next-door neighbors' outdoor patio. We ducked beneath a clothesline as Dinora told us, under her breath, that the neighbors were religious and sometimes sacrificed animals. Then once more we were inside, back to the living room, where Abuela was craning her neck to get another look at us.

"I'm going to take the girls upstairs now to show them their rooms," Dinora said. "So there's no need breaking your neck trying to listen in on the conversation."

Abuela paid no attention and continued to stare at us as we strapped on our packs and ascended another steep staircase.

"She's never seen the upstairs," Dinora said. "We built it a year ago, but even then she was having problems walking. Still, though, she always wants to be included. She reminds me of a giraffe, stretching her neck to see where I am, what I'm doing. She's a very nosy person, and she can be very bossy too. You know, I only had one child because she told me not to have any more. I was the good daughter, and I always listened to her."

"Do you have a lot of siblings?" I asked.

"Two sisters and two brothers, but one sister's in Miami. The other comes over with her husband to visit every few days, and one of my brothers is good, but the other, he just comes over and falls asleep in the rocking chair when it's his shift to keep Abuela company." Dinora made a clucking sound with her tongue and shook her head disparagingly. "I'm the youngest, but ironically I'm the one in charge now."

Dinora showed us our bedroom—a glossy white tile floor and crisp, creased white bedsheets, two closet sets with some shelves for books, and even an air conditioner against the wall. Everything was so tidy and clean that I almost forgot about the disorder and dirt outside.

There was one other bedroom, occupied by an American who was studying organic agriculture, and there was the bathroom and a small kitchen and dining room, where sunlight poured in through the open window. One more flight of steps led to the rooftop, where a bedsheet and several tank tops flapped in the slight breeze. Salsa and rock and bolero music emanated from every crevice of the city. Old men stood on the rooftops looking out at the sparkling blue sea, and I took in the panoramic view of Havana, looking west to the Roman columns at the entrance to the University of Havana and then north to the omnipresent line in front of Coppelia ice cream parlor. I turned clockwise toward the skyscraper of Hospital Hermanos Ameijeiras. Then at the conclusion of my 360-degree spin, I came across a bright scribble of color in the cement-gray heart of Centro Habana. A few blocks from Dinora's house, the buildings were painted in jigsaw-puzzle pieces of red and blue, yellow and white, and green and black, as if a painter had tested out her palette on the side of a building.

"What's that?" I asked Dinora.

"Callejón de Hamel. It's an alley dedicated to the Afro-Cuban religion from Africa. In the 16th century, Cuba imported slaves from Africa, and they brought their religion with them."

From conversations with Alfredo, I'd learned about the Afro-Cuban religion, a mix of Cathólicism and the Lucumí religion of Africa's Yoruba people. I knew that Santería, as the Afro-Cuban religion was often referred to, was now practiced by many Cubans, both of Spanish and of African descent. But from what I'd seen, the demographics of Santería followers were similar to those of the Revolution's supporters—it was the older generations that were the true believers. Alfredo's mother and grandmother were religious and celebrated an extra birthday each year on the date that they'd been assigned a patron saint. In order to "make their saints," as people said in Cuba, Santería disciples, or *yabos,* had to undergo a yearlong purification ritual. This involved three months spent eating from a mat on the floor and using the same plate each meal so that it wouldn't be contaminated by anyone else. Among the many other regulations imposed upon *yabos* was a rule against looking at themselves in a mirror or cutting their hair for a year. *Yabos* could not venture outside between dusk and dawn, in case something dangerous was lurking in the darkened air. They could not play dominoes with their friends or partake in other social gatherings for fear that they might be tainted by the impurity of those who weren't making their saints. *Yabos* could wear only white clothes, but prior to 1992, when being religious was illegal in Cuba, people were afraid to wear their white outfits outside, so they waited until they returned home from work. Then, in the relative safety of their houses, they hid out in their nurselike attire.

Alfredo went to the Santería birthday celebrations but felt little connection with the religion. Several years ago, to satisfy his grandmother, he'd had his cowry shells read, a Santería tradition not unlike the turning over of tarot cards. A *babalawo* tossed the shells and, once they settled on the table in front of him, told Alfredo his fortune.

"The *babalawo* said bad things would happen if I drank alcohol or wore dark colors or swam in the sea. But I like to drink rum, and I like to wear black sometimes, and I love going to the beach," Alfredo told me. "So that was the end of my religious experience."

"Are you religious?" Amy asked Dinora.

"No," Dinora said. "I was baptized as a Catholic, but I was eleven when the Revolution triumphed, and three years later I volunteered in Cuba's Literacy Campaign. I went to eastern Cuba to teach the campesinos how to read. And I don't know, something in me changed then. I saw their lives and how religious they were and how much poverty they lived in, and when I returned home, my faith was gone."

On the neighboring rooftop, two boys tossed cement pebbles onto the street, and Dinora paused for a moment to shake her head at them.

"It's dangerous," she called out. "You could hit someone, and from this height . . ." Instead of finishing her sentence, Dinora made a common Cuban gesture. She shook her wrist so that her index and middle finger slapped together, making a loud, clear snapping sound, a feat of hand acrobatics that signified the onset of something terrible. The boys nodded solemnly and took to staring out over the rooftops like the old men.

"Anyway," Dinora continued, "my mother was always religious, not political. Her family was wealthy and lived on a big estate, and she fell in love with one of their farm workers, who was a communist. This was during the time when communists were persecuted here, but my mother married him anyway. In bed, she forgot he was a communist, and he forgot she was religious."

Amy giggled, and I couldn't help laughing too.

"It's true," Dinora said. "That's how passion is; it's apolitical. You know what we say here in Cuba—the only thing that isn't rationed is sex."

Dinora smiled, pleased with her explanation. "Well, there you have it," she said. "Cuba in a nutshell. So, do you want a tour of the neighborhood now?"

Amy and I nodded, and Dinora spent the next hour guiding us through the main streets of Centro Habana. We walked through Callejón de Hamel, where the jigsaw paintings transformed into swirling trees and silhouettes of women, floating faces, suns, and poems about the trials of life. Lampposts, rather than serving any utilitarian purpose, also became part of the artscape, decorated with plants and yet another bust of José Martí.

The sun was unrelenting, so we stopped at a street pizza stand for some guava juice after Callejón de Hamel. Amy went to pay for the drinks, but Dinora quickly pulled out her change purse and insisted on treating us.

"When you have so little, it's a luxury to be able to give someone else something," she said.

I wondered how it was possible that Dinora could make such a statement. Was I not understanding her use of the word "little," or had she never entered another Cuban's house—for example, Liudmila's, where everyone slept in one room, and to treat someone to a bus ticket, which was a fraction of the cost of a guava juice, meant you would have to forfeit your own ride home that evening?

"To tell you the truth, I got you the guava juice partly for selfish reasons," Dinora said as she handed us our sugary pink drinks and we crowded under the tiny street pizza awning, relishing the pocket of shade.

"What do you mean?" I asked.

"Sometimes I feel embarrassed to be walking down the street with foreigners," Dinora said. "I don't want people to think that I'm hanging out with you because I want something, that I'm a *jinetera*. Now I buy you something, and they see we are friends."

Dinora took us into the neighborhood *chopping*, which smelled of Freon and blood. Unlike the *chopping* near Hotel El Bosque, this store sold not just dried goods but also dairy and meat. The meat sat in Styrofoam trays wrapped in plastic, just like in the U.S., but here the meat—like the mud-coated *boniatos*, or sweet potatoes, in the farmers markets—was displayed without disguise, delivered floating in its own red soup. In the checkout line, the cashiers used rags to wipe up the blood that seeped out onto the stainless-steel counter over which everyone's food passed. The juice boxes and package of pasta that Amy and I bought stuck to the plastic bag the cashier placed them in, and I made a mental note to wash my hands after unloading the groceries.

On our final stop, at a farmers market around the corner from Dinora's house, she said she needed to go home because her feet were hurting.

"All the shoes sold here are defective," she said, sighing and staring distastefully at her high-heeled espadrilles. *"Bueno, es Cuba."* She handed us a key to get back into the house and left us to explore the market on our own.

We bought a *zapote*, a wet, sugary fruit that tasted like a fig, and a *guanabana*, a green prickly fruit whose milky white flesh tasted like suntan lotion. Amy found a grapefruit so big that I didn't even recognize it at first, and a vendor wearing a Michigan baseball hat got so excited when Amy told him that Michigan was her home state that he gave us a free bagful of bok choy, okra, and green peppers.

"Next time you come back, I'll give you a letter for my niece who lives in Michigan," he said, not even discouraged when Amy told him she wouldn't be going home for another month.

I too had received several letters from both Cuban friends and strangers I'd met on the street—letters to relatives in Miami and Las Vegas and small midwestern towns I'd never heard of. Sometimes people told me what was in their letters—a plea for money or a query about a pair of glasses promised but never delivered. But most often the letters were given to me without a word as to their contents. They were simply placed in my hands with an apology for the missing envelope or stamp.

Walking through Havana my first week, I had noticed that there were no mailboxes in the streets and no mail slots in the doors.

"How do people get their mail?" I asked Alfredo.

"The mail person comes by and whistles outside your house if you have anything," he said. "And then you go out and get it."

"What if you're not home?"

"Oh, well, then maybe your neighbor will pick it up for you," Alfredo said, temporarily perplexed. "Yes, I think that's right, because I remember once, a few years ago, the woman next door to my mother got a letter from her son in Tampa, but she wasn't home, so my mother had to go get the letter."

I asked Alfredo if he'd ever received a letter.

"I don't think so," he said. "Why would someone take the time to write when they could just walk over to my house and tell me what they needed to?"

"But what about bills? Like for electricity or library fines?"

"Then someone comes to your door to collect the money," he said. "It's not like this in the U.S.?"

I tried to imagine what Alfredo would think if he could see the piles and piles of junk mail and advertisements and nonprofit solicitations for money that always awaited me when I returned from my travels. I wondered what he would think of the weekly missing children notices that arrived in my mailbox. Or the sweepstakes offers. Or the concept of coupons. It made my head spin to try to imagine Alfredo in my world.

And when I saw him my first evening at Dinora's, standing at the bottom of her massive marble staircase, he seemed oddly out of place there too. He looked off balance and small, shadowed and shrunken by the enormity of the house's entrance.

Amy and I had asked him and Liudmila to come over for dinner, excited to finally be able to invite them to do something that didn't involve money and didn't, consequently, make them feel embarrassed for their lack of it. I was excited to have them over to our house, where, unlike at the hotel, no one would look at them funny or tell them they had to wait downstairs. And Alfredo wouldn't have to put on his Argentine accent to ask for me over the phone.

But when I heard the doorbell ring and ran down the first flight of steps to greet Alfredo, I found Dinora and a small, shirtless man, olive-skinned like Dinora, staring down at Alfredo from the top of the steps.

"He says he's a friend of the girls'," Dinora told the man, a doubtful expression on her face.

"He's here for a dinner," I said as I walked over. In that moment I remembered that Alfredo had asked me to tell Dinora that he would be coming. It had seemed a strange request in a country where people just stopped by without invitation and without calling to make plans in advance. Nonetheless, I tried to rectify the situation now.

"There's one more friend who should be here soon," I said. "Is that okay?"

"Oh, of course," Dinora said. "This is your home now. Come on up," she said, motioning to Alfredo and stepping back so he could see me. The man stepped back too, but Alfredo looked at me uneasily until I came over to the top of the staircase and smiled at him. As he got closer, I could see sweat streaming down his face despite the dim coolness of Dinora's stairway.

"You just never know," Dinora said when Alfredo reached the top. "All sorts of people come knocking on our door. Once this drunk man came by, and when I opened the door, he tried to walk right in. Can you believe that? I had to chase him out."

I shook my head, mimicking Dinora's disbelief. I introduced Alfredo to the man who introduced himself as Luis, Dinora's husband. Luis shook Alfredo's hand and Dinora kissed Alfredo on the cheek. Everything seemed so normal that I had difficulty understanding what had just transpired.

Abuela twisted her neck from her rocking chair in the living room to get a glimpse of Alfredo.

"Okay, *Mimi,*" Dinora said. "You can meet the young man too."

"Is this your *marido?*" Abuela asked excitedly.

"My husband?" I repeated. "No, he's just a friend."

This time Abuela responded with such a whirlwind of words that I couldn't make out any of them.

"What's that?" I asked.

Alfredo laughed. "She said, 'I can sense that there's more going on here.'"

I laughed too, unsure of what else to do. It was becoming apparent to me that Cuba was a country of matchmakers, a place where love and commitment came with a speed that scared me and came with much less anxiety and reflection than I poured into such matters.

As I was considering this, the doorbell rang, and this time I went over to the top of the stairs to save Liudmila the family stare-down. When Liudmila saw me, she ascended the steps quickly, and once she reached the top, she removed her hand from behind her back, holding up a creamy white *mariposa*.

"For you and the *señorita* Amy," she said. She watched as I inhaled the flower's dizzying scent of vanilla and jasmine and added, "There's a very rich perfume that comes from the *mariposa*, but it's also very expensive. It's only sold in the dollar stores."

Dinora nodded sympathetically, the ice now broken as she leaned forward to kiss Liudmila's cheek in greeting. Liudmila smiled when I introduced her to Alfredo and, as we climbed upstairs behind him, she gave me the thumbs up sign.

Upstairs, Amy was cooking beans on the stovetop. We had planned to make *potaje,* a Cuban black-bean soup poured over white rice. It was one of the better dishes served at Hotel El Bosque. But after a full afternoon of sorting through the bulk black beans and rice from the farmers market as Dinora had instructed us to do, tossing out the pebbles and bits of dirt, we realized that we didn't know the first thing about how to make *potaje.*

Now Liudmila came over to inspect the meal, lowering her head to sniff the contents of the large pot.

"It needs onions," she said.

Alfredo came over to get a whiff for himself. "And garlic," he added, stepping back to think some more. "And salt and oil too."

"And don't forget the sugar and cumin," Liudmila said.

Within a matter of minutes, Liudmila and Alfredo had kicked us out of the kitchen and had taken over the dinner preparations. Trying to regain some sense of usefulness, Amy and I started preparing mojitos at the dining room table. Without being too obvious, I tried to eavesdrop on Liudmila and Alfredo's conversation, distilling out their words from the general evening hubbub that surrounded us—the sounds of salsa that floated in through the window and the clinking of the neighbors' silverware as they ate their dinners.

At one point, I thought I heard Alfredo singing, and I stopped my fervent *hierba buena* crushing to look up.

Alfredo was hunched over the sink, scrubbing out a pot while Liudmila poured the *potaje* over beds of rice that lay in perfect circles on our plates.

"*Sabe lavar, sabe planchar, sabe coser, sabe cocinar. Mi casa, limpia y bonita.*

¡Qué maravilla es ese papá!" Alfredo sang in a sweet, lullaby voice. "To know how to wash, to know how to iron, to know how to sew, to know how to cook. My house, clean and beautiful. How marvelous this father is!"

"Did you make that up?" I asked, smiling at his ingenuity in substituting *"papá"* for *"mamá"* in what I'd assumed was a traditional Cuban housewife's song.

"No," Alfredo said as he laid the pot on a dish towel to dry. "It's from a cartoon I used to watch on TV when I was little."

"It's still on," Liudmila said. "The government started it after the Revolution because they wanted to change men's attitudes."

"Wow," Amy said. "Why don't we have cartoons like that in the U.S.?"

Liudmila brought over our *potaje,* and Alfredo gathered all the vegetables in front of him and then stood huddled over them with his back to us in what looked like a very uncomfortable position. Before he began to chop, he looked at us over his shoulder and said, "No peeking, this is a surprise."

Ten minutes later, he turned around, a trickle of sweat once again running down his forehead. He carried over a tray containing one of the more beautiful salads I had ever seen. Unlike the salads I usually made at home, where everything was chopped and then randomly tossed together to prevent the cohabitation of like vegetables, Alfredo's salad was laid out with intention, an edible painting of harvest day. There was a bed of lettuce framed by slivers of green bell pepper and dotted with curlicues of white onion. Paper-thin tomato slices delicately overlapped like a row of collapsed dominoes, and in the center, Alfredo's arrangement of the final vegetable made me blush. In all capitals, he had spelled out my name in red bell pepper.

"See," he said proudly, "nothing about love, just your name."

Liudmila winked at me and Amy giggled, and we toasted our mojitos to the end of our program and Hotel El Bosque, and to the start of what I called our "new, real life" in Cuba.

After dinner, Amy and Liudmila headed out for a walk along the Malecón, and Alfredo and I went up to the rooftop. We sat on two low-lying lounge chairs and looked out over the city.

"Do you think it's okay that I'm here this late?" Alfredo asked.

I reached for his wrist to read the time on his watch. It was only ten o'clock.

"I'm sure it's fine," I said. Maybe it was the *"¡Qué maravilla!"* song, or the salad, or maybe it was just Alfredo's subtle reference to my letter and the implication that he was attempting to change, but I felt more attracted to him this evening than I ever had before.

I leaned over and kissed him. "Don't worry," I said. "We're safe here."

But soon Alfredo leaned backward, and his lounge chair collapsed, sending a cockroach slithering out from under it.

"Are you sure I'm safe?" Alfredo asked, laughing.

"Maybe we should move inside," I suggested.

"Okay," he said, but I noticed a hesitancy in his voice.

In my room, I shut the door and sat down on the bed, and Alfredo looked at me anxiously from across the room.

"What's wrong?" I asked.

"Maybe I should be going," he said. "I don't know, what if Amy comes back?"

"She won't be back for a while. Liudmila is a good talker," I said.

I stood up to walk over to him, but once again, as if on cue, something disrupted us. Someone was knocking on the door. Alfredo jumped, and then the door opened a crack to reveal Luis's head peering through. From his small view space, Luis could see only me.

"Is the guy still here?" he asked. "I want to go to bed soon, and I need to lock up."

Alfredo walked to the door.

"I'm leaving now," he said.

"Oh, okay, fine," Luis said. "Thanks."

After I heard his footsteps descend the stairs, I turned to Alfredo, who looked ready to bolt.

"What was that about?" I asked him.

I was surprised by the expression on Alfredo's face, which was now closer to anger than to anxiety.

"I knew it. From the minute I walked in here, I knew it," he said.

"Knew what?" I asked. "Do you think he thought you were going to spend the night?"

"What he thought was that I don't look like him," Alfredo said, pinching at the skin on his arm to emphasize its color. *"Es racismo."*

I was taken aback by this implication. During my time in Hotel El Bosque, I had been schooled in the nuances of tourist apartheid, but this sort of racism had nothing to do with skin color. Every Cuban—black, white, or *mulato*—had been stared at suspiciously and treated in an equally offensive manner at Hotel El Bosque.

When experts came to speak with us in the hotel conference room in the evenings, an equal number of blacks and whites represented the different professions. And walking the streets that surrounded the hotel, I'd seen no signs of racism—or at least not racism as it existed in the U.S., with its segregated neighborhoods. In Cuba, blacks lived next door to whites.

"I don't think this is racism," I said to Alfredo. "Maybe Luis just doesn't feel comfortable having strangers in his house."

"And what are you?"

"But that's different," I said.

"How?" Alfredo asked. "Aren't you a stranger too?"

"But I'm a renter."

"Well, then that's just a different type of racism, because I would never have the money to stay here."

While I felt annoyed that he had jumped to such a damning conclusion after only a brief encounter with Dinora and Luis, I also knew that Alfredo was right about his not having the money to rent a room at a *casa particular*. Together, Amy and I were paying twenty-five dollars a day, essentially seven hundred and fifty dollars a month, for a shared room in a house. That was the going price in San Francisco, but there, the room probably would have come with a phone line, the kitchen with hot water, and the bathroom with a full shower, not just a drain in the floor next to the toilet. In other parts of Latin America, where the salary was substantially higher than Cuba's twelve dollars a month, I had never paid as much as seven hundred and fifty a month for a room. It was yet another detail of the Cuban economy that I didn't understand.

Alfredo kissed me quickly as we headed down the stairs.

"Lea, *no te pongas molesta,*" he said. Don't be angry. "But I know what I'm talking about. You've been living in a hotel for a month, *una vida plastica*. A plastic life. Outside of Hotel El Bosque, there are many problems in Cuba. Most tourists don't see them, but now you will. And you should listen, and you should take notes so you can write a good story and tell people what's really happening. You said at dinner that now you would have a new, real life in Cuba. So here it is," Alfredo said as he opened the door to leave, revealing the dark street still filled with people milling about and miniature, malnourished dogs sleeping on doorsteps. He spread his arms wide, like a conductor readying his orchestra for the overture.

"Welcome, Lea," he said, "to the real Cuba."

9

The Real Cuba

In Hotel El Bosque, there had been twenty-four-hour electricity, but life in the real Cuba, I soon learned, involved blackouts that came like clockwork every Monday. They arrived just before sunset and lasted anywhere from two to four hours.

Alfredo told me that during the Special Period, people often went without electricity for up to eight hours each day. And then, when the electricity came back on, it often returned with such a surge, at such a high voltage, that it broke people's appliances; once, it even caused sparks to fly out of his father's refrigerator.

By now, Cubans were so used to the blackouts that they ceased to say anything when they happened. They just reached for their matches, lit their candles as if preparing for an elegant dinner party, and went about life as usual. Since rooms in Cuba were often poorly lit because light bulbs were expensive, the flickering candlelight wasn't a big change. The most noticeable difference was actually not a visible one. It was instead the absence of salsa, a deadening silence that overtook Havana as everyone's radio shut off.

In Cuba, blackouts were planned events. Like school lunches, the blackout schedules were posted by zone in the newspaper every day. Blackouts were organized by the government as a way to decrease electricity costs and cope with shortages. Only hospitals and hotels and government offices were spared the *apagones.*

Soon I got used to the lack of light, keeping a matchbox in each room in our upstairs flat and making sure to carry my flashlight if I was going to be in the street during an *apagón.*

I learned this trick a few days after Amy and I moved into Dinora's house. It was a late afternoon preceding a near moonless night, and I was running along the Malecón. I'd planned to go for a short run but was drawn in by the romance of the seawall—the crashing surf and the fishermen throwing out their lines, the schoolgirls sitting on the edge clacking their feet together as they stared out across the deep blue infinity. Just a few strides into my return run, as the sun dropped below the curve of the Caribbean, turning the water from indigo to black, the electricity went out. I had never been outside when this happened, and the darkness was so intense that I couldn't see the outlines of buildings or decipher the edge of the sidewalk from the thoroughfare of 7th Avenue.

When there was light, Havana was an easy place to get around in, so easy that I'd never even bothered to buy a map. In Vedado, where I spent most of my time, the wide numbered and lettered streets ran on a diagonal grid, dead-ending into the sea at their northern tips. Near Dinora's house there were clusters of smaller, named streets. I decided to ask one of the invisible people, whose guarded footsteps I could hear all around me, for help.

Like a prayer to an unknown god, I called out to the darkness, asking the opaque sky, "Excuse me, could you tell me what street this is?"

My question was followed by a resounding thump directly in front of me.

"*¡Dios mío, como me asustaste!*" a woman's voice called out beneath me. My God, how you scared me!

I knelt down and felt a head of short, wiry hair and then a hand reaching for my own. I pulled the woman up and apologized profusely.

"It's okay," she said. "I'm not hurt. Now, where are you headed?"

"Animas," I said, "between Soledad and Aramburo."

"I'm passing right by there," she told me. "We can help each other."

We walked together, hand in hand, like mother and daughter out for an evening stroll. The woman talked to me about the heat and the shortage of cooking oil this week. When we reached Animas, I heard her rustling around in her pockets.

"Ah, here it is," she said, scratching at something in her hand, and then she held up a lit match. She waved it in front of the door next to us to reveal the house number. We were right next door to Dinora's house.

In this brief moment of light, I realized the woman was quite old, and I offered to walk with her to her house, but she just laughed.

"I'll be fine," she said. "I have walked this way in the dark many, many times."

"Es Cuba," I said, and she laughed once more, leaning forward to kiss me goodbye, smelling of sea salt and sidewalk.

I was surprised by how quickly I fell into the rhythm of life at Dinora's. My stay at Hotel El Bosque seemed like a distant memory in another country. I had difficulty remembering what it must have been like to wake without the shouts and laughter of children from the *círculo infantil,* one of the low-cost daycare centers started after the Revolution, which convened below my bedroom window.

I showered to the raucous concert of fruit and vegetable carts screeching their way into the farmers market at the corner of Soledad and Animas. As March wore on, the weather, impossible as it seemed, grew even hotter, and I began showering at least twice each day, like Cubans did. The slick white tile of the bathroom floor transformed into a swimming pool that I had to mop up after each shower, since the shower itself was distinguished from the rest of the bathroom floor, not by a ledge or curtain, but only by a drain. At first the shapeless shower had scared me, but soon I grew to enjoy its freeform feel, like an indoor waterfall in the heart of the city.

I would stand in the middle of the bathroom with water squirting out of the wall and chickens squawking at the market below the open window, and

I would feel happy. After showering, I would wash my clothes in the bathroom sink and then hang them on the rooftop clothesline, where the blistering sun and wind whipped them dry in less than half an hour.

Dinora had a washing machine downstairs, but it often exploded, spewing out a river of soapsuds all over the dining room floor. As with her shoes, Dinora blamed the washing machine's malfunctioning on Cuba.

"There's no place here that sells automatic soap for washing machines," she said. "So I have to depend on a foreigner bringing me laundry detergent as a present, or I have to wait for Nitza to return from her travels."

Nitza came home from Argentina in the middle of my first week at Dinora's. Amy and I were sitting in the living room, talking with Abuela, who was always waiting for us when we returned from school. Because it had been more than a year since Abuela had been strong enough to climb down the stairs and leave the house, she was full of questions about life outside. She asked about our classes and the people we saw in the neighborhood, the produce at the farmers market, and the temperature in the street. She was always excited to talk to us but rarely remembered our names. Instead, she took to calling us *"La Gorda"* and *"La Flaca."* The Fat One and The Thin One. On afternoons when I came home without Amy, Abuela would ask me, a concerned expression on her face, *"¿Donde está La Gorda?"*

On the day Nitza came home, Abuela knew before anyone else.

"Nitza's back," she called out excitedly. "I just heard a car in the street."

Even though Dinora's house was in Centro Habana—literally the center of the capital city—car sounds were not common here. In a country where most people went everywhere by foot, the rumble of an automobile engine could generally be attributed to the one person on the block who owned one.

"Nitza's boyfriend has a car," Abuela told us and then lowered her voice to confide, "But he's going bald. I think he's too old for her."

I walked over to the top of the steps to see Nitza, but her packages preceded her. When Dinora yanked the rope to open the front door, a pile of boxes poured in, followed by a dark-haired and, yes, balding man who looked like he was in his early forties. He carried one of the larger boxes upstairs, and then Nitza, a short woman in a tight, pink-and-white flowered dress, lifted another and slowly ascended the long staircase.

Close up, I could see her resemblance to her parents. Her long hair was the same shade of brown as Dinora's, and she had Luis's wide shoulders and slightly stocky frame.

"New boarders?" she asked, leaning forward to kiss Amy and me.

"They're here for two weeks," Dinora said. "And then they're going to travel around Cuba. *¡Ay, qué rico!*" Dinora sighed the same sort of dreamy sigh that Liudmila and Alfredo made whenever I talked to them about my travel plans with Amy.

"How was Argentina?" Amy asked Nitza.

"Oh, like it always is," Nitza said with a nonchalance that stood in stark contrast with Dinora's wanderlust. "I met some friends for lunch. I went out to clubs at night. I went shopping."

At the mention of shopping, Dinora walked over to Nitza's pile of packages, which was growing bigger by the minute as the boyfriend trudged up the steps with yet another load of cardboard boxes.

"You bought the TV?" Dinora asked, and Nitza nodded. "And the bed sheets?" Nitza nodded again. "And fabric for clothing? And soap for the washing machine?"

"Yes, *mimi*," Nitza said, exasperated. "You can look at everything. But I need to take a shower now and get ready for tonight. Rey and I are going dancing."

"*¡Ay, qué rico!*" Dinora sighed again.

Rey, Spanish for "king," kissed each of us goodbye—his face warm and clammy from his workout—and Nitza retreated into her bedroom. Dinora looked around as if at a loss for what to do next.

"Is anyone hungry?" she asked. "Lea? Amy? Luis is cooking dinner."

Although meals weren't included in our rent, Dinora was always inviting us to eat with the family. At first I'd felt shy about accepting, but she was so persistent, and the food was always so much better than anything Amy and I managed to prepare.

Luis was a good cook and, unlike Dinora and Abuela, who looked at me with a mixture of skepticism and wonder as they asked me, at every meal, to reiterate the reasons behind my diet, Luis never questioned my vegetarianism. And on many occasions, his cooking had saved me from going hungry.

Luis made a delicious *ajiaco* soup with ingredients that I never would have considered combining, such as noodles and plantains and lemon juice and potatoes. He loved to cook, and whenever he was home, he was in the kitchen stirring a pot of beans or frying up a pan of pork. After meals, he dutifully collected the dishes to wash, refusing any help from Amy or me.

After Alfredo's *"¡Qué maravilla es ese papá!"* performance, I was no longer surprised to see a Cuban man in the kitchen, but it did surprise me one day when I asked Dinora about machismo and she said, "I don't even know where to begin."

"Machismo is one of the biggest problems we have here," she said. "Luis is better than most husbands. At least he helps me around the house and he cooks, but still, when he leaves the house, he doesn't like to tell me when he'll come back. It's subtle, but it's still a form of machismo. I never learned to drive because of it. Luis said I couldn't, so he got his license instead, and then he got in an accident, and that was the end of our car. And whenever he's around his brothers, they don't include me at all. I remember the first and last trip I took to visit his family. One day Luis and his two brothers decided they wanted to go buy beer, so they all just left without me, because they felt women should stay in the house. They left me alone for hours in this house in this city where I didn't know anyone. Can you believe that?" Amy and I shook our heads sympathetically. "But then, I should've expected that. Luis is from Santiago, *oriente,*" Dinora said, an expression of distaste on her face.

Even though eastern Cuba was the birthplace of the Revolution, and Santiago was a celebrated and well-touristed city, people from Havana still spoke disparagingly of its residents. They called them *guajiros,* country bumpkins or, oddly enough, *palestinos,* Palestinians. Once, after a policeman had stopped Alfredo in the street, asking for his ID card, I heard Alfredo mumble under his breath, *"el santiaguero estúpido."*

"My neighbor married a *santiaguera,*" Alfredo told me once. "She moved up to Havana to live with him, and for the first month, everything was fine. But then the second month, she invited her brother, and the third, her mother. And they didn't do anything. They just sat around the house, waiting for my friend to bring home his paycheck every month. Everyone from Santiago is just looking for an easy ride to Havana."

Yet in a way that struck me as very Cuban in its incongruity, Alfredo still wanted to go to Santiago, and never missed an opportunity to bring up my trip. Because I couldn't decide for sure whether I wanted him to come, I continued to put him off, saying Amy and I hadn't finalized the plans or dates yet.

Really, I was worried about the new turns our relationship might take while traveling. Things had definitely changed for the better since the night I gave Alfredo my letter. To my surprise, not only had he folded it up to carry with him in his wallet next to a passport photo of me, but he'd also memorized the letter as if it were a love poem. Now, when he got that glazed-over look in his eyes that usually signified a rush of *piropos,* he would instead recite portions of my letter.

Unfortunately, the one aspect of our relationship that didn't seem to change was Alfredo's continued sense of unease in Dinora's house. Often, he felt so uncomfortable that he'd ask me to meet him outside at a prescheduled time. On International Women's Day, he met me on the corner of Animas and Soledad to give me a mahogany carved flower with the dedication, "To Lea, with all my heart," written on the back. When I invited him in, he asked if we could walk around outside instead.

I studied the family for signs of racism, but I couldn't find any. They seemed like genuinely good people, and I felt much more comfortable in their house than I ever did at Hotel El Bosque. Even though I told Alfredo that Dinora and Luis regularly asked how he was and when he would come by again, Alfredo insisted that they were racists.

"You can't understand because you're not Cuban," he told me one night as we walked along the Malecón.

"Well, maybe we shouldn't be together then, because I'm never going to be Cuban," I responded, frustrated with the way our arguments always seemed to circle back to the same irreconcilable differences.

"You Americans are very difficult," he said. "You think you can just come in somewhere and understand everything in a month."

"I never said I understood everything," I retorted. "And what I say has nothing to do with my being American. I'm a person, not a country."

But some days I did see what Alfredo was talking about. Some days I understood that I would never truly comprehend Cuba. I could see that, for as much as I could study its history and stand in its lines, I would only be able to do so as a tourist. And because of this, I couldn't really understand Alfredo's life either.

I didn't tell him this, though. It was a victory I wouldn't allow him. As our relationship developed, I discovered a stubbornness within myself that I hadn't before realized existed. Sometimes our relationship seemed like one long argument that each of us was too proud to let go of, even when we knew the other one was right.

10

El Bombo

When Alfredo told me his father had won *el bombo,* or the Cuban lottery, I misheard him and thought he said his father had won *el bombón,* or a box of chocolates, also a rare prize in Cuba.

I had never heard of *el bombo* before. In other Spanish-speaking countries, there was *la lotería.* But I had read that gambling and lotteries of any sort were illegal in Cuba.

"Well, there's no chocolate involved, but even so, this is a special type of lottery," Alfredo said, laughing at my misunderstanding. His forlorn expression, which had lingered on his face since we met outside the symphony half an hour earlier, faded into a smirk, something that under other circumstances might have been mistaken for a smile.

We were sitting in a taxi headed toward Alfredo's father's house in the Residencial Almendares neighborhood near the airport. We had planned this visit a few days earlier so I could interview Alfredo's paternal grandmother, who lived with her husband and Alfredo's uncle, half-sister, father, and father's second wife. Now, given this latest news about *el bombo*, our visit took on an unanticipated urgency.

El bombo, unlike U.S. lotteries, elicited a mix of emotions ranging from joy and excitement to sadness and fear. *El bombo* wasn't about money—Cuba didn't charge any to play, and it didn't give out any to the winners. Instead, *el bombo*, created in 1996, granted 20,000 Cubans permission to move to the U.S. each year.

Alfredo's father, who wanted an easier life for himself and his family, had mailed the U.S. Interest Section his application for *el bombo* in 1997. When he didn't hear anything, he reapplied in 1998. Months, and then years passed, and still he didn't hear anything, and so his friends stopped asking if he'd be moving to the U.S. Eventually Alfredo too assumed his father would always be in Cuba. But this morning, just as Alfredo was heading out to work, his father called to tell him the news.

"He said he could be leaving within two months," Alfredo told me as our taxi approached the José Martí International Airport and drove parallel to its runway. Alfredo's father had tried to leave Cuba once before, during the infamous 1980 Mariel Boatlift, by which 125,000 Cubans had fled to the U.S. via the port of Mariel. It all started when a Cuban bus driver crashed his bus through the gates of the Peruvian embassy, demanding political asylum. The Cuban police asked the embassy to hand over the *contrarevolucionario*, but the Peruvian authorities refused. News spread quickly throughout the international community, and soon, U.S. President Jimmy Carter extended an open invitation to any oppressed Cuban who wanted to come to the U.S.

Fidel responded in kind. Not only would he allow all willing Cubans to leave the country, he announced, but he would also encourage the more oppressed contingents of Cuban society—including those who inhabited the jails and mental institutes—to do so.

But even before the inmates arrived at the Peruvian embassy, news of the planned exodus spread through the streets of Havana. On the first day of the eleven-day Mariel exodus, Alfredo's father went on his midday work break and met several friends who were on their way to the embassy.

"They asked if he wanted to go along," Alfredo recounted as our taxi turned off the main road and entered a neighborhood with wide streets and small, tidy front lawns. "My father went to check it out, and he decided that he wanted to leave too. So he came home to get my mother and sister and me, but my mother didn't want to go."

"Did you?" I asked.

"I was only seven years old," Alfredo said. "My whole life was Cuba, so I'm sure I wouldn't have wanted to leave, but I wasn't asked. I was at school then. And everything I'm telling you now, I don't even know exactly how I learned it. These are just things I've come to know through the years."

"Do you know how your father felt when your mother said she didn't want to go?" I asked. "Is that why they got divorced?"

"No," Alfredo said. "They stayed together for a few years after that, but two of those years my father spent in prison, because ten days after he'd gone to the embassy, he was arrested."

"Why?" I asked, shocked both by the trauma of Alfredo's story and by the calm manner in which he recounted it. "What did he do wrong? Wanting to leave? Going to watch people leave when they were told they could go? It doesn't make any sense."

"Es Cuba" Alfredo said, shrugging his shoulders.

With this disclaimer, Alfredo directed the taxi to stop in front of a two-story cement house with a mutt basking in a sunny spot on the lawn. We climbed a set of steps up to a balcony, where an older black man sat reading in a rocking chair. Other than students at the University of Havana, where I was taking Spanish classes, this man was the first Cuban I'd seen with a book.

Even though Cuba boasted a literacy rate of 98 percent, the highest in Latin America, few people seemed to take advantage of this special skill they possessed.

When Amy and I joined Alfredo on the symphony's regular Sunday trip to the beach, we brought bottles of water and books while everyone else just brought rum, which they drank straight out of the bottle. When the rum was gone and the conversation, a mix of gossip and good-natured teasing, had also run dry and the sun had hit its noonday high, people retreated beneath the shade of a palm and busied themselves with sifting sand through their fingers.

"Don't Cubans like to read? Don't you?" I asked Alfredo once. I was surprised that, for all the questions about writing that Alfredo had bombarded me with when we first met, and for all the poet–revolutionaries who peopled the country's past, Cubans still preferred contemplating sand to reading a book.

"What is there to read?" Alfredo asked. "Have you ever been in a book-store here?"

I had. In fact, I had visited several, searching each time for something to differentiate one from the next. Each bookstore had the same musty shelves of revolutionary history and the poetry of José Martí. For children, there were comic books of Che and Fidel fighting in the Sierra Maestras. And for those desiring fiction there was a special literature section with novels by Tolstoy and Dostoevsky. The only American authors whose work I'd seen were Edgar Allan Poe and William Kennedy.

Regardless of the author, all books were packaged in the same bland single-color cover, a variation in font the only design detail. The vertical titles on the spines were written from bottom to top, so that in order to read them when browsing in a bookstore, people had to tilt their heads awkwardly to the left.

At Alfredo's father's house, I saw that the older man in the rocking chair was reading an English engineering text.

"Lea, this is Alipio, my grandfather," Alfredo said as the man closed his book and stood up to give me a kiss.

From a previsit prep session Alfredo had given me a few days earlier, I knew that Alipio had studied engineering through a cultural exchange at MIT in the 1950s, and I also knew that he wasn't really Alfredo's grandfather.

"He's been married to my grandmother at least since I was born," Alfredo had told me as he attempted to outline his family tree. "But my real grandfather lives somewhere in the La Vibora neighborhood. I don't really know him. I've only seen him two or three times."

"Does he live with another wife?" I asked.

"No, he never remarried, but he has been with many different women, even when he was with my grandmother, which is why she divorced him."

"Was it unusual for people to divorce back then?" I asked.

"Maybe," Alfredo said. "You should ask my grandmother. She did it three times. Now she's with her fourth husband."

When I heard this story, I knew immediately that I wanted to interview this grandmother. Even though Alfredo couldn't tell me definitively whether all this divorcing and remarrying was considered scandalous at the time, I couldn't imagine that it was the norm, especially not for women. I envisioned Alfredo's grandmother as a rebel of sorts, a strong woman who would demand her due and who would have been one of the first to answer the call of the Revolution.

Juana Rosa González didn't disappoint me. After her husband conversed excitedly with me about politics and engineering in rapid but not entirely intelligible English, Alfredo and I walked into the house to find his grandmother waiting for us. She sat at a large glass dining room table with two revolutionary medals laid out in front of her.

Juana was a small, light-skinned black woman. Her long gray hair was braided and then wound into a bun, which was fastened with a turquoise and silver barrette. She wore a white-and-blue flowered dress and sat beaming out at us from behind a pair of large glasses that engulfed the top half of her face.

"Ask me anything you want," Juana instructed me as she patted the chair next to her. "But I should warn you that I'm seventy-one years old, so some of my memory is faulty."

I asked Juana how her life had changed since the Revolution.

"Well, before the Revolution, when I was younger, I studied to be a teacher, but it was unusual for women to study, and even more unusual for them to work," Juana said. "On top of that, being black, there were few opportunities. My mother was black, but I had some luck because my father was Spanish, and he had a high post in the army. We weren't rich, but we weren't so poor that I couldn't study."

"When you were studying, did you know that you wouldn't be able to get a job?" I asked.

"Yes," Juana said, nodding her head solemnly. "But I also just felt within me that something was going to change. When I was growing up, there was a sense of unrest. I did what I was expected to do. I left my studies and married at nineteen. I've been married ever since." I thought Juana might add something here about her divorces, but instead she ran her hand over the two polished medals that rested between us like miniature gilded coasters.

"When I was thirty, the Revolution came, and I finally became a teacher," Juana said proudly. "These medals are for my service in the Literacy Campaign, and this certificate is signed by Fidel." Juana pushed a yellowed piece of paper in my direction, and I nodded approvingly at the scribbled autograph across the bottom.

I remembered Dinora mentioning that she too had participated in the 1961 Literacy Campaign, during which more than one hundred thousand Cubans had moved out to the country to teach the peasants to read. At the time, nearly one quarter of Cuba's population was illiterate.

"For three months, I taught the peasants how to read. But, *pobrecitos*, they didn't even know how to write their names. They would sign with their thumbs." Juana held up her own thumb, staring at it sadly. "Can you imagine that? This was only forty years ago. My students were so grateful, and I still keep in touch with some of them. One is a lawyer now, and another is a doctor, and many have died. But at least they died decent, natural deaths, unlike some of their teachers."

"What do you mean?" I asked.

"The CIA killed them."

"The CIA?" I asked, not sure if I'd really understood. "You mean the CIA in the United States?"

"Yes," Juana said. "They didn't want the Revolution to succeed, so they made up stories to scare the peasants. They told them we were there to hurt them, not to help, and they paid them to kill the teachers. Some of them they hung from trees, and others they drowned in ponds."

"I've never heard anything about this," I said, too shocked to know what else to say.

"Well of course not," Juana said, laughing. "I doubt they'd teach you about this in your history classes in the U.S."

I nodded my head solemnly. "But how do you know this is true?" I asked. "I mean, how do you even know about it?"

"It's in some declassified documents that the U.S. released recently. When you go home, do some research, and you'll see for yourself," Juana said. "And while you're here, there will be lots of people willing to tell you more." Juana paused before adding quickly, "But honestly, I don't like to talk so much about these things. I've never liked the political. *Es sucia en todas partes.*" It's dirty everywhere.

While I contemplated this statement, Alfredo, who had been sitting out on the balcony with his grandfather when I began the interview, walked through the front door holding a bottle of rum in his hands. He was followed by a half dozen other people, each with something in hand. A large woman in a purple-and-black striped spandex body suit, a common fashion in Cuba, plugged in a boom box while a teenage girl still in her mustard-yellow school skirt set down a bowl of popcorn and started to dance to the jerky rhythm of Los Orishas, a Cuban rap band now living in Europe.

Alfredo walked over to me with a man in a sea-blue tank top that showed a surfer riding a rainbow-colored wave above the words "Atlantic Ocean."

"This is Lea, dad," Alfredo announced, and then I saw the resemblance. Alfredo's father was lighter-skinned and had green instead of brown eyes, but they both had the same thin frame and the same soft voice.

"So you're here to celebrate with us?" Alfredo's father asked.

"Sure," I said. During my conversation with Juana, I'd forgotten about *el bombo.* "Congratulations," I said. "Are you excited?"

"I'm getting there," Alfredo's father said. "It's still hard to believe. Yesterday I was talking to my friend who delivers the mail, and he said, 'You know you won *el bombo,*' and I just laughed. I said, 'Yeah, right,' and he said, 'No, come over to my house. I'll show you. I have the notice there,' and he did. But then when I went home and told my wife, she didn't believe me either."

Alfredo's father motioned to the big woman in the spandex body suit who was now dancing with a man with a baby on his shoulders. "Milagro, come here for a minute," Alfredo's father called out.

I had so many questions I wanted to ask Alfredo's father. I wanted to know about his time in prison and, even though Alfredo told me it hadn't affected his father's career, I wanted to know what life had been like afterward. But tonight was obviously not the time to have this conversation.

Milagro recited for me her own story of *el bombo* disbelief, and then she grabbed Alfredo's father by the hand and they slid into a smooth salsa on the makeshift balcony dance floor. Alfredo looked over at me, waiting for a cue.

"Okay," I said and I saw his face break into that open, overflowing smile that he always wore when he danced.

We danced off to the side of everyone else, just a little slower and a little clumsier too. Sometimes I felt like the only person in Cuba, tourist or native, who couldn't salsa. Alfredo was embarrassingly patient with me, as were all the Cubans who'd tried and failed to teach me how to circle my hips and move my feet to the rhythm of the music.

Tonight, after three songs, Alfredo took a break to nurse his stomped-on foot, and I, looking for consolation, asked him if he'd ever had a friend who couldn't salsa. Maybe there had been some bookish girl in his grade school, I thought, or a klutzy third cousin somewhere in Cuba.

"No," Alfredo said shaking his head. "It's just you and Fidel."

"Fidel?" I asked laughing.

"People criticize him for that," Alfredo said. "And for not being married. Well, there are rumors that he's married, but if so, no one knows who his wife is. People say he's so focused on the Revolution that he's lost touch with the details of daily Cuban life."

Alfredo put his hand on my shoulder for balance as he stood on his sore foot. "I think I need to sit down," he said. "Do you want to have a drink with me?"

We moved into the living room and spent the evening drinking rum and chatting with Alfredo's numerous relatives as they passed through. Soon the rum disappeared, and as the hours passed, I kept expecting someone to make a run for food. I hadn't eaten since lunch, and it was now after ten. The few kernels of popcorn I'd devoured earlier were not enough to counter the dizzying effect of the rum. But everyone else seemed caught up in their dancing, and beyond that, I knew there probably wasn't money to buy food, so I decided to just drink lots of water while sitting on the sofa, a safe distance from the salsa dancing, my stomach rumbling to the rhythm that my feet had rebelled against.

11

Idioma Ruso, Profesora

When I came home from class the day after *el bombo* party, Dinora was standing in the living room, talking on the phone. As I made my way up the final set of steps to my bedroom, I called out *"Hola"* in greeting, but with one swift wave of her hand, Dinora simultaneously shushed me and motioned for me to come over.

As I got closer, I saw that she wasn't actually talking on the telephone but rather had her hand over the mouthpiece and was eavesdropping on someone else's conversation. Dinora held up her hand, indicating for me to stay put. I stared at the television, which had the volume turned off. Fidel, in his trademark olive-green fatigues, raised his arms as his lips moved rapidly. Inset in the left corner of the screen was a photo of Elián González in his trademark thinker pose, and in the right corner of the screen was a woman signing for the deaf.

After a few minutes, Dinora returned the telephone receiver to its cradle, just seconds before Nitza's door burst open.

As always, Nitza looked as if she had just received a beauty makeover. She wore eye shadow and lipstick, and her hair was neatly sprayed in place. Every time I saw her, she seemed to have on a new outfit, and this afternoon she was wearing a black evening gown.

"Wow," I said. "Where are you off to?"

"Oh, nowhere really," Nitza said. "Just meeting up with some friends. Same old, same old."

"What friends?" Dinora asked.

"Oh, *mimi*, whoever shows up," Nitza said, growing irritated. "I'm going over to Margarita's if you have to know."

Nitza walked cautiously in jerky steps over to the staircase, and after the final clunk of her stiletto heel had faded into the slam of the door, Dinora turned to me.

"That," she said dramatically, "was a lie."

"How do you know?"

"Well, what I mean is it's not the whole truth. I just heard Nitza talking to her boyfriend. She is going over to Margarita's now, but then she's meeting up with Rey later tonight."

"So?" I asked, adding, "You really shouldn't eavesdrop."

"I know," Dinora said, her voice softening. "I'm just worried about her. Do you know how she met Rey?"

"No, how?"

"*En una botella.* She was on the side of the road hitchhiking, and he gave her a ride. I think she was impressed because he has a car. I think she likes him because he has money, but I just don't get a good feeling about him. Her old boyfriend was so nice."

"Dairon?" I asked. Among the regular cast of characters, including neighbors and relatives and vegetable vendors invited in for a glass of *guanabana* juice, I had noticed one repeat visitor passing through Dinora's house every day. Dairon was a dark-haired man in his midtwenties. At first I assumed he was a friend of Nitza's, but then I noticed that he often stayed on when she went out in the evenings. Sometimes Dairon helped Luis with cooking, and other times he spent hours rocking in the living room alongside Abuela, listening attentively to her every mumble.

"Dairon and Nitza lived together for seven years, since they were both seventeen, right here in Nitza's bedroom," Dinora said. "I invited him to live here because I knew they were together, and he's such a sweet boy."

"What happened?"

"Everything was fine at first when they were both just students. But when Nitza became a flight attendant, because she was actually earning money, she wanted to go out at night, to go to clubs and concerts. But she always had to pay for Dairon, because he's a doctor and he doesn't earn very much."

"Nitza earns more as a flight attendant?" I asked.

"She earns dollars," Dinora said.

"It sounds like a foreigner–Cuban relationship," I said. "I think that was a problem at first with Alfredo and me, but now we just try to do things that don't cost money."

"Oh, and how was your meeting with his father last night?" Dinora asked. "I stayed up until midnight waiting for you, but then I got tired."

"I got home late," I said. "It ended up being like a party. Alfredo's father found out the day before that he had won *el bombo.*"

"I have a friend, a nurse, who won that in 1996," Dinora said. "She moved to Miami with her children and husband. But she works so much that she never gets to see her husband, and her children have already moved out and live in different cities. Now she's trying to get permission to come back to Cuba, but her children and husband want to stay." Dinora shook her head. "I don't blame her," she said. "I know that things are bad here, but her life in the U.S. is no life I'd ever want. Your kids moving away and no one left to take care of you when you grow old . . . she told me that old people get sent away to live with other old people there. Is that true?"

"Sometimes," I told her. "Everyone in the U.S. is just raised to be so independent. . . ."

"I think it's wrong," Dinora interrupted. "For us, it's not logical or humane to put your parents away like that."

"What happens to old people here who don't have relatives?"

"Well, then they have no choice but to go to a home, but here, at least the homes are free, and if you have any living relatives, the government will pay you so you can take time off to take care of them. That's what they're doing for me. You should write about that when you write about Cuba," Dinora said, and then suddenly added, "When are you going to interview me?"

"You want me to?" I asked, surprised. When I'd told Dinora, on the first day we met, about my plan to write something about women in Cuba, she turned visibly nervous.

I was taken aback, since all the other Cuban women I'd spoken with had candidly told me their life stories, readily sharing with me their criticisms of the government. The only thing I could attribute Dinora's fear to was a small three-letter sign on her door that read "CDR."

CDRs, or Committees for the Defense of the Revolution were Revolutionary watchdog groups on each block. In the U.S., I had heard them described as Fidel's spies, people to make sure no one was engaging in any counterrevolutionary activities. From what I'd seen in Cuba, the CDRs appeared to be more like apartment managers, collecting money to set up communal gardens, taking complaints about faulty electrical wires and much-needed house repairs. Luis was the block's CDR president, and once a week, from 10 PM to 2 AM, he paced his block, making sure all was safe. I knew there was more to the CDRs than I'd been able to ascertain in my short time in Cuba, and I could only assume that it was something somewhere in this gap in my knowledge that was scaring Dinora.

"I'd love to interview you," I told her now. "I don't have to include anything that makes you feel uncomfortable, and, of course, I can always change your name in my story."

The bit about her name seemed to calm Dinora, and her facial expression shifted from concern to excitement.

"Okay," she said, smiling as she settled onto the couch. I sat in the armchair across from her. "Ask away."

I ran upstairs to grab my notebook, and when I returned, Beatriz, another friend of Abuela's from the *círculo de abuelos,* was shuffling Abuela into the living room to sit in her favorite rocking chair.

Beatriz leaned over to kiss Abuela on the cheek and said, "I'll see you tomorrow, sweetie."

"Nice woman," Dinora commented after Beatriz left, "but very Revolutionary."

"And you're not?" I asked. I couldn't quite figure Dinora out. She vacillated from downright pessimism about the situation in Cuba to simplistic idealism, imagining that another TV or a new bedsheet could fix everything. And now, after her initial anxiety over my Cuban women story, she chose to discuss the Revolution as our first interview topic.

"I'm not anti-Revolution, and I'm not anticommunist, but I'm also not communist, because that means not to fight for yourself and for your own happiness. I've fought for so many years. Look at my hands," Dinora demanded, holding them out in front of her. I looked, anticipating scars but seeing only smooth, olive-colored flesh.

"I worked in the countryside for the Revolution," Dinora continued. "But now, everything I have is from my husband and my daughter, because they get paid in dollars. That's not socialism. If you ask me, I'd call it capitalism. I used to think differently. I thought we were all in this together. Now, though, I think you have to look out for yourself. I used to live like this," Dinora said, standing up and placing one hand on each side of her face. She paced back and forth in the living room, repeating, *"Idioma ruso, profesora. Idioma ruso, profesora."*

"I was like someone with blinders on," Dinora said. "All that mattered in my life was teaching Russian at the university. That's what the Revolution had given me. I worked for thirty years as a professor, imagining that my life would always be that way, and now I'm a housewife."

"But I thought you stopped teaching to take care of your mother," I said. "That doesn't have anything to do with the Revolution."

"In 1994, when the collapse of the U.S.S.R. really began to take its toll on Cuba, there was no more demand for Russian classes," Dinora said. "And all the Russian professors began scrambling to learn Italian and English and Portuguese. I studied English, but there were already enough English teachers. Entering the university in those days was like entering a morgue, because everyone was so depressed. My boss hung himself. The economy had changed so that people in tourism were being paid in dollars, and I felt like my friends were using me because they knew Luis earned dollars. People didn't have soap, so they had to wash with salt."

Luis wandered into the living room with El Dormido, The Sleeper, as everyone referred to Dinora's brother, who dozed off during his daily shift with Abuela.

Dinora picked up a copy of Isabel Allende's *Casa de los Espíritus* from the coffee table.

"Please don't take this the wrong way," she said, "but I'm an impatient person. It comes from anxiety, so if you don't mind, I might read while you ask me questions."

"An American who stayed here left this," she said, flipping absently through the pages. "Even though the author writes about Chile, it's the same life as here—a small life, a hard life in an underdeveloped country. The only difference is that our campesinos aren't exploited anymore, but who knows, maybe I'd feel differently if I were still one of them, if my family hadn't moved to Havana when I was little."

"Why did you move?"

"*Mimi*," Dinora said to Abuela, who was trying to read the *Granma* but still squinting, even with the newspaper less than an inch from her face. "Why did we move?"

Abuela said something that I couldn't make out.

"Oh, right," Dinora said. "Well, I told you that was during the time when communists like my father were persecuted. Some people came with a gun one day, so we left."

Abuela returned to her *Granma,* and I marveled at the matter-of-fact tone with which Dinora discussed such traumatic incidents.

"Tell me about the Literacy Campaign," I said.

"It was difficult, and I cried sometimes," she said. "But I taught for the full eight months, because I believed in the Revolution. The campesinos were very good to me, and I liked them a lot. Every night, I'd read to the old people from the book *History Will Absolve Me*."

History Will Absolve Me was Fidel's eighty-one-page court defense of his failed 1953 assault on Batista's military barracks in Santiago.

"I told the *campesinos* something that I still believe strongly today," Dinora said. "I told them that they should try to learn something new every day. It's a beautiful thing. I still try to do it, and when I go to sleep, I try to think about what I've learned this day." Dinora's eyes took on a distant look as she continued.

"Afterward, when the government asked me to write down my dream in life, I wrote that I wanted to study foreign languages. For the next few years, I studied and taught Russian, and then when I was twenty-three, I got a telegram saying I'd received a grant to go to Russia for five years."

"Is that where you learned your lullaby?" I asked. The previous Monday, rushing out of the house during a blackout to meet Alfredo, I had passed Dinora sitting with her eyes closed by a candle on the coffee table, singing a sweet, soft hymn in a language I didn't understand.

"Yes, I know lots of Russian songs," Dinora said proudly. "I was in a Cuban chorus in Moscow. It was directed by Frank Fernández, who's now a famous pianist here. He was very cute when he was younger, and I had such a crush on him."

"Did you like Russia?"

"I did. I'd never left Cuba before, so it was all a wonderful, new experience, even though it was colder in the winter than I ever imagined any place could be. What I didn't like were my studies. My grant was for engineering, which I didn't have any interest in, but life isn't a paradise, and you have to take from it what you can. Actually," Dinora added, "I've lived a fortunate life. I hate cooking, and here I have this husband who cooks for me. Before I met him, all I ate was chocolate."

"When did you meet?"

"Is the story you're writing going to be for or against Cuba?" Dinora asked suddenly.

"It's neither," I said, startled. "It's just . . . a story."

"Okay, then," Dinora said. "We met during my fourth year in Russia, in this town called Sochi, which was near the Black Sea. We met in August, and we spent twenty-four days as friends. September 12th was the first day we had sexual relations, and then on September 24th, I asked Luis his plans for the future, and he said, 'To get married to you,' so we did. After eight months, I was pregnant with Nitza."

"What was your wedding like?"

"We just had a few friends come, because most of the people we knew were in Cuba. I didn't even tell my family about our marriage until we came home."

"Why?" I asked. "Why didn't you wait until you were in Cuba to get married?"

"I was afraid of losing the moment," Dinora said, looking down at the book in her lap, which she hadn't touched since announcing her intention to read it during our interview. El Dormido had left by now, and Luis had retreated to the kitchen to cook dinner. There was only the creak of Abuela's rocking chair as the sun dropped, submerging the balcony in darkness.

Dinora's voice sounded scratchy against the surrounding silence. "I got married in Russia," she said, "because that was my moment of happiness, and I think the most important thing in life is to realize when your moment arrives."

12

The Latino Lover

For the rest of the day following our conversation, the urgency of Dinora's final declaration stayed with me. That night I slept a fitful sleep, haunted by my impending return to the U.S.

I had one of those traveler's nightmares, which I had suffered many other times in many other places. I dreamt that for some unnamed yet nonetheless urgent reason I had to rush home at a moment's notice. But then once I got to California, like a dream within a dream, everything turned to slow motion. Each time I attempted to move forward with my plans to return, my movements became so labored and languid that I couldn't complete any of the many preliminary steps—purchasing a ticket, packing, making it to the plane on time—that were necessary for me to get back to Cuba.

Generally when I woke from similar nightmares, I saw how silly they were and easily shrugged them off, knowing that return was always possible.

My nightmare in Cuba was different. I knew that if ever there had been the remotest likelihood of my dream's anxiety-ridden scenario taking place, it would occur on an attempted return to Cuba.

Through my program, I had received a piece of paper from the U.S. Treasury Department stating that I was officially allowed to be in Cuba, but I knew that if I tried to return on my own and got caught, I could be fined up to fifty-five thousand dollars.

But really my reasons for wanting to stay in Cuba were more basic than a fear of being caught trying to return. I wanted to stay simply because I was happy.

I was happy with my revamped relationship with Alfredo. We moved more slowly now, and in this space of calm, everything I liked about him—from the way he always remembered to ask what I'd been saying if he interrupted me to the way that not just his lips but his whole face took part in his happiness when he smiled—came into a finer focus.

I was happy too with my easy rapport with Dinora. When I thought back, beyond the complaints, to everything that she had told me during the short week that I'd known her, I found that her words had an unassuming wiseness to them, a poignant quality that reminded me of poetry.

And from my first day there, my happiness with the routine of my life in Centro Habana continued to grow. In the absence of our program's field trips, Amy and I created our own. She researched classes at different dance schools in Havana, and I spent my afternoons wandering the streets, sampling the pickings at pizza stands and making new friends along the way.

One day while waiting for my pizza at a stand on San Lázaro, a tall, deep-black Cuban man decked out in red and brown African-print pants and no shirt approached me. As if he already knew me, he asked how I was enjoying my stay and if I had plans to travel. He greeted the woman working at the street pizza stand and, speaking quickly, handed her some coins. We talked for a few minutes, but before I was able to ask who this beautiful man was, the small white dog he was walking started tugging at its leash. The man gave me a quick kiss on the cheek before disappearing down the bright alley of Callejón de Hamel. When I turned back to the pizza stand, the woman working there handed me a pizza.

"For me?" I asked. "But I haven't even ordered yet."

"Oh, no, it's a treat from Harold," she said, motioning to the space where the man had stood moments before. I walked down Callejón de Hamel to thank Harold, but I couldn't find him, and I never saw him again.

Life in Cuba was a lesson in this sort of unexpected, undemanding kindness. Outside of the classroom, I still felt that I was learning something new each day, just as Dinora had recommended her reading students do.

When I woke up on the morning after her story about finding one's moment, I realized that it was here in Cuba that I had found mine. I told Amy that I wanted to stay for another month, and she smiled mischievously.

"I'd been thinking I wasn't ready to leave either," she said.

When I told Alfredo, topping off my announcement with an invitation to travel to Santiago with Amy and me, he got so excited that he did a little dance in the middle of Linea and D Streets, snapping his fingers and swinging his hips to his invented rhythm. We were standing in front of the symphony, surrounded by a crowd of people waiting to hear Frank Fernández, the famous Cuban pianist whom Dinora had had a crush on in Russia.

Earlier in the day, I had invited Dinora to the concert, and she had become as animated as Alfredo was now.

"Oh, I'd love to go," she had said, sitting straight up in her bed and clapping her hands joyfully like a child. "I haven't seen Frank play for years." Dinora paused for a moment before adding, "I feel like I haven't gone out for years."

I had passed by Dinora's room on my way to meet up with Liudmila that morning and then again when I'd returned home in the afternoon. Both times Dinora had been lying lifelessly on her bed, reading her Isabel Allende book in a futile fight with her nightstand fan, which, anytime Dinora loosened up her grip of the book, began flipping the pages by itself. Each time this happened, Dinora would swat at the empty air as if trying to catch an invisible fly. Then she'd stiffen up, angrily clutching together the pages of the book as she turned her back to the fan.

It was too hot to turn off the fan, and there was no air conditioner. Once, unaware of the frustrated rant my question would release, I had asked Dinora why, since Amy and I had an air conditioner in our room, she didn't invest in one for herself.

"Ay, Lea," she had said sighing. *"La vida aquí es tremenda lucha."* Life here is such a struggle. "Do you know how long it took me to save up for your little air conditioner? Two years."

"Two years? How much did it cost?" I asked.

"Two hundred and fifty dollars," Dinora said, leaning back in her seat at the dining room table as if exhausted by the thought of all this money. She pointed to the thick sliding wood-panel door of the room I shared with Amy. "Do you know how much that cost?"

"No."

"Seven hundred dollars." Dinora drew each syllable out like my Spanish teacher at the university did when introducing a new word.

Dinora picked up a bouquet of plastic sunflowers that sat in a vase on the table and waved them in front of me.

"Three dollars?" I ventured.

"Hmph, try five," Dinora said. She picked up a placemat.

"Ten?"

"No, only five," Dinora said, sounding disappointed.

"But doesn't the rent money you make cover these expenses?" I asked, confused. Dinora had two rooms that she rented out on a regular basis. Even if both of them were only occupied half of the time, she'd be bringing in more than seven hundred and fifty dollars each month, which was fifty times the monthly salary of an average Cuban. And in addition, Dinora had Luis's and Nitza's dollar salaries.

"But there are taxes," Dinora said. "Anyone who has a private business has to pay taxes. Isn't it like that in your country?"

"It is," I said. "But how much are your taxes?"

"I have to pay a hundred dollars each month for each room I have available to rent, whether I rent it or not," Dinora said. "And everything I buy for these rental rooms has to be top-of-the-line, because that's what you foreigners are used to. No one would stay here if they had to live like a Cuban, without hot water or a telephone or a washing machine. Your room's the only one with an air conditioner, so now I have to save up two hundred and fifty dollars to buy one for the other room. And when I installed your air conditioner, the other girl who's staying here complained, because she was paying the same price without an air conditioner, so I had to lower her rent."

"Why didn't you just raise the price of the room with the air conditioner?" I asked.

"Oh," Dinora said, startled by the suggestion. "Well, I never thought of that. Cuba's a socialist country. We don't know about the capitalist way of thinking."

After accepting my invitation to the Frank Fernández concert, Dinora had told me she was going to shower and would be ready in half an hour.

I went upstairs to do the same, but when I returned to Dinora's room, she was still lying in bed, although she had now abandoned her book and was staring absently at the ceiling.

"What happened?" I asked.

"My sister called right after you left," Dinora said. "She can't come over tonight, and it's her night to watch Abuela."

"What about Nitza or Luis?" I asked.

"They're on a flight to Cancún. They won't be back until tomorrow."

"And your brothers?"

"They don't have phones, and they both live far away. If I walked over there and back, we'd never make the concert."

"We could catch a taxi," I suggested.

"Oh, no," Dinora said. "It's okay, I feel a headache coming on anyway. It's probably best that I just stay home."

At the symphony, Alfredo invited me to sit with him in the tech crew's balcony, and while he prepared the lights, he detailed for me all the places he wanted to see during our travels. He told me about El Cobre, a famous church in Santiago that his grandmother had always wanted to visit.

"Do you have a camera?" he asked.

I nodded.

"Well, I'm getting paid next week, so I'll buy some film to take photos of El Cobre for my grandmother," Alfredo said, and I could hear the echo of pride that always filled his voice when he was able to pay for something.

I leaned over and kissed him and he rubbed my back with his right hand as he put on his headphones with his left and then flashed on the lights, setting a rainbow of colors swirling across the stage.

"What color should I use for the spotlight when Frank Fernández comes out?" he asked.

"Purple and then maybe a quick splash of orange," I said jokingly, but to my surprise, Alfredo shined an amethyst light in front of the piano and then, as Frank Fernández made his appearance, Alfredo switched to a yellow-orange glow that lit the way to Frank's bench.

"Not bad," Alfredo said, laughing. "Maybe you have a talent you haven't discovered yet."

Applause broke out as Frank sat down and struck the first key. His fingers released a wave of soft, smooth sound that seemed to cast a spell of calm over the theater, and soon I was swept away by the romance of it all.

"This music makes me feel like we're in another world," Alfredo said. "Another time."

I wrapped my arms around him, and we sat silently holding each other throughout the first half of the performance. As the theater emptied out for intermission, Alfredo took off his headphones and turned to me, his eyes earnest and unwavering.

"Tengo ganas de estar solo contigo," he said. I want to be alone with you.

Since that first evening at Dinora's house, I had been thinking about this too, wondering what would have happened if Luis hadn't interrupted us. I had been speculating on what shade of brown Alfredo's skin would be beneath his clothes, untouched by the scorching city sun. I had been imagining what it might feel like to wake with him by my side. Did he sleep in place, or flip positions during the night? Did he snore?

"I want to be alone with you too," I said, repeating Alfredo's ambiguous phrase. I was surprised that he, who always seemed so direct about his feelings and desires for me, would choose now to revert to such vague vocabulary.

"Really?" Alfredo asked, every feature of his face breaking into smile. "You do? Tonight?"

"Okay, but where?"

"I'll find out," he said. "I'll be right back." He took off running down the balcony so quickly that his *pañuelo,* tucked loosely into his back pocket, fell out onto the floor. I walked over to retrieve it and saw Alfredo stop at the end of the balcony to talk to a coworker. I half expected them to look over in my direction and giggle or high-five each other, but they just conversed in hushed voices.

Alfredo returned, still smiling, a few minutes later. He showed me a scrap of paper with an address in Vedado written on it.

"He told me this is a good place," Alfredo said.

"Okay," I said, still willing, but feeling a little awkward now. It seemed that our decision to be alone, whatever that might entail, should be a more private affair. I hoped that we wouldn't have to pass by Alfredo's coworker on the way out.

I glanced around for escape options as Frank Fernández finished his final encore piece. I felt relieved to discover that there was a balcony exit directly behind me. I could leave this way, unnoticed, and wait outside the symphony for Alfredo while he helped move the piano and clear off the stage with the rest of the tech crew.

But Alfredo stood up just as I did. He gently placed my purse on my shoulder and took my hand in his.

"Let's go," he said.

"Don't you have to clean up?" I asked.

"Darien said he'll cover for me," Alfredo said, smiling as he *psst psst*-ed in the direction of his coworker, who in turn waved at us and called out, "Get out of here."

We took the elevator down to the lobby and walked out of the symphony, past the crowds, and into the dark, dark Vedado night.

I tried to imagine where we might be going. I hadn't heard of any hotels that allowed both Cubans and foreigners, and I wondered if Alfredo's definition of "being alone" together included spending the night together. Did Alfredo need to call his house to say he wasn't coming home? Should I call Amy so she wouldn't worry about me and so Dinora wouldn't stay up waiting? And most importantly, did Alfredo have a condom on him? I could only assume that since he'd been the one to suggest we be alone together, he would also have the condom.

Finally I decided to stop analyzing everything, to stop being "so American," as Alfredo would've said, and to just let the night unwind as it would. If there were no condoms, then we'd truly just have to be alone with each other in a way that didn't involve sex.

We walked mostly in silence until Alfredo stopped at a two-story cement house with a street-front balcony. There were no lights on, and it was impossible to make out the number. Alfredo backtracked to the house we'd just passed, where a bedroom light illuminated a big "34" on the door. Alfredo held his now crumpled piece of paper up to the light.

"I think that's it," he said, pointing to the darkened house. "We're looking for number thirty-six."

"But it looks like maybe they're, umm . . . closed." I didn't know if this was the right word, since this structure in front of us was obviously a house, not an operating place of business.

Alfredo looked at his piece of paper once more. Above the address was the name Lucia. Alfredo walked over to the darkened house and called out "Lucia," once, and twice, and then a third time. Each time, Alfredo drew out the final syllable more, so that the woman's name lingered in the moist night air. I had seen people do this before for second-story friends who had broken doorbells, but that had always been during the day, not at one in the morning.

"Hmm," Alfredo said, perplexed when no one answered. "Well, let's just go knock."

We circled the house looking for a door and ended up walking into a garage where there were no cars, only an old man curled up and snoring in a rocking chair.

"*Oye, tío,*" Alfredo called out. "Listen up, uncle" was a common form of addressing older people.

"Huh?" the old man said, letting out a loud snort as he woke.

"We're looking for Lucia," Alfredo said. "Do you know where she is?"

The old man pointed a bony finger toward a dark corner of the garage, where there was a staircase. As in a game of blindman's bluff, we made our way up it. At the top step, a motion-detector light flashed on, and Alfredo reached toward the door that stood in front of us. His knock was followed by a trail of feet running around.

A woman, presumably Lucia, opened the door, and a little boy scurried out from behind her. Lucia was a chunky, light-skinned woman with a friendly face.

"Come in. Have a seat," she said, patting at a bench in front of us. "Let me prepare the bed."

We sat down while Lucia disappeared around a corner. Her son ran around a little more and then, exhausted, plopped down on my lap. I patted his head, and Alfredo smiled at me. For the first time since he'd suggested that we be alone, I caught a glimmer of nervousness in his eyes. I was happy when Lucia returned and her son jumped up to greet her. Lucia motioned for him to sit down again after Alfredo and I had stood up.

Lucia showed us to our dimly lit room behind the kitchen. A framed painting with an abstract design encircling the number "6" hung on one wall, and a tennis racket adorned another. A Jesus figurine was nailed to a back wall behind the bed. Lucia walked over to a small nightstand and clicked on a radio. We all stood silently for a beat, listening to the staticky salsa song. Then Lucia clicked the radio off and said, *"Una hora, tres dólares."*

Alfredo must have done some sort of *negocio* earlier in the week, because to my surprise, he pulled out three dollars from his pocket and handed it to Lucia, who smiled at us as she left the room and closed the door behind her.

I sat on the pillowless bed, which creaked so loudly I was afraid it might give out beneath me.

"Come here," Alfredo said, motioning for me to stand up. He put the radio on and flipped through the stations until he found one that came in clearly. It was playing "Mambo #5." "A little bit of Rita is all I need," sang Lou Bega.

I walked over to Alfredo, and he folded his arms around me, encompassing me in his familiar warmth.

"Do you feel okay?" he asked.

I nodded and leaned in to kiss him.

When we fell back onto the bed this time, it cried out once more but stayed intact. We tossed our clothes on the floor, the only space there was, and I tried not to think about what they might be landing on. Alfredo crawled to the end of the bed and kissed my toes.

"What are you doing?" I asked.

"Don't you remember that I promised you that some day I would kiss every spot of you, starting at your big toe?"

I laughed and lost myself in our romancing. I had meant to ask about condoms once it became obvious that that was where we were heading, but Alfredo moved up my legs quicker than I'd imagined.

"I don't have a condom," I announced suddenly.

"I don't either," Alfredo said, sitting back on his knees. "But it's okay, I've been tested for everything."

Although I believed Alfredo, knowing that, to combat the AIDS epidemic in nearby Haiti, Cubans were routinely tested for HIV and other STDs, I still shook my head.

"I'm sorry," I said. "It's nothing personal, but I just don't have sex without a condom."

"But what did you think we were coming here for?" Alfredo asked.

"To be alone," I said, attempting humor.

Instead of laughing, Alfredo looked at me with an expression so sad and pained that I thought he might break out into tears at any moment. "Lea, please," he said, overenunciating each syllable. "I'm Latino."

I burst out laughing. "Alfredo, you're not going to explode if we don't have sex tonight," I said.

Alfredo didn't speak but instead continued to stare at me with his plaintive, pleading eyes.

"And if that's what you wanted, why didn't you bring a condom?" I asked. "What do you usually do?"

"Usually?" Alfredo repeated. "Lea, I don't know what type of person you think I am, but I'm no *mujeriego*."

"But you have been with a woman before?"

"Well, of course," Alfredo said, offended again. "But I've only had one serious girlfriend, and she always got the condoms."

I didn't feel like getting into a political discussion now, but I was surprised by Alfredo's attitude. I would have thought that after the Revolution, birth control would no longer have been just the women's responsibility.

"What about you?" Alfredo asked.

"Well, I've bought condoms," I said. "I even brought some with me, but they're at Dinora's."

"I wasn't asking about that," Alfredo said, quickly glancing down, as if unsure of whether he wanted to continue with his question. "I was asking about your relationships. Have you had a lot of boyfriends?"

"No."

"Have you ever cheated on a partner?"

"No, have you?"

"No," he said. "Never."

"The last person I was involved with had an open relationship with his girlfriend," I told Alfredo. "Do you know what that means?"

He shook his head, and I tried to explain, but it was futile. I might as well have been speaking in English. I knew that multiple partnering went on in Cuba, but the difference, of course, was that here it was clandestine, or supposedly so; not consensual.

A knock at the door interrupted my thoughts.

"Fifteen more minutes," Lucia called out.

Alfredo looked at me, a panicked expression on his face. "I don't want to spend the night without you," he said. "I just want to sleep by your side. But . . ." Averting his eyes once more, Alfredo picked his pants up from the floor and emptied the pockets for me, revealing only one peso.

"I can pay," I said.

Alfredo kissed me on the forehead and started to dress himself.

"Give me seven dollars," he said. "I'll go negotiate, but I think that should be enough."

I turned the radio off and switched on the fan beside it, and I crawled under the threadbare, soapy-smelling sheet to wait for Alfredo.

When he returned, he gave me the thumbs up sign and settled down on the bed beside me. We talked a little more, about relationships and our families, and then, without realizing it, I must have fallen asleep, because the next thing I knew, the sun was creeping in through the open blinds, and Alfredo's watch read 6:05.

I knew we hadn't gone to sleep before three, but I felt fully awake and anxious to leave before Lucia came knocking on our door once more. I nudged Alfredo, who rolled over to embrace me.

"Buenos días, mi amor," he said.

With a little convincing, I managed to get him up, and we dressed quickly and left the house on tiptoe.

"So is that where Cubans go to be alone?" I asked Alfredo once we were out in the street.

"No," he said. "That's a private *posada*. It's illegal. That was Lucia's *negocio*. Cubans go to a government *posada* that charges in pesos."

"Why didn't we go there?"

"I didn't think you'd like it."

"Have you ever been to one?"

"Once," Alfredo said. "There was this girl in my neighborhood who had a crush on me, so I invited her to get a drink, and when we were at the bar, before we even finished our beers, she said, 'Let's go to a *posada*.' But I didn't like it. There weren't even sheets on the bed."

"It doesn't sound very nice," I said.

The morning was quiet and the streets stiller than I'd ever seen them before. I'd only once before been up and out this early, and that was during the week, not on a Sunday morning, when everyone was still asleep. Now there were no cars out, and it felt like we had Havana all to ourselves.

We walked home on streets I'd never seen before, and Alfredo gave me an impromptu tour, pointing out the house where he used to take drumming lessons.

"My teacher died of a heart attack right before you arrived," he told me. "And I haven't been able to find another one who will accept payment in pesos."

"But I thought education was free," I said. "Couldn't you just go to the university and take a class?"

"You know, everything in Cuba has a but," Alfredo said. "Education is free, but first you have to be accepted into the music school, and I don't have that type of background, so I have to take private classes, and everything that's private costs."

We walked past a cement building with a sculpture of a woman and child out front, and Alfredo told me it was a children's hospital.

"My sister used to work there," he said. "She's a nurse."

"Where does she work now?"

"Oh, well now she's working in tourism," Alfredo said, and I thought of Nitza. "She studied a lot of languages to work in medicine, so it made tourism an easy transition."

Down the street a bit, Alfredo showed me where he had studied Italian and Portuguese several years ago.

As we approached Dinora's, I asked Alfredo, "What are you going to do today?"

Alfredo held his hand out, palm up, and counted on his fingers as if checking off items on a to-do list. "Only three days until we leave for *Santiago,*" he declared. "I think I'll start packing today."

"So soon?" I asked.

"Well, I've never packed before," Alfredo said defensively. "It might take me a while."

"Okay," I said laughing. "But I probably won't pack until the night before we leave."

"Well, just make sure you pack well," Alfredo said, a sly edge to his voice.

"What do you mean?"

"I mean," Alfredo said, raising his eyebrows suggestively, "don't forget anything that we might need some night."

"Oh," I said, feeling the blood rise to my cheeks.

Alfredo smiled at me, a childlike smile that reminded me of the first night we'd kissed outside Hotel El Bosque, except that instead of looking to his lucky star on this hot Havana morning, when the sky was as starless and blue as the sea, Alfredo was looking only at me. As the eastern sun beat down on my neck and the vegetable carts rumbled over the potholes of Animas Street, signaling the start of morning in Centro Habana, I stared straight back.

13

The Legal Illegal

On the day of our departure for *Santiago,* Amy and I hid out in the shade of Dinora's house, doing some last-minute packing while we waited for a phone call from Alfredo. From the relative cool of our bedroom, I looked out through the wooden louvered blinds and watched the heat waves slither across the faded asphalt.

"It's only going to be hotter in Santiago," Dinora said as she poked her head into our bedroom for what must have been the tenth time in the past two hours. I was passed out on the bed, dehydrated and exhausted after a quick one-story climb to the rooftop clothesline to collect my laundry.

I pulled myself up into a semislouch and leaned back on my elbows to look at Dinora. I was beginning to feel she didn't want us to leave.

"I've also heard that there are more *jineteros* in Santiago than anywhere else in Cuba," Dinora said, pointing the broom in her right hand at us. "So you girls should be very careful."

Dinora was cleaning the house, a task she usually immersed herself in wholeheartedly, scrubbing at the kitchen counter and reordering the dishes we'd put away the night before while Marta mopped the floor. Marta was an older woman who came over to clean and smoke, often leaving a spotty trail of cigarette ash along the bathroom floor. But other than this oversight, Marta was as immaculate as Dinora. Once she found my mud-stained running shoes under the bed and scrubbed them until they were so spanking clean I barely recognized them.

I had at first mistakenly assumed that Marta was a maid. Dinora, though, was quick to correct me.

"She's a cleaning helper," she said, sounding irritated. "Not a maid."

I tried to determine what the distinction might be. I knew that Marta also ate meals with the family, something I'd never heard of a maid in the U.S. doing. But still, I didn't understand why Dinora had been so offended by my assumption.

When I told Alfredo, he laughed. "You probably scared her," he said. "Maybe she was afraid of getting in trouble."

"What do you mean?" I asked.

"Maids are illegal in Cuba," Alfredo said. "They were outlawed after the Revolution."

"So what would happen if someone found out Dinora had a maid?"

"Probably nothing," Alfredo said nonchalantly.

"Then why would she be worried?"

Alfredo shrugged his shoulders. "Because it *is* illegal," he repeated. "But as you can see, in Cuba there's always a way."

Unfortunately, Alfredo's optimistic explanation didn't extend to our attempts to get to Santiago by either of Cuba's two bus lines, by plane, or by rental car. The Astro peso buses—which charged foreigners in dollars and took seventeen hours to complete the six-hundred-mile journey—had no air-conditioning and were rumored to break down frequently. The marginally faster fourteen-hour Viazul tourist/dollar buses, like the airplanes, reserved only a handful of peso seats for Cubans, and all of them were all sold out several months in advance. Panautos rented only cars that were stick shifts, which neither Amy nor I could drive; and Alfredo didn't have a license. Alfredo did, though, have a neighbor who had told us the day before that he could *resolver* some bus tickets for us.

"Jimmy does this as his *negocio*," Alfredo had told us, smiling at the cleverness of his plan. "He knows the Astro driver, so he can get us a special deal—three tickets for just fifty dollars. That's twenty dollars off what you and Amy would have to pay if you bought just two Astro tickets on your own, and it's seventy dollars off what we'd all have to pay to ride on Viazul."

I remained silent for a beat, envisioning our Astro bus breaking down in the middle of nowhere and us being stranded for hours, or perhaps days.

"I could give you thirty-five pesos," Alfredo continued encouragingly. "That's what it would cost me to ride Astro on my own, so this way it would be like I was paying for my ticket."

He looked at me expectantly, his smile wavering as I hesitated to respond.

"Okay, that sounds good," I finally lied, sacrificing my better judgment for the sake of Alfredo's pride.

"Great," Alfredo said. "I'll give you a call around eight-thirty tomorrow morning to let you know what time Jimmy gets the tickets for."

But the following day, eight-thirty came and went, as did nine and nine-thirty, and by ten, despite my decision to put aside my skepticism and just let things unfold as they would, I was beginning to feel anxious. I wished I could call Alfredo but, to be closer to me, he had recently moved into his mother's house in Centro Habana, where there was no telephone.

"What do you think happened?" I asked Amy. "What if his neighbor just took our money?" The night before, we had given Alfredo fifty dollars for our three one-way bus tickets.

"Maybe one of us should go down to the bus station to look for him, and the other should wait here," Amy said. Before I could respond, Dinora stopped by for her every-ten-minutes check-in and offered up another demoralizing Santiago statistic.

"Did you know that machismo is worse there than in Havana?" she asked.

"No," I said wearily. "Dinora, are you trying to convince us not to go?"

"Oh, no," Dinora said. "Of course I'll miss you, but really I'm just trying to prepare you. You know, not everywhere is like Havana."

The phone rang, and I felt relieved for the interruption.

"Lea, it's Alfredo," Nitza called up. "But please be quick. I'm expecting a call from Rey."

Dinora wrinkled her face in distaste and dismissively waved away Nitza's comment as I went to retrieve the phone.

"Where are you?" I asked Alfredo.

"At a pay phone near my mother's house. Jimmy's still at the station, but I know there's a bus that leaves at noon, so I think we should just head over there to meet him."

Dinora helped us do a final sweep of our rooms, and then she accompanied us down the first flight of steps. Her eyes looked watery as she hugged us goodbye. Luis was at work, Abuela in bed for her afternoon nap, and Nitza, despite the heat, had her head stuck under a hairdryer in her bedroom. Dinora looked sadly around her empty living room.

"Well, at least you'll be here for another month afterward," she said.

Alfredo was waiting for us outside with a wobbly *bicitaxi* in tow. He stuffed our packs under the driver's seat and sat down on the tiny two-person bench in back.

"I don't think we're all going to fit," Amy said. Alfredo laughed.

He handed me his pack, a tattered red duffel bag that Dinora had lent him, and he patted his lap for me to sit down. Amy squished in next to us and, from the balcony above, Dinora called out, "Be careful. Call me if anything goes wrong."

And then we were off, our driver breathing so heavily that I was certain it would be only a matter of minutes before he demanded we get out. But somehow he kept pedaling, and we chugged through the congested Centro Habana streets so slowly that we were passed by old women walking home from the farmers market, loaded up with all their fruits and vegetables. It seemed to me that in the time it took us to clear a city block, we could take in the better portion of a game of dominoes.

Alfredo didn't seem bothered by our dawdling pace. Rather, he seemed to be enjoying the ride. Unlike the shiny, yellow, eggshell-shaped *cocotaxis* that accepted only U.S. dollars and sat at the corner of 21st and O Streets, waiting to transport tourists from the Hotel Nacional to the hot spots of Havana, our rusted, black, skeletal *bicitaxi* could still be hired in pesos, qualifying it as a Cuban form of transport. But its twenty-peso, or one-dollar, cost was literally a hundred times that of a ride on the *camello,* so Cubans used the *bicitaxis* only on special occasions.

Today, like a prince in the lead car of a parade, Alfredo waved at his fans as we pedaled through these neighborhoods that comprised the entire geographic fabric of his life.

"¿Qué bola, socio?" he called out as we passed his Uncle Elpiri's ice cream stand. In greeting, Elpiri waved an empty ice cream cone at Alfredo, motioning for us to stop for a scoop.

"No, no ahora." Alfredo yelled out, as if there wasn't enough time for Elpiri to serve all three of us triple scoops before our *bicitaxi* struggled up the block. *"Voy pa' Santiago."*

Next, we passed the medicinal-plant man who, in the mornings, before the sun got too intense, sat out near Parque Trillo to sell cooking and medicinal herbs, as well as honey in beer bottles with the labels peeled off. Alfredo had taken me here during my first week at Dinora's as part of a tour of the black-market vendors of Centro Habana. He'd shown me how, by knowing which nondescript door to knock on, I could get strawberry soy yogurt or mangoes or rationed bread, which actually wasn't so bad, for less than half the price of what it cost in the dollar *chopping* stores.

"So none of these are legal businesses?" I had asked Alfredo.

"Bueno, son legales pero son illegales," he answered. They're legal but they're illegal. I raised my eyebrows at him. "Except for the mangoes, these are all legal businesses," he told me. "In a sense. The honey is legal, but not for foreigners to buy. The soy yogurt is legal, but only for children and the elderly, and the bread is legal, but only one piece per person per day with the ration book. After that, you can buy as much as you want for a peso each, but that's all illegal."

"So we could both be fined?" I asked Alfredo.

"Well, technically yes, but no," he said.

Alfredo told the medicinal-plant man, too, that we were going to Santiago, and then he asked our driver if he could stop on the next street to run into his grandmother's house and say goodbye. By this point, our driver was so drenched in sweat, it looked as if there was a sprinkler beneath the little awning above his head.

"I'll be right back," Alfredo said as he jumped off the *bicitaxi*, which rose an inch or two in his absence.

"Say *'Hola,'* to your grandmother," I said.

Alfredo looked at me with an odd expression.

"*¿Hola?*" he asked. "*¿O que le mandas un beso?*"

"Oh, yeah, tell her I send a kiss," I said. I still hadn't quite mastered the affectionate Cuban way of greeting people.

While Amy, I, and the *bicitaxi* driver sweated under the shade of a blossoming almond tree, I looked at a SE PERMUTA sign posted on one of the neighbor's houses. This was the equivalent of a FOR SALE sign in the U.S., except that in Cuba, where owning a house was considered as basic a human right as free health care and education, and where earning money off basic human rights was considered a crime, "For Sale" got translated to "For Trade."

As Alfredo might put it, people in Cuba owned their own houses, but then they didn't. People didn't pay rent, so from my capitalist perspective, it seemed that they must own their homes. But ultimately it was the government who held the deed, which was another reason why houses could only be traded.

When Alfredo returned from his grandmother's, he took one look at our exhausted *bicitaxi* driver, paid him his dollar, and said, "We can just walk the rest of the way."

Half an hour later, we arrived, parched and salt-streaked, in front of the bus station where Alfredo announced, "I know a special drink that's perfect for a day like this."

We followed him down a dirty backstreet that smelled of rotting yeast and composted orange skins. We stopped in front of an open kitchen window, where a man with thick, earthy hands pushed a green, bamboolike branch through a rotating cylindrical machine that churned out a chalky white liquid.

"*Dame tres,*" Alfredo ordered the man, who set three overfull glasses on the windowsill for us. Alfredo reached for one and ingested its contents in one long, fluid gulp as excess juice streamed down his hands. Following his

lead, Amy and I wrapped our fists around the two remaining messy concoc-
tions and quickly downed them. Imagining something like Alka-Seltzer, I
was surprised by the drink's silky sweetness.

"What is it?" I asked.

"*Guarapo*," he said, slapping down three pesos to pay for the drinks. "It's
the juice of the sugarcane."

"Where did you get all this money?" I asked as we left. Normally, Alfredo could afford his own drink if it was in pesos, but not three drinks plus a
bicitaxi ride.

"My grandmother gave me five dollars," he said. "And I have two dollars
of my own when that runs out."

I was going to pay half of Alfredo's expenses on the trip, and Amy, declaring, "he's my friend too," had offered to cover the other half. But there
had been no discussion of this with Alfredo. As was the custom in Cuba, we
danced around the issue of money.

Now, as we entered the bus station, I hoped that Alfredo's friend would
come through with the tickets so that we could start our travels on an equal
footing, with this first leg of our journey already paid for.

"How do you say *emocionado* in English?" Alfredo asked me as Amy
headed off to the bathroom and we dropped our bags in the bus station, using them as pillows to sit on.

"Excited," I said. "Are you excited?"

"Yes, and a little nervous too," he said, smiling shyly at me.

"Why?"

"Well, we didn't see each other at all yesterday, and sometimes when we
go a while without seeing each other, I feel nervous when I see you again."

"You shouldn't," I said. I wanted also to add that I sometimes felt the same
way—a shortness of breath and a certain shakiness when I saw Alfredo after
an absence—but I was not as brave as Alfredo, and I couldn't bring myself to
admit this to him. So instead, I leaned over and kissed him on the cheek.

When Amy returned from the bathroom, we went searching for Alfredo's neighbor Jimmy, and we found him huddled against a railing with
two other men.

"Wait here," Alfredo instructed us as he rushed over to the group. I watched the four of them interact, Alfredo every now and then waving his arms about in a way that seemed equal parts excitement and frustration.

Alfredo looked like a Rasta leprechaun, decked out in his favorite outfit but my least favorite—green-and-black plaid golfer's shorts and a neon-green T-shirt advertising the German beer Bavaria, which I'd never even seen in Cuba.

Before the collapse of the Soviet Union, Cubans had gotten their clothes for minimal prices from the *bodegas,* but now they were on their own to piece together something presentable. Alfredo had a few new shirts from the New England and Minneapolis symphony orchestras, which had played at his theater, but the majority of his clothes were hand-me-downs left by strangers passing through the island.

Alfredo's clothes contained logos for products and places that he knew nothing about. He wore his Habitat for Humanity and Nike T-shirts with equal indifference, unaware of the disparate histories behind the concepts they advertised. Even though Habitat for Humanity, minus its Christian beginnings, sounded like a program that could have been developed in Cuba, few Cubans had ever heard of it. Like Nike, it was an American entity, subject to the travel and trade limitations of the U.S. embargo.

Consequently, both T-shirts were rare commodities in Cuba. Unfortunately, the ugly Bavaria ones weren't, and I'd actually seen several other Cubans wearing them. Now I watched the decal of a yellow frothy beer ripple across Alfredo's T-shirt as he gesticulated animatedly at Jimmy and the two middlemen. Finally, the foursome separated, with Alfredo heading outside and Jimmy coming over to us.

"I'm sorry," Jimmy said, slouching down into a cracked plastic seat both Amy and I had avoided sitting in. "It doesn't look like it's going to work out."

"What do you mean?" Amy asked.

"Well, I thought I could get you on the noon bus," Jimmy said, "but it's full, and the driver I'm friends with is out sick."

"Aren't there any other buses?" Amy asked.

"There are a few, but it's too late to get a ticket now."

"Where did Alfredo go?" I asked.

"He went to see if he can find anyone who can help you guys out."

I sighed, perhaps too audibly, and Jimmy put his hand on my shoulder. *"Es Cuba,"* he said.

"Yes, but I thought that also, as Alfredo says, 'In Cuba, there's always a way,'" I said, irritated.

"Don't be angry with him," Jimmy said. "He was just trying to help out. You know he's really in love with you. He talks about you all the time."

I blushed. Even though Alfredo had already told me this on his own, hearing it from a stranger seemed to somehow make it more real and, oddly, intimate.

Alfredo continued to run around searching for tickets, and by the time he returned, at nearly three o'clock with a *taxi particular* offer that, at one hundred dollars, was more than either our Astro or Viazul options, Amy and I were so anxious to get out of the bus station that we quickly agreed. We walked outside, where a man leaning against a dented gray Russian Lada waved us over.

"He can take us to Bayamo in his car," Alfredo said. "It's only an hour from Santiago, and it'll be quicker than a bus."

"Is this legal?" Amy asked.

"Well, it's legal for him to drive to Bayamo, because he has a driver's license, but," Alfredo said thoughtfully, "he may not exactly have a license to carry passengers so . . ."

"Let me guess," I interrupted. "It's legal, but it's also a little illegal."

"Oh, yes," Alfredo said, smiling. "Good, you understand."

The driver, who introduced himself as Darien, helped us load our packs into the trunk, and then we were off. A few blocks into our journey though, Darien pulled over without explanation in front of an off-white stucco house. With the key still in the ignition, he got out and ran up to knock on the front door, returning to the car with another man at his side.

"This is my brother, Ramiro," Darien explained. "He's coming too."

As Amy vacated her shotgun position and squished into the backseat with Alfredo and me, Ramiro stuck a salsa tape into the cassette player, and we took off once more. The Lada drove smoothly and almost speedily for the first half hour of our trip, but then Darien shifted into a lower gear as we approached the potholed country roads lined with scattered palms and mango groves and ramshackle farmhouses, with a stray chicken or turkey pecking around the premises.

"It looks just like Havana *campo*," Alfredo said, sounding surprised. The Havana countryside was as far as Alfredo had been outside Centro Habana. During the past year, while he worked at the symphony, Alfredo had traveled vicariously through the musicians' retellings of their tours to Mexico and Martinique and Minneapolis. Since he'd met me, Alfredo had taken to regularly grilling me about the countries I'd traveled to, asking about the food in each one, the people, the landscape, the weather.

I had always wondered why Alfredo never left Havana. International travel was next to impossible for the average Cuban, but most Cubans, like Europeans, received a minimum one-month vacation. Alfredo could have used this time to see other Cuban cities.

"All my family's in Havana," Alfredo said now as we yelled to hear each other over the blasting salsa music. "So I wouldn't have anywhere to stay in another city."

"What about an Islazul hotel?" I asked. I knew that *casas particulares* like Dinora's would be too expensive, but Alfredo's mother worked at Islazul, a Cuban travel agency that ran a chain of hotels of the same name.

"But that's only for *personas destacadas*," Alfredo said. "For baseball players or government officials or for employees who've done something outstanding at their work and their boss says, 'Here's a pass to go stay in this hotel in Santiago for a week.'"

"So regular Cubans don't even get to travel in Cuba?"

"Not unless they have family to stay with."

"So what do they do for their vacations? What do you do for yours?"

"This is my first vacation in two years," Alfredo said. "Most people only take their vacations because their bosses say, 'Look, you've got to take some time off,' because, really, there's nothing to do. People use vacations to do *negocios, para resolver algo.* When I was younger, I used to go out to the country to buy cheap fruit and meat and sell it for more in Havana, but that's not exactly a vacation."

We passed by a billboard, which read No NECESITAMOS AMOS, We

Don't Need Owners, and I pulled out a little pocket notebook where I'd been keeping a list of billboard propaganda, the previous one being, "Two hundred million children sleep in the streets each night. Not one of them is Cuban."

Alfredo sighed. He didn't understand my fascination with all these political slogans, but in comparison with the rest of the world's commercial propaganda, I found Cuba's proud billboards refreshing. En route to Cuba, I'd stopped over in Cancún, where I had been greeted with a row of English billboards. The first one read AMERICAN EXPRESS SPOKEN HERE, and the second—a photo of a thick slab of steak—announced VEGETARIANS GO HOME.

Now, as I jotted down my latest Cuban roadside jingle, Darien slowed the car until it came to a clunky, resounding stop in front of a small yellow house. Ramiro jumped out, leaving the passenger door open as he ran over and knocked on the door, soon disappearing inside. Within minutes he stepped back out with a young woman in a crisp white halter top, and the two ran excitedly over to the car.

"This is my girlfriend, Milagro," Ramiro said. "She's going to come too."

Milagro leaned forward to kiss my cheek, and then she waved at the air as if to pass along the greeting to Alfredo and Amy, who were beyond her reach. Ramiro sat in the passenger seat again, and Milagro sat on top of him. She took out the salsa tape and stuck in a Spanish techno cassette. She bopped along to the music as we pulled back onto the highway, and soon, she passed back a half-empty bottle of rum.

We bumped our way past bicyclists and roaming bulls and, every once in a while, a broken-down car. If baseball was the national pastime in Cuba, I decided that pushing decrepit DeSotos and Chevys across the highway must be a close second.

Just after sunset, we stopped once more; this time in front of a row of farmhouses.

"Our parents' house," Ramiro announced. "We can have dinner with them."

We followed Milagro and the brothers inside, where we were introduced to the father, who, as if he'd known all along of our visit, quickly made room at the table. An older woman pulled back a sheet hung over the doorway of a doorless bedroom and exclaimed, "¡Tenemos visita!" The mother brought out black beans, rice, pork, and a cucumber-and-tomato salad, and we all sat down to eat.

Darien narrated our meal with tales of his and Ramiro's trips transporting Cubans up and down the island, and afterward, the father took us into the backyard for a dessert of fresh coconuts knocked right off the tree. Their sweet juice dribbled down my chin and onto my shirt. My shorts, which had been ironed (Dinora had insisted) and white when we'd left Havana, were now wrinkled and speckled with black dots that looked like grease. But the moon was nearly full and the night silent except for the snort of the family's piglet, and I was happy that we hadn't been able to catch a bus after all.

14

Living History

At the bus station in Bayamo, among a swarm of flies and in air as thick as gelatin, Alfredo announced that he wanted to go back to Havana.

It was seven in the morning, and after more than five hundred miles and fifteen hours of driving, we were all suffering from exhaustion and crankiness. During the final hour of our taxi ride, Amy and I had discussed our travel plans for Santiago. We'd both spent the past month highlighting in our guidebooks the places we wanted to see. To save space in my backpack, I had ripped out the pages on Santiago, which thoroughly irritated Alfredo.

"You Americans," he said, shaking his head disparagingly "In Cuba, people respect their books. No one here would ever deface one like that."

I sighed and continued scribbling notes in the margins of my severed guidebook pages.

Alfredo leaned over to see what I was writing. "When are you going to tell me what that book says?" he asked.

Giddy from my lack of sleep, I held the pages up close to Alfredo's face.

"What, you mean you don't understand?" I asked, but Alfredo didn't find my joke amusing.

"It's my country, but that's not my language," he said, shaking his head solemnly.

Sometimes it still amazed me that Alfredo didn't speak English—that we had gotten as far as we had in our relationship without a native language in common.

Now, in the Bayamo bus station, as Alfredo announced his desire to go home, I realized that there was still a lot that wasn't being communicated, much of which had nothing to do with our different languages.

"Do you know what a *zero a la izquierda* is?" Alfredo asked me when I questioned him about his sudden decision to leave. The three of us stood in the sweltering heat outside the Bayamo bus terminal, dirty, hungry, and futilely swatting at the flies.

"Tell me," I said, as Alfredo pulled out his *pañuelo* to wipe a streak of sweat off his forehead, "What is a *zero a la izquierda?*"

Alfredo pointed to Amy and motioned for her to move closer to me.

"It's like you two are there," he said, standing off to the side. "And I'm always over here to your left, by myself. You're always speaking to each other in English, and it feels like you're telling secrets. It feels like you've already got your plans for the trip, and all I can do is sit here and do whatever you've chosen, because it's like just my being here is a burden to you. And this isn't right," Alfredo concluded indignantly, looking directly at me. "No one should be made to feel like this, especially not someone's boyfriend."

I stood, letting the flies gather on my head, as I contemplated Alfredo's accusation, shocked by his bitterness and embarrassed by the partial truth in his words. I had not been telling secrets, but during our very long and circuitous journey to Bayamo, I had been unable to avoid thinking about how the trip would have been easier if Amy and I had just caught a dollar bus straight to Santiago.

"Maybe we should discuss this alone," I told Alfredo and then looked over at Amy, who nodded and walked inside the bus station.

"Alfredo, I'm sorry," I said. "I want you to be here."

Alfredo raised his eyebrows at me.

"I didn't mean to make you feel like a *zero a la izquierda*," I said.

Alfredo averted his eyes until I tilted his face with my hand so that he was forced to look directly at me. "I want to travel with you. If you'll stay, Amy and I can speak more Spanish around you, and I could even give you English lessons if you want."

Alfredo leaned in to hug me, and I felt the damp sweatiness of his T-shirt and the comfort that always came from being embraced by his thin yet sturdy frame.

Aboard our bus, Alfredo filled Amy and me in on the history of Bayamo. All I knew was that in the lyrics of Cuba's national anthem, *los Bayameses* were being told to run to battle.

"This is where the first war against Spain began, in 1868," Alfredo told us. "Carlos Manuel de Céspedes freed all his slaves, rebelling against Spain's colonial government. Then the Spanish captured his son and said they'd kill him unless Céspedes surrendered. But," Alfredo paused dramatically, "Céspedes said that all Cubans were like family to him, and he couldn't sacrifice the entire family's freedom to save one son's life."

"So what happened?" Amy asked.

"The Spanish killed his child."

"That's terrible," I said.

"That's one of the reasons I don't like politics," Alfredo said. "Because everything becomes political, even your own children."

"Wasn't Céspedes also killed by the Spanish?" I asked.

"He was, just a few years after his son, but before that, *los Bayameses* could sense that they were going to lose, and they were a proud people, so rather than let the Spanish destroy their city, they burnt it down themselves."

"Do you think something like that could happen today?" I asked. "If Fidel died and the U.S. tried to invade Cuba?"

"I don't know," Alfredo said shaking his head. "But I can tell you that the day Fidel dies, it's going to be total chaos here. That's not a day I want to be in Cuba."

꾼ᪿꙮꙮ

At the Santiago bus station, we called Martín, the dirty blond–haired, pale-skinned owner of the *casa particular* where we had reserved rooms. He picked us up in his mint-green Chevy. As we drove through the uncongested, hilly streets of Santiago, backed by evergreen mountains, I noticed that, although people hung out on their balconies as they did in Havana, no one was dumping their wastewater onto the sidewalks. Santiago seemed so clean and tranquil in comparison to the capital city, which had twice as many people and twice as much dirt and chaos. Tall, lanky palm trees sprouted up between the red-tiled roofs of the brightly colored houses.

"Santiago was the colonial capital of Cuba," Martín told us proudly as we passed by a grassy outcropping with a giant bronze statue of a man gripping at the neck of a rearing horse.

"This is the Plaza de la Revolución," Martín said. "And that's Antonio Maceo."

In Havana, on my way to the Malecón, I often passed a similar, smaller statue dedicated to the distinguished *santiaguero* who fought in both of Cuba's Wars of Independence, serving alongside José Martí in the second one. Like Martí and Céspedes, Maceo too was killed by the Spanish, as were his father and several of his brothers. In accounts I'd read of Maceo's life, the authors always mentioned that he was a *mulato,* a significant detail in a country whose majority population was black but whose leaders (with the exception of former President Fulgencio Batista, a *mulato*) were always white. Even now, in Fidel's revolutionary government, there were few blacks in office.

It did, however, seem fitting that Santiago had a *mulato* general, since there were more blacks here than in any other Cuban city. Briefly, when I had encountered this tidbit of trivia in my guidebook, I had recalled Dinora's rant against Santiago and wondered if it might have had something to do with this statistic.

I hoped that maybe, surrounded by so many Afro-Cubans, Alfredo's accusations of racism would be one less issue that would come up between us in Santiago. At his insistence, when I called Martín from Havana, I had warned him that Alfredo was Cuban.

"Great, no problem," he'd said.

When I'd relayed this to Alfredo, he had seemed comforted. But I hadn't mentioned to Martín that Alfredo was black. Secretly, I had hoped that Martín would be black too.

We ate dinner our first night with Martín; his wife, Esperanza; and their two grown children, Usnavy and Yinette, who, with their eclectic, educated backgrounds, rounded out the picture of the model Cuban family—the one that got by and somehow even thrived despite the shortages; the one that held true to the cultural and academic ideals of the Revolution.

Esperanza and Martín taught math and geology, respectively, at the local university, and Usnavy studied German and supported himself by working as a track coach and a tattoo artist. At the dinner table, he slowly rotated his arms like two shish kebabs being barbecued to show us his symmetric swirls of serpents and roses. Alfredo stared at the spectacle with wide, bulging eyes, as though he were witnessing the emergence of an alien life form.

"Did you do that yourself?" he asked, a painful expression on his face.

"Yep," Usnavy said proudly. "People here don't really like them, but my girlfriend lives in Germany, and there, everyone has tattoos."

I looked at Alfredo, and, seeing the shock on his face, I imagined him envisioning a country full of serpent-covered people.

Yinette's story was a little tamer, although equally diverse. A former model, she was now studying English and trying to decide whether to pursue a career in law, medicine, or journalism.

"They all fascinate me," she said, laughing at her indecision. "I wish I didn't have to limit myself to just one profession."

After dinner, Usnavy and Yinette invited us to a friend's party, and we walked with them beneath a full moon that cast its glow like a spotlight along our trail as we passed one single-family house after the next. Here there were none of the hideous Russian cement high-rises that filled in the open spaces between the crumbling colonial houses of Havana. In fact, the only sign of the Soviet influence came in the form of a row of faded red letters painted on the peeling, powder-blue door of a barred and abandoned house. The out-dated propaganda read ¡QUE SE FORTALEZCA Y PROSPERE LA AMISTAD SO-VIÉTICO CUBANO! Long Live the Soviet–Cuban Friendship!

When we arrived at the party house, we found everyone dancing, and to my great delight, they were dancing merengue, the less intricate, eastern sis-ter of salsa. I could dance merengue, which had no fancy spins and was es-sentially the same few steps repeated over and over. Merengue originated in the Dominican Republic and, perhaps because of this geographic distinction, proud *habaneros,* Alfredo included, tended to dismiss it as too basic, some-thing best fitted to the simple-minded *santiagueros.*

Off to the side of the merengue dancers, a small group had formed a cir-cle around two guys, one of whom was dangling a *pañuelo* in the air. When he let go of it, the other guy, as if heeding the command of an angry drill ser-geant, dropped to the ground in a pushup position, catching the *pañuelo* in his mouth on the way down. Everyone in the circle cheered.

"¡Qué bobería!" How stupid! Alfredo said to me under his breath.

When the *pañuelo*-catcher stood up, he saw us huddled on the outskirts of the circle and motioned for Alfredo to come over. Alfredo shook his head, a sheepish expression on his face. But this seemed only to egg on the members of the *pañuelo* circle, and soon they were all shouting, *"Te toca a ti,"* and gesticulat-ing wildly, a crazy hand dance with no rhythm, for Alfredo to come over.

Alfredo shook his head once more, but one of the dancers grabbed his arm and pulled him in. Alfredo turned, giving Amy and me one last, helpless glance before the dancers asked his name, and soon the infamous *pañuelo* was being released to the chant of "Alfredo, Alfredo."

Alfredo caught it on his first drop pushup, and everyone applauded and patted him on the back, encouraging him to do it again. He mastered the catch a second time, his initial grimace was now replaced with the full-on smile of the initiated. I left Alfredo with his new friends and wandered off with Amy to see what was happening in other parts of the party. The meren-gue music had been replaced with Michael Jackson.

Everyone broke out into her or his individual dance moves, and the sin-gle guys in the group started making their romantic moves. I saw several of them eyeing Amy.

"*¡Qué fuerte!*" said an attractive, dark-haired guy, equating Amy's size with physical strength. He grabbed Amy's hand and then shook his body like a slinky in front of her, up and down in smooth, fluid motions. Amy was a good dancer and quickly picked up on her partner's rhythm, swinging her hips in time while the suitors who hadn't gotten to her fast enough looked on jealously.

One of them made his way over to me and, excited to finally be able to take part in the dance scene at a Cuban party, I obliged by doing my free-form sway that always made Alfredo laugh. My partner looked at me curiously for a moment, but then he smiled.

"I like how you dance," he said. "It's very . . . different."

I couldn't tell whether he was being facetious or not, but I didn't step on his foot once, and when he caught me off guard and spun me around, I just went with it and didn't get tangled up like I usually did. When my partner started the slinky move, I heard a high-pitched yelp, like that of a small animal being attacked, coming from the side of the dance floor. I turned to see Alfredo running over from his *pañuelo* circle.

"She's mine," he said as he jumped in front of me, spreading his arms out as if I were a basketball he was guarding from an opposing team member.

My dance partner took one look at Alfredo's menacing glare and backed off without a word. I stared at Alfredo in disbelief. I glanced around the dance floor and was relieved to discover that no one else was paying much attention to our drama, immersed as they were in their own dancing and mate-seeking.

Alfredo patted my shoulder gently and started dancing as if nothing had happened, but I was no longer in the mood. I walked away, toward the back of the house, looking for a space to be alone and collect my thoughts. I found a bathroom and stood there staring at a mirrorless wall until I heard a knock on the door. I opened it to find Amy and Alfredo standing on the other side.

"I think we're gonna go," Amy said.

"That's fine with me," I said, avoiding eye contact with Alfredo.

"Well actually, Jorge, that guy I was dancing with, wanted to go for a walk," Amy said quickly. "But I don't know if I want to be alone with him yet, so I was thinking maybe we all could walk back to the house together."

I nodded, and Alfredo stood motionless. We walked home in silence as Amy and Jorge spoke in hushed voices in front of us, parting ways at his house just a few blocks before our own.

Inside our *casa particular,* Alfredo wished Amy goodnight and headed straight for the bedroom.

"Is everything okay with you two?" Amy asked me as we stood in the hall. I was about to launch into the whole story, but then Alfredo abruptly stepped out of the bedroom.

"Machismo," I whispered in Amy's ear as I hugged her goodnight. "I'll explain tomorrow."

Alfredo waited for Amy to retreat into her bedroom, and then he said, a nervous waver in his voice, "I have to ask for a favor."

"What?" I asked, imagining that he was going to request that I didn't talk to any other men at parties. Instead, Alfredo motioned for me to go back into the bedroom with him. He walked over to the worn duffel bag Dinora had lent him and pulled out a toothbrush.

"I brought this," he said, pausing for a beat, "but I forgot my toothpaste."

"That's it?" I asked incredulously. "That's all you wanted to tell me?"

"Well," he said, "and to ask if I could share your toothpaste while we travel."

I laughed, not knowing what else to do. I pulled the toothpaste out of my backpack and shook my head as I handed it to him.

"Really, Alfredo," I said. "I think we should be talking about what happened tonight, not about toothpaste."

"Okay," he said, grabbing his towel and toiletries. "But let me take a shower first."

I wrote in my journal while I waited for Alfredo to finish showering, and by the time he returned to the bedroom with his towel wrapped around his waist, I had figured out exactly what to say. For a moment I was distracted by his beauty, his dreadlocks shiny and glistening with beads of water and his skin such a deep brown with a blush of red from the heat of the shower.

"I don't belong to you," I told him as he sat down next to me on the bed. "And it's not right to just rush in and tell the person I'm dancing with that I'm yours."

"But didn't you see how he was trying to get close to you?" Alfredo asked.

"It doesn't matter," I said. "You have to trust me. If I need your help, I can ask you for it."

"Did you want him to get close to you?" Alfredo asked, confused.

"No," I said, "but if he had gotten romantic, I just would have told him no. Don't you know that?"

"I do," Alfredo said, pausing, "but I guess I just get scared sometimes that you'll find someone else."

"But if that's going to happen, then it'll happen either way," I said. "You can't try to control who I interact with."

Alfredo nodded, staring down at the bed like a scolded child. He put his head on my shoulder, and I felt my anger begin to fade.

"You shouldn't worry that I'm going to find someone else," I said, "because I want to be with you."

Alfredo tilted his head to look up at me.

"Me too," he said.

He nuzzled his nose against my neck, and I pulled him in toward me. We lay down together, and after Alfredo had kissed the entire surface of my face, he edged his way down my body, stopping at my waist to look up hesitantly.

"Did you bring the condoms?" he asked. I nodded and reached over to the nightstand to pull one out of my cosmetic bag.

As we tumbled around on the bed, I ran my fingers along the taut, smooth skin of Alfredo's back, and I could feel the beads of sweat on his face as we kissed. Warm, humid air blew in through the louvered blinds, and I remembered something that a former professor of mine had said to me once when I'd asked about her recent visit to Cuba.

"Too hot," she had said, shaking her head in disbelief. "I don't know how anyone has sex there."

The next day, we escaped the heat by heading to a nameless, pebbly beach where I floated on my back in the turquoise sea, letting the gentle waves massage my travel-weary muscles. The reflection of the sun danced in rivulets around me as I reflected on all that had happened in the past day and a half.

Fifteen hours ago, I had been at a party in Santiago, fending off Alfredo's *machista* assault, and fifteen hours before that, I had been fending off flies in Bayamo. Fifteen hours earlier still, I had been in the Havana bus station, unable to respond in kind to Alfredo's confession of being nervous around me after an absence.

Now we had spent the night together, and this new intimacy, combined with the trials of our travels and everything leading up to our being at this beach in this moment, made the scene seem even sweeter.

But once I got out of the water, I felt my calm dissipating. Next to where Amy lay reading a book beneath a shady palm, I sat down to write in my journal, and Alfredo sat next to me, snapping apart twigs from the *uva caleta* tree overhead, reminding me of someone cracking their knuckles.

Save for the night at the *posada privada*, most of which we had spent sleeping, Alfredo and I had never been together for more than six hours straight. And now, as I felt my irritation increase with every twig he snapped, I worried that maybe forty-five hours was my limit.

I knew that the stillness, this seaside silence I so valued, wore on Alfredo just as the constant motion and always-on nature of Cuba could sometimes make me seasick ashore. Recalling the sand sifting ritual, which Alfredo and his symphony coworkers had employed on our trip to the beach outside Havana, I wished now that there was another Cuban here to entertain him—preferably under a different, distant palm.

"Alfredo, why don't you go for a walk?" I suggested. "You could even take some photos," I offered, handing him my camera.

Alfredo had never owned a camera but had once taken a photography class where, along with forty other cameraless students, he had listened with longing as the teacher lectured about lighting and camera angles.

Now Alfredo's face brightened at my proposal, and he dropped his twigs. He gently extended a pair of cupped hands to receive my scratched and travel-beaten automatic camera. He disappeared for nearly two hours, during which I took two swim breaks, read three chapters in my book, and started a new entry in my journal. When Alfredo finally approached, he swaggered across the sand with his hands behind his back. When he reached me, he used his left hand to pull up his too big boxers/swimming trunks and, with his right, revealed a wide-brimmed straw hat, a *sombrero santiaguero*. He placed it on his head and beamed as it, also too big, slid down to his nose.

"Where'd you get that?" I asked, laughing.

Instead of answering, Alfredo put his sombrero on me and quickly snapped my photo.

"Hey," I said, swatting at him with the hat.

"Don't worry. It'll be a good photo," he said knowingly. "I wanted to capture the expression on your face in that moment, the way you were looking at me when I put the hat on you."

"How did I look at you?"

"Like a writer," Alfredo said. "Like you were trying to figure me out, like you were looking for the best adjective to describe me with. My *guajira* writer."

Not used to hearing Alfredo utter the word *guajiro* without the adjective *estúpido* attached, I smiled and repeated my first question.

"I got it from *mis amigos guajiros*," Alfredo said proudly.

"You have *amigos guajiros?*"

"I met them in a bar near where we got dropped off," he said. "When I was walking by, they called out to me, and guess what they offered me?"

"What?"

"A Hatuey beer!"

Ever since our arrival in Santiago, Alfredo had been hoping to come across this once popular malt that had mysteriously disappeared from all the bars in Havana in the mid-1990s. Today it was only available in eastern Cuba, the land of its namesake Taíno Indian chief.

In 1512, the original Hatuey had been captured by the Spaniards, who informed the chief that he would be burned at the stake in their largely successful mission to rid the island of its indigenous people. A priest offered to baptize him first, thereby shoring up his admittance to heaven. Hatuey asked the priest if heaven was where the Spaniards went when they died, and when the priest nodded, Hatuey promptly replied that he would rather go to hell.

Just as I had done at Dinora's house in Havana, Alfredo and I now easily settled into a routine in our new residence in Santiago. In the evenings, while Amy went out with one of her several suitors, Alfredo and I would sit on the front steps beneath the Spanish-tile overhang of Esperanza's roof, surveying the street life like an old Cuban couple. A slight breeze would ripple through the thick, hot air as a bicyclist pedaled by in slow motion, chatting with a neighbor as he passed. Always, there was the soft swish of someone's broom sweeping the sidewalk and at nightfall, an old man selling mangoes would parade his blushing yellow-and-red fruits beneath the purple-streaked sunset.

When darkness came, we would retreat inside for English lessons. While I had long ago given up on trying to roll my *r*'s, hoping instead that people would excuse my poor pronunciation and employ contextual comparisons to understand me, Alfredo insisted on repeating each new word I taught him until he obtained the perfect pronunciation. At the end of our lessons, he would smile shyly and say, in English, "Thank you, my love."

Before bed, Alfredo, ever the cleanliness-obsessed Cuban, would take his third shower of the day. Recently I had discovered that not only had he "forgotten" his toothpaste, as he'd told me our first night in Santiago, but he'd also "forgotten" his soap. I knew that the average Cuban didn't have access to dental floss or cotton swabs, but the *bodegas* still sold soap at reasonable rates.

It was not until Alfredo and I took our first shower together in Santiago that I had discovered the reality. When I saw Alfredo reach for Amy's bar of white Dove soap from the U.S., I realized that the *bodega* rates were not reasonable enough to enable families to buy more than one bar of soap at a time. Alfredo had "forgotten" his soap at home so that his family could shower in his absence. I had been too shocked to say anything during that first shower, but the second time that I saw Alfredo reach for Amy's much-diminished bar of soap, shrunken from Alfredo's many showers, I offered him my liquid soap.

"I'm not going to wash my hair now," he said.

"No, it's soap," I said.

"It is?" he asked. "But it's liquid."

"Don't you have liquid soap in Cuba?" I asked.

"Oh," Alfredo said, a glimmer of recognition crossing his face. "We have *gel del baño,* but it's only sold in dollar stores."

The whole incident made me so sad that I tried to put it out of my mind, but Amy asked me, an awkward waver to her voice, "Do you think Alfredo has been using my soap? I hardly have any left, and I noticed some of his hairs on it. I was just wondering," she added quickly. "Not that I mind."

"I don't think so," I said carefully, slowly, trying to feign thoughtfulness. "Probably what's happening is that so many people are using the shower that the water keeps washing away your soap. But I'll tell Alfredo to watch where his hairs fall."

For several of our first days in *Santiago,* we went museum-hopping around this birthplace both of the Revolution and of many of its martyrs. As exciting as it was to see the origins of all the history I had heard about in Havana, each day I could also feel myself falling deeper into the dizzying onset of information overload.

By the time we walked into the Museo Lucha Clandestina, Museum of the Underground Struggle, at the start of our second week in town, everything began to blur over. We wandered through halls plastered with black-and-white photos of armed and bearded revolutionaries, each one indistinguishable from the next, and I noticed Amy's eyes glazing over and strange words emerging from Alfredo's mouth. When I listened closer, I discovered that he was mumbling, to no one in particular, "*mierda,* shit," like someone with a mild condition of bilingual Tourette's syndrome.

"What's going on?" I asked.

"I'm tired of all this propaganda," he said.

"Okay, I'm getting a little tired too," I said. "Maybe we should skip Moncada."

The Moncada barracks, which had been attacked by rebels on July 26, 1953, today housed a school and the Museo de la Revolución. This was the last museum on our list, but now I worried that visiting it might put Alfredo over the edge. To my surprise, though, Alfredo appeared insulted by my suggestion that we call our afternoon of revolutionary reenactments quits.

"We can't miss Moncada!" he exclaimed. "It's the start of the Revolution."

"But I thought you thought it was all *mierda,*" I said.

"Yes, but this is Mon-ca-da," Alfredo said, emphasizing each syllable as he reverted to that unflagging Cuban patriotism, which coexisted alongside an equally fierce sense of frustration with the current state of things.

We walked onto the grounds of Moncada just as school was letting out, and children in their red, white, and blue *pioneros* uniforms ran in crazy zigzags in front of the mustard-colored fortress. Although it was riddled with bullet holes, rumor had it that these weren't the originals. After the attack, Batista had filled in the holes, and after Fidel came to power in January of 1959, he reopened them, commemorating the Revolution's far-from-victorious first battle, which has since become a celebrated event.

Despite the loss of 69 of Fidel's 105 soldiers (originally there were 123, but 18 of them got lost on the drive down from Havana and missed the battle), who split up to attack Moncada and another site in Bayamo, July 26 is now a national holiday and is marked by one of Fidel's marathon speeches. I had never understood the reasoning behind the celebration, and the trip to Moncada's Museo de la Revolución left me only more confused as we examined exhibit after exhibit of stiff, blood-soaked uniforms detailing the murder of captured revolutionaries.

"Well, it was a failure," Alfredo explained. "But in its own way, it was also a success. *¿Entiendes?*"

I nodded my head, knowing that to press Alfredo any further would only elicit more elusive responses, reminiscent of his previous "legal–illegal" descriptions of maids, private businesses, and *taxis particulares* in Cuba.

So I continued walking through the museum, determined to find an answer in something written on one of the display panels. Ultimately though, the explanation came not in anything posted in front of me but in the act of stepping back from what I considered reasonable and true.

I realized that I had been defining success in the most literal way—a triumph in battle. Instead, the July 26 attack had been considered a victory precisely because of the gruesome details of its failure. It was a success in retrospect, just as Fidel had predicted it would be in his *History Will Absolve Me* court defense of his attack.

At the trial, a young journalist named Marta Rojas had smuggled in photos showing that sixty-one of the rebels had been tortured to death. Although twenty-six-year-old Fidel and twenty-five of his captured compatriots were still immediately sent to prison, the photos revealed Batista's lies about the battle. They caused the public to rally around the rebels, to form El Movimiento Revolucionario 26 de Julio, which in turn forced Batista to release the prisoners on May 15, 1955, after they had served just twenty months of their fifteen-year sentence.

Just as I had originally been confused by the Moncada defeat–success, I often found myself equally perplexed by the contradictory mix of motivations behind Alfredo's behavior, so seemingly personal on the surface and so very political and closely connected at their core to a recent history I was only just beginning to understand.

On our last day in Santiago, while descending La Gran Piedra, a 4,000-foot-high rock with an edge-of-the-world feel to it, Alfredo commented on the beauty of the deep green, unobstructed forest, and then he tossed an empty water bottle into it.

We had just cut over to a side trail to escape the tourists streaming down from the monolith, so only Amy and I had been witness to Alfredo's littering. It seemed such bizarre behavior, given his obvious appreciation of this wilderness that, for a moment, I was stunned into silence.

But turning to see the astonished expression on Amy's face prompted me to take action. I picked up Alfredo's water bottle from the side of the trail and returned it to him.

"Why'd you do that?" I asked.

"What am I supposed to do with it?" Alfredo responded, looking blankly at the dented, dusty bottle in his hand. "You want me to carry this all the way down the mountain and then on the taxi back to the bus station and on the bus back to town?"

"You can't just throw things in nature," I said, looking over at Amy, who nodded encouragingly. "You just keep it until you find a trash can."

"But I can already tell you there's not going to be one anywhere near here," Alfredo said. He looked around at the pebbly, potholed trail, which was deserted except for a tiny, one-room schoolhouse where chickens and children played together on the perimeter of a fledgling vegetable garden.

"Now if we were still on the tourist trail," Alfredo added, "that would be a different story."

"What do you mean?" I asked.

"Haven't you noticed that the government always puts out trash cans for the tourists but never for the Cubans?" Alfredo asked, the irritation in his voice growing with each word. "Haven't you noticed that this country, whose independence all these *santiagueros* died for, is now just for tourists?"

"Pero no tiene sentido," I said, a phrase meaning "It doesn't follow," which I had recently learned and now frequently employed in arguments with Alfredo. "It's not right that there aren't trash cans for Cubans, but you're only destroying your environment by tossing your trash outdoors."

"Here," Alfredo said, handing me back the water bottle. "If you feel so strongly about it, then why don't you carry it?"

"Fine," I said. "That's what I always do when I'm traveling and can't find a trash can."

"Ah," Alfredo said, as though my comment had spurred an epiphany. "But there you go. You're a traveler here. I'm a Cuban."

"Alfredo, you know, not everything's political."

"Who mentioned politics?" he asked. "I hate politics."

"I give up," I said in English. Amy laughed, and Alfredo mumbled something that sounded very much like the familiar, *"Americanos."*

15

El Bloqueo Internal

We drove back to Havana in a slick, black, air-conditioned Toyota with Ralph, an Israeli-born New York taxi driver whom we'd met in Santiago, at the wheel. Ralph told us he'd come to Cuba on a whim, cutting short his two-week Jamaican vacation because someone had told him there was "good ganja" in Cuba. Now, having discovered that there was barely even any bad ganja to be found on the island, Ralph, or El Loco as Alfredo referred to him, wanted out. He had offered to share a rental car back to Havana, and we had quickly agreed to this impromptu road trip, being otherwise faced with the unpleasant prospect of another squished and sweaty *taxi particular* ride along the inland highways of the island or an equally unappealing marathon bus trip.

Save for the purchase of a thirty-dollar tankful of black-market gasoline, of which, several miles down the road, we discovered contained at least 50 percent water, the rest of our two-day drive transpired without incident. We sped past pineapple groves and flaming fields of sugarcane, burnt to make them sweeter and easier to harvest. When the hot, uninhabited land gave way to small towns, Ralph would take a long puff off his cigar and shout out the window, to both people and passing dogs, *"¡Cuba Libre!"*

Alfredo joined in occasionally, while Amy, her breaths falling and rising to the rhythm of the potholes, managed to sleep through the whole performance. Minus Amy's snoring, the scene reminded me of a grainy black-and-white clip I'd watched on Cuban TV of Fidel riding atop a tank in January of 1959, waving at his fans during the rebels' five-day victory parade from Santiago to Havana.

I wished that, like Amy, I could have slept through Ralph's reenactment, but unfortunately every time I managed to settle into a comfortable cranny in the car, Ralph's cries pulled me out of my slumber. So I stared straight ahead, trying my best to ignore his outbursts.

"The way you are regularly," Ralph told me as I pondered the cloudless, sun-streaked sky, "is how I am when I'm stoned."

Once we arrived at the Panautos office in Havana, Ralph, who was flying to Jamaica the next morning, announced, "This time tomorrow I'll be sitting in my air-conditioned hotel, puffing away on a big fat one."

I watched Ralph walk away along the curve of the Malecón, where the late-afternoon sun glittered across the Caribbean. Young couples, beaten-down old men, and skipping schoolchildren crowded the sidewalk—all of them except Ralph heading to their various destinations without haste. A car chugged by, releasing a cloud of diesel, and Alfredo raised his hands in the air, his fingers curved inward as if to capture the contamination.

"La Poma," he said affectionately, invoking Havana's nickname. "Oh, how I've missed the pollution."

I laughed as Amy fanned her face with her hand, trying to dissipate the oily residue hovering in the air.

"I can't believe we're finally back," Alfredo said. "I have so many stories to tell people. First, I'm going to visit my grandma, and then," he said smiling mischievously, "I'm going to put on my *guajiro* hat from Santiago and stop by the theater. Everyone's going to completely crack up."

I laughed at the image of Alfredo entering the dim, air-conditioned theater in his wide-brimmed straw hat.

"Well, have fun," I said. "And give your grandmother a kiss from me."

"Okay," Alfredo said as he lifted his duffel bag onto his shoulder. He stood hesitantly as if unsure of what to say next. "So . . . should I call you tonight and we can go for a walk?"

"Sure, that sounds good," I said, but in truth it sounded strange. This nightly walk, preceded by the phone call had been our evening routine ever since I moved into Dinora's. Now though, given the intimacy and constant contact of our past two weeks, the idea of calling each other in order to see each other suddenly seemed stilted. It felt like a step backward, from living with a boyfriend to just dating him. And I worried about whether, with no more endless nights to discuss everything before we drifted off to sleep side by side, we would lose the tenuous sense of understanding we had found during our travels.

Several blocks from where I said goodbye to Alfredo, I was enveloped in the familiar chaos of Animas Street, where I busied myself greeting neighbors and dodging stray wadded-paper baseballs.

I imagined the excitement that would dance across Dinora and Abuela's faces when they saw Amy and me. I looked forward to a leisurely afternoon sitting in the fan-swept cool of the living room, recounting our adventures.

But when we arrived at Dinora's house, it was Nitza, not Abuela, who stood peering out the balcony at us, and rather than Dinora, it was Marta, the cleaning helper, who pulled the door string to let us in. We climbed the stairs and entered the living room, which was completely quiet and with fewer people in it than I'd ever seen before.

"Abuela's not well," Marta said. Nitza came in from the balcony, looking worn out and anxious.

"My mother is visiting her at the hospital," she said. "I can't even go because I'm waiting for Rey to come drive me to the airport. I have to go to Mexico in three hours. My father's been there all week, and tomorrow he has to go to Chile for another week."

"What's wrong with Abuela?" I asked.

"We don't know exactly," Marta said. "It all just happened so suddenly. One day she was sitting here in her rocking chair watching TV, but when I came over to help her into the dining room for lunch, I took her right hand and it was as cold as ice. She said it felt numb and she felt dizzy."

"It's a circulatory problem," Nitza said.

"How long has she been in the hospital?" Amy asked.

"About a week. And every day, she's asked when you two would be coming back." Nitza glanced at her watch. "You should go over and see her now. There's still an hour left of visiting hours."

Amy and I dropped our bags in our room and headed back into the street. We zigzagged through the congestion of Centro Habana until we reached the imposing, milky-yellow tower of Hospital Hermanos Ameijeiras, which I looked out at from my bathroom window each morning and night as I showered.

Inside the San Lázaro Street entrance, Amy and I stood in an elevator line reminiscent of the one to get into Coppelia. Here, though, everything moved a bit faster, and the mood was surprisingly more festive, with people carrying boom boxes and precariously balanced plates of steaming food—all of which they clutched to their chests as they rushed the elevator doors each time they slid open.

After half a dozen rounds of this stop-and-start game, Amy and I made our way into the elevator and up to the 20th floor, where we landed, conspicuously empty-handed, in one of those dingy, nondescript hospital hallways.

Abuela was in room 54 with three other female roommates. Two were black, and one was white. Two were young, and one was old, like Abuela. It was as if the hospital had preplanned the race and age makeup of everyone to create a balanced mix of patients.

Each woman's space was separated by a drawstring sheet similar to those I'd seen in hospitals in the U.S. But unlike in U.S. hospitals, all the sheets here were pulled back, adding to the communal atmosphere, and each bed had personalized, brightly colored sheets. Abuela was the only one with a TV, a small portable one whose volume was turned down low, although the noise level in the room was as loud as that of several televisions turned up full blast. Visitors milled about, chatting with everyone present, and I had trouble distinguishing which guest belonged to which patient.

Abuela was asleep, so Dinora gently nudged her as she waved us over.

"Look who's here," she said to Abuela.

Abuela blinked her eyes and beamed at us, releasing a rush of words, not one of which I could understand.

"*Mimi*, you have to speak slower for the girls," Dinora said, but Abuela just continued smiling. She reached past a plate of rice and beans to touch Amy's face, and Amy leaned in to kiss her cheek.

"How are you?" I asked.

"I'm good," she said, placing a bandaged hand in mine and once again mumbling something indecipherable.

"She said it's starting to feel better, and maybe in a few more days, she'll be able to come home," Dinora said. Lowering her voice, she added, "Honestly, I think she could have come home several days ago. By the time she leaves, it'll have been nearly two weeks, and all for a little circulation problem in her hand."

"But why would the doctors keep her here if it wasn't necessary?" I asked.

"They say they just want to be certain, monitor her a little more," Dinora said, sounding irritated.

I thought about my few visits to U.S. hospitals, where the emphasis had always been on getting the patient out as soon as possible.

"But that's not necessarily a bad thing that the doctors want her to stay longer," I said.

"Yes, but it is a bad thing," Dinora said wearily. "*No es fácil*, Lea. It's not easy."

"What do you mean?"

"Abuela being here doubles all my work. When the U.S.S.R. collapsed, the hospitals really suffered. Not one of them closed, but now they have nothing, so everything you see here—I brought it all. The TV, the food, even the sheets and towels."

"Everyone has to bring their own food to the hospital?" I asked.

"They don't *have* to," Dinora said, scrunching up her nose in distaste. "But the food here is so disgusting that no one wants to eat it."

"It's the same in the U.S.," I said.

"Yes, but at least there, everyone has a car to bring the food."

"Well, people don't usually bring meals to the hospitals in the U.S.," I said.

"No?" Dinora asked. "Why not?"

"I don't know," I said, looking over to Amy for help.

"Maybe it's not allowed," she suggested.

"Or maybe people are just too busy," I said.

Dinora looked at us with an odd expression on her face, narrowing her eyes as though examining alien life-forms. But then, anxious to return to her own story, she continued.

"Here, three times each day, I have to carry Abuela's meals through the dirty streets, trying my best not to trip on anything but also going as fast as I can so the food will still be warm," Dinora said, pausing to look down at Abuela, "because if it's cold, she won't eat it."

Abuela waved her bandaged hand in the air excitedly, which I at first interpreted as an angry gesture directed at Dinora. Then, though, I saw Dairon, Nitza's ex-boyfriend, walking in the door.

"Is he her doctor?" I asked, remembering Dinora's story about how Nitza had ultimately broken up with Dairon because he could never pay for anything with his doctor's salary.

"Dairon is just here to visit," Dinora said as she handed him an index card–sized scrap of paper. "It's switch-off time."

"Switch-off time?" I asked.

"This paper allows one person to stay here all the time, even after visiting hours," Dairon said. "I'm going to spend the night."

"Really? But where will you sleep?" I asked. There were a few chairs but no spare beds in the room.

"He's going to sleep right here with me," Abuela said, patting the bed with her good hand. "Nitza's loss is my gain."

We all laughed, but I noticed that with the mention of Nitza's name, Dairon's laugh seemed to shrink and turn slightly off-key, like the wavering voice of a singer who has just missed the high note.

For the next several days, between Abuela's meal shifts, alternating overnights at the hospital, and the start of my final month of classes at the university, Dinora and I hardly saw each other. I learned about Abuela's condition in snippets that Dinora would deliver to me, sweating and out of breath, as she rushed past me in the street.

"They're taking off the bandages tomorrow," she told me one afternoon near the farmers market. We stood covering our noses to ward off the stench of rotting banana peels and sour, discarded *panadería* yeast, which spilled over from a nearby dumpster.

"Her hand is warming up," Dinora informed me a few days later at a *churro* stand on Aramburo Street. "These are her favorites," she said as she purchased half a dozen of the rough, sugary treats. "I buy her one every day at home."

Finally, as Dinora had predicted, Abuela was released from the hospital two weeks after she'd been admitted. That afternoon, as Dairon, El Dormido, and a stream of Abuela's other friends and relatives stopped by to visit, Dinora and I finally got to sit down in the living room for that catch-up talk I'd imagined having when I returned from traveling the previous week.

"So tell me, how were the *santiagueros*?" Dinora asked expectantly. "Did you see what I was warning you about? Were there a lot of *jineteros*?"

"There were a lot of *jineteros* in the touristy part of town," I said. "But we didn't spend much time there."

"What did Alfredo think?" Dinora asked.

"He might not admit it, but I think he liked it. He even made friends with some *santiagueros*. And the family we stayed with was really nice. Professors," I said, adding the final detail for Dinora's benefit.

"Hmm," Dinora said, unconvinced. Then, changing the subject, she asked, "Did I tell you that my twenty-fifth wedding anniversary is next week, and we're going to have a party here?"

I shook my head.

"When Luis called from Chile the other day and I told him you were back, he said to be sure to tell you to invite Alfredo."

"Really?" I asked, surprised. I knew that Luis and Dinora had warmed up to Alfredo after that first night. Often they insisted he join them for a cup of coffee and some conversation when he stopped by to see me. But Alfredo, while never refusing their invitations, had remained so cautious and critical of Luis's and Dinora's overtures, and so adamant in his insistence that they were racists, that I felt caught in the middle, never quite sure what to believe.

Now Dinora further confused the situation by following up her party invitation with a suggestion that Alfredo spend the night the next time he came over. Stunned, I found myself staring at Dinora.

"He's your boyfriend," Dinora said. "And he seems like a good person. I just want you to be happy while you're staying here, to feel like this is your home. I've fixed up that extra room next to where you and Amy are, but there's no one there now. I was thinking that whenever it's empty, you and Alfredo could use it."

"Thanks, that sounds good," I said, nodding and grateful for Dinora's offer but also a little embarrassed to be having this conversation with her.

"I've been trying to think about how this could all work," she continued. "And I think it'll be fine as long as you don't tell anyone about our arrangement."

"What do you mean?" I asked. This was beginning to remind me of renting my bike at Hotel El Bosque, and I half expected Dinora to inform me of a hidden camera in her living room.

"It could just create some problems if people knew," Dinora responded cryptically. She paused before continuing. "I told you about taxes, right? That I have to pay a hundred dollars each month for every room I have available to rent out, even if I don't rent it."

I nodded.

"So, I was thinking," Dinora said slowly. "Since I don't have anyone lined up to rent this new room yet, maybe I just won't report it now."

"Can you do that?"

"Well, if no one knows . . ." Dinora said. "So what I've been thinking is that when Alfredo sleeps over, he should leave early in the morning, like before eight, so no one sees him and starts making calculations and wondering if I have a new room."

"Do other people even know how many rooms you have to rent out?"

"Maybe. You never know," Dinora said. "And also it's not official, but it's looked down upon to have Cubans stay at *casas particulares*."

"Why?"

"Well, everyone knows that a Cuban couldn't afford a *casa particular* himself, so it means he's staying with a foreigner," Dinora said, "and those sorts of relationships definitely aren't encouraged."

"But don't worry," Dinora added quickly. "I think my plan will work. While you were traveling, I thought about it a lot. It was nice to have something to think about other than Abuela. I've just been so anxious, and I missed having you and Amy here to talk to. Just sitting with you now, I feel calmer already. And I know it's a little late to say this," she said, leaning over to kiss my cheek, "but welcome home."

Dinora's calm, unfortunately, was short-lived. Just a few hours after our talk, while I sat in my bedroom doing homework, she poked her head in the doorway, flustered and worried once more.

"Lea, excuse me, are you busy?" she asked hesitantly.

I shook my head and motioned for her to come in.

"I just went to the hospital to get the prescription slips for Abuela's medication, but it's not available at any peso pharmacies, only at the international pharmacy, in Miramar," Dinora said, pausing for a breath. "So I was wondering if you would mind coming with me, because Nitza gave me money for it, and I can pay for the taxi for us, and it really shouldn't take very long."

"Sure, I can come," I said, confused by the meaning of Dinora's whirlwind of words. "But why is it that you want me to come?"

Dinora looked out at my louvered blinds' splintered view of the clustered rooftops of Centro Habana and sighed.

"Cubans aren't allowed to buy medicine in the international pharmacies," she said. "I can go in with you, but you'll have to hand the pharmacist the money."

"Are you sure?" I asked. "But why would a doctor give you a prescription for a medicine you're not allowed to buy?"

"Because it's the medicine Abuela needs," Dinora said. "And everyone knows that in Cuba, there's always another way."

The pharmacy was a small, unthreatening gray building on Avenida 41, but just looking at it made me anxious. Dinora, however, seemed confident and simply walked inside and directly over to the pharmacist. Without wavering, she handed over the prescription slip and pointed to me.

"This girl needs her prescription filled," she said, and I understood that it was my role to play the non-Spanish-speaking tourist befriended by a helpful *cubana*. The pharmacist nodded, and while she retreated to the back of the pharmacy, Dinora passed me an underhand bill. I wrapped my fingers around it and, trying to behave as casually as possible, examined the contents of the glass case in front of me. Here lay all the hygienic, cosmetic, and dental goods I hadn't seen since leaving the U.S.—albeit at higher prices than they were back home. There was dental floss for five dollars, a box of tampons for ten dollars, and a tiny tube of sunscreen for fourteen dollars. I looked longingly at the dental floss, having used up mine the previous week. But now, as I recalled how Dinora had shown me a spool of thread she used sparingly for flossing, I felt extravagant for even considering the purchase.

When the pharmacist returned and announced that the medication was twenty dollars, I opened my hand and was relieved to see Andrew Jackson's face unroll onto the counter.

Then we were out on the street once more, hailing a taxi while Dinora complained of the heat and an incessant pain in the arch of her foot, as if she'd already forgotten about the whole fantastic pharmacy scene.

On the ride back to Centro Habana, Dinora remained uncharacteristically quiet, and I tried to contain my curiosity about what had just happened, in case such matters should not be discussed in the presence of strangers.

"So, what did you think?" I asked once we were alone back at the house, where Dinora stood at the kitchen sink, filling her pink plastic pedicure tub with hot water to soothe her feet. "It wasn't so bad after all, was it?"

"No," she said. "In the end, most things here work out. It's just tiring to arrive at that place. You have to always be alert, always fine-tuning your plan."

"But why is it like this with the pharmacies?" I asked. "Why can't Cubans get medicine there?"

"I know it probably sounds terrible to you," Dinora said as she carried the tub to the living room, where she sat on the sofa and submerged her feet in the steaming water. "For a while I used to feel that way too, especially because before the collapse of the U.S.S.R. it wasn't like this. But now tourism is our number-one industry, and because of the U.S. *bloqueo,* Cuba can't get most of the medicines it needs. So the government has to make sure that the little medicine we do have is available for the tourists. Who would come here if they knew that there would be no medicine if they got sick?"

"But what about the Cubans? Shouldn't you come first?"

"Yes, in theory," Dinora said. "But the tourists' money subsidizes so much in Cuba—our education, our health care. Look, my mother was in the hospital for two weeks receiving excellent care, and we didn't have to pay one peso."

I wondered whether Dinora had forgotten that, just a week earlier, she had criticized the doctors for keeping Abuela for so long.

"But then, when Abuela got out," I said, testing Dinora, "for a week's worth of medication, you had to pay more than most Cubans earn in a month."

"That's true," Dinora said, switching positions. "I guess you could say that there are two *bloqueos* in Cuba—*un bloqueo external y un bloqueo internal.*"

"Could Nitza ever get you the medicine? As a doctor?"

"Well, if she was actually working as a doctor then she'd never be able to afford it," Dinora said, releasing a quick, sharp laugh. "Besides Abuela, that is the other thing that I was worrying about while you were traveling."

Dinora lifted her feet out of the tub of water and laid them atop a towel-covered footrest. As she spoke, she gave herself a pedicure, accenting our conversation with the delicate *click-clack* of her toenail clippers.

"While you were gone," Dinora continued, "Nitza got a phone call for a medical assignment." Dinora paused dramatically and looked at me with expectant eyes.

"And?" I asked.

"And?" Dinora repeated. "*And* these phone calls are just going to keep tormenting Nitza until she makes up her mind about her career."

"But hasn't she already made up her mind?" I asked. "Isn't she a flight attendant?"

"Well, yes, but that's because of the economic situation, but eventually that has to change. Then Nitza will want to be a doctor again, because being a doctor has always been her dream. But if you spend five years outside of your field, you lose your title."

"What if Nitza left her job now and started working as a doctor? With Luis's salary and renting rooms, wouldn't you be able to get by?"

"If Nitza were a doctor now," Dinora responded without even pausing to think, "we wouldn't have our TV, our second floor. You wouldn't be here. Now Nitza gets to travel and see the world, but there's a law that says that doctors can't travel."

"But what about those who are posted in other countries?"

"That's for work, and they have to return home the minute they finish their assignment. I want Nitza to be free, and I want her to have a better life than I've had."

"Do you think Nitza will have a better life than you've had so far?" I asked.

"Her life has been much better than mine was before the Revolution," Dinora said. "Nitza has had everything—love, clothes, food. She's studied. Her parents are both educated. If I had had someone to direct me, like I did for Nitza, maybe my life would've been better. Maybe I would've studied literature instead of engineering. All I did, I did alone."

"But what about her life now?" I asked.

"Sometimes I think it's very good," Dinora said. "Nitza knows more of the world than I ever will. She has money to do the things she wants. Last week she even received a permission card so that in a few years she can buy a car. But then other times, all I can think about is how she had always wanted to be a doctor, and then I get confused about what I think. Then I just don't know anymore."

16

The Cuban Cinderella

About a week after Abuela's homecoming and two weeks into my own return, life in Havana settled back into its usual sweet, stagnated pace. The only decipherable difference I could make out since my trip was that all the tomatoes in town had disappeared. In their ruby-stained crates at the farmers market there were now pyramids of avocados, so large and smooth-skinned that I hardly recognized them as the fruit I made guacamole with in California.

In the same simple way that the passage of spring into summer had been marked only by a change in produce, I noted an equally subtle transformation within myself. As Alfredo and I drifted off to sleep one night in Dinora's extra room, without either one of us stopping to point it out, I realized that I'd responded to his nightly "I love you" not with my usual "Mmm . . ." followed by an embrace but with an "I love you" of my own.

At some point between our travels and the present moment, while I'd been worrying about transportation or Abuela or any combination of other things, I had fallen in love with Alfredo.

I loved how sensitive he was, to his own emotions and to the politics of the world he lived in. I loved the delicate, rich brown fold of his eyelids as he slept at night. And, although it had intimidated me to the point of irritation when we first met, I had grown to love the way Alfredo so openly expressed his feelings for me without fear of appearing vulnerable. He made me want to live my life more bravely.

For the first few days after I told Alfredo I loved him, his permanent smile and the intensity of this emotion seemed enough to sustain us. But then, in a way that wasn't at all subtle, I realized that despite all the clichés and pop songs testifying otherwise, love was not always enough. Certainly, it wasn't a synonym for compatibility.

Our relationship reminded me of a tango where we stepped back just as we came together. Were a choreographer to write out the pattern of our part-nering, it would have read something like: Argue, get hurt, withdraw, approach, discuss animatedly, discuss calmly, appease, and then begin all over again.

Was my inability to truly understand Alfredo—or at least foresee how he might respond to a given situation—a result of our differing languages and cultures? Or was it the climates we came from and the skin colors we wore? Was it our disparate economic and political backgrounds? Or was it simply just a clash of personalities?

Because there were too many variables to isolate and label any one as the root of our miscommunication, I decided to eliminate the only variable I had control of—my participation in our arguments. For one night, I decided, I would humor Alfredo, assuming that whatever he did came from a place of good intentions. Essentially, I would act as if I understood him and see where that left us at the end of the night.

The evening I chose for my experiment was the birthday of a classmate, an Austrian woman who invited me to join her and her friends to celebrate along the Malecón. When I called Alfredo at his work to see if he wanted to come, he hesitated and then asked if he would be the only Cuban.

"I'm sure Barbara has Cuban friends," I said, "and if not, I'm sure she'd be happy to have a Cuban there. But whatever you decide to do, I'll understand."

"I want to come," Alfredo said, no echo of reservation remaining in his voice. "I want to be with you."

I smiled as I hung up the receiver, pleased with the positive start to the night. I wondered how many of our previous disagreements could have been avoided if I had just been more sensitive to Alfredo's concerns.

There were two other Cubans among Barbara's group of friends, and I could see that Alfredo was enjoying himself as we all sat along the Malecón talking. But then as the sun started to set, Barbara suggested we get something to eat, and Alfredo tensed up.

While traveling, because he was hungry and didn't have the option of going home for a free dinner at his grandmother's, Alfredo had gradually gotten over his embarrassment of being paid for. But tonight, at Restaurante Hanoi, a government-run peso eatery whose offering of rice and beans and fried chicken seemed more Cuban than Vietnamese, Alfredo sat uncomfortably in his seat, staring blankly at the menu. Even in pesos, the meals here cost a good two days of Cuban wages.

I looked at the other two Cubans to see how they would react and was surprised to find them unfazed. They ordered their meals like everyone else, and when the bill came and was divided among the foreigners, they continued the conversation they'd been having with Barbara, acting as if this being taken out to dinner on their friend's birthday was completely normal. Alfredo, on the other hand, had eaten in silence, averting his eyes when the bill arrived.

Although I wasn't surprised by his behavior and in many ways admired his pride, I still sometimes wished that Alfredo didn't take everything so personally. Tonight, though, I was determined not to harass him about his behavior.

After dinner, one of Barbara's foreign friends bought a bottle of rum, and we returned to the Malecón, where we watched a young boy with a fishing rod staring intently into the deep, black sea.

"*Oye, socio,*" Alfredo called out. "Have you caught anything yet?"

The boy shook his head and walked over to us. Up close he looked even younger and smaller than he had from a distance. He wore a torn baseball cap, and there were deep bags beneath his eyes.

"I haven't caught anything yet, but I have all night," he said, swaying as he chuckled to himself. He was giddy in the way of the very old and the very sleep-deprived.

"I fish every night until six in the morning," he said. "And then I go home and sleep for an hour, and then I go to my job at a cement factory."

"What about school?" I asked, eyeing the boy skeptically. His story sounded made up, like a case study of child labor from the days of Batista.

"School?" the boy asked. "I don't have time for school. I'm the oldest of four kids, and I have to help support the family."

"Pobrecito," Alfredo said as the boy returned to his lonely post by the sea, not so far from a kiosk selling beer and soda and cigarettes to foreigners.

"Do you believe that?" I asked.

"I do," Alfredo said solemnly. "Life is difficult here, Lea."

Alfredo looked over at the kiosk and then asked, "Do you have some *fula*? I'm going to buy him a soda."

I handed Alfredo a dollar bill and watched as he brought the boy the soda and affectionately patted him on his frayed baseball cap. I smiled at him when he returned, but Alfredo looked at me for a second as if he didn't recognize me.

"Why aren't you wearing my necklace?" he asked. On Valentine's Day, the one-week anniversary of our meeting, Alfredo had given me a necklace with a rainbow of Indian beads. He had a matching one, which he slept and showered in. But I always took off jewelry before showering or sleeping, not always remembering to put it on the next day.

"I wore it yesterday," I said.

"I didn't see it," Alfredo replied matter-of-factly. He looked around him once more, but this time instead of fixating on the fisher boy, he focused on Barbara and her friends.

"I want to leave," he said abruptly.

"Okay," I said, breathing deeply to quell my growing irritation. I was going to remain calm until Alfredo's misplaced outrage settled and he had no one to share it with but himself and no choice other than to face up to the motives behind his behavior.

I walked over and told Barbara we were heading back while Alfredo sat waiting on the ledge of the Malecón.

"Where is your house?" Barbara asked.

"Centro Habana."

"Oh, great, mine too," she said. "I'll walk back with you, and I think Charlotte lives there too."

It ended up that everyone lived in or near Centro Habana, and they were all ready to go. I waved Alfredo over to join us, but after just a few minutes of walking with the group, he announced, "I want to walk down another street, just you and me."

"But I want to walk here," I said, momentarily forgetting my vow not to argue.

"Why does everything always have to be what you want?" Alfredo asked.

"It doesn't," I said. "Let's go down another street."

I told Barbara we were going to stop by a friend's in Habana Vieja, and luckily no one offered to follow us this time.

Trying to steer the conversation away from the approaching argument, I asked Alfredo if the fisher boy had told him where he lived. I was imagining shadowing him for a day and a night and writing an article that I would title, "The Young Man and the Sea."

"He didn't tell me where he lives," Alfredo said, "but what I do know is that I've never met anyone who had someone offer them a house to stay at for free but turned it down to stay at a *casa particular.*"

"Alfredo," I said, shocked at his mention of an issue I thought we'd resolved more than a month ago. "I told you I really appreciated the offer to stay at your house, but I like the independence of having my own floor and not living directly with a family."

"But when we traveled, you didn't have that independence," Alfredo protested. "In Santiago we shared the bathroom with the whole family, and that didn't bother you."

"But that was only for a limited time," I said.

"Well, my invitation was too," Alfredo said. "It's not like you're going to live in Cuba forever. You're free to leave whenever you want."

I looked at Alfredo, who stared back at me defiantly. "Maybe you can't understand because you're not like me," I said. "But it makes me feel vulnerable to get too close to you. That's what's been comforting to me about being at Dinora's because if I want to be alone for a night, I can."

"How can you say you have independence here?" Alfredo asked. By now we were in front of Dinora's, and Alfredo stared up with contempt at the thick wooden door. "I don't call independence someone telling you that if you want your black boyfriend to spend the night, he has to be out by eight in the morning like he's some sort of embarrassment to the family."

"Alfredo, I don't like that you have to leave early either, but that doesn't have anything to do with your being black," I said. "I already told you it's about *casa particular* taxes."

"I don't know what your definition of independence is," Alfredo continued as if he hadn't heard anything I'd just said, "but the only way I see it fitting with your reality is if you define it as independence from me and my family."

Alfredo took one last intense look at me and then, to my surprise, he leaned over and kissed me on the lips. It was only a formality, though, as passionless and automatic as a knee jerk at the doctor's office.

"*Buenas noches,*" Alfredo said, and then before I could formulate a response, he was off, a lone shadow quickly engulfed in the darkness of Animas Street.

Inside Dinora's house, I tiptoed up the stairs and into my bedroom, where Amy lay on top of her sheets, curled up in the fetal position against the cool metal of the air conditioner. I grabbed my journal off the nightstand between our beds and carried it into the extra room. Here, sitting on the bed where Alfredo and I had spent the last few nights together, I realized that, as much as I did care for him and as much as we'd been through together, we just were not compatible as a couple.

In the process of writing down these thoughts, I saw suddenly and clearly the impetus behind what had transpired tonight and what had, in fact, been happening all along since that first evening when Alfredo and I met outside Hotel El Bosque. Regardless of whether I responded nonconfrontationally or argued back at Alfredo, he saw our conversations in terms of the predetermined roles he had scripted for each of us—I was the oppressive white American and he was the oppressed black Cuban. All this time, I realized, we had not just been arguing, traveling, sleeping together as two people, but as two races, two nations. We had been carrying with us the bitter, twisted history of racism, as well as that of an international feud that was stronger than each of us and older than both our lifetimes.

At 5:45 AM, as the sun began its ascent over Havana and the rooster that always patrolled the tamal stand at the farmers market let out the first of his morning *cock-a-doodle-doo*s, I finally set my journal down and returned to the bedroom for a long overdue sleep. I slept solidly until 2:30 when I was woken by Amy's rummaging through her dirty clothes pile.

"Sorry," she said. "I didn't mean to disturb you. When did you get in last night?"

As I recounted what had happened, she came over to sit next to me on the bed.

"You know," she said, "I like Alfredo a lot, but I've always noticed, especially when we were traveling, that he does . . . well . . . see things in his way. I mean, we all do, but Alfredo has a lot of pride. I think maybe he doesn't even realize how he's being with you, but I know you've tried a lot to work things out, and I think it makes sense if you don't want to spend your last week and a half fighting with him."

I nodded, pleased to have my thoughts validated, but also sad that Amy, who knew so well the details of my relationship with Alfredo, hadn't seen fit to propose a different solution. I sat silently for a moment, still exhausted after my nine hours of sleep. As I stood to stretch out, I heard the doorbell ring downstairs.

"Amy, is Lea there?" Dinora called up cheerily. "It's Alfredito."

I sat back down and pulled the bed sheet up around me.

"Do you want me to tell him you're sleeping?" Amy asked.

"Yeah, that's good, and don't let him come up here either."

"Okay, I'll guard the staircase," Amy said, laughing.

She returned a few minutes later looking somber.

"He wanted to come up anyway," she said, "but I told him I didn't think he should. He said for you to call him at the theater. He was on his way to work."

"So late?" I asked.

"He didn't look too good," Amy said, adding softly, "Maybe he had trouble getting to sleep too."

After I showered and dressed, I toyed with the idea of returning to the safe solitude of my bed, wondering what would happen if I just claimed to have come down with some rare strain of narcolepsy, leaving me conveniently bedridden for the remainder of my time in Cuba. Yet, while I knew that Dinora would enjoy attending to me, I also knew that I needed to face Alfredo.

I had just heard Nitza, the family phone hog, hang up, so I rushed downstairs to grab the phone before Dinora could decide to call a friend, or before one of her next-door neighbors got embroiled in one of their lengthy phone conversations. Via an intricate maze of wires, Dinora had rigged up an extension enabling her next-door neighbors, who had not yet been assigned phone service by the government, to share her phone. This was, of course, illegal, and also, of course, quite common throughout Cuba, where the phone-to-people ratio (5 to 100) was one of the lowest in Latin America.

The phones connected by this intricate extension system had the same telephone number, which meant that the neighbors, not knowing that I was on the phone, would often pick up in the middle of a conversation to make an outgoing call.

"*Oye, estoy hablando,*" Hey, I'm talking, I'd yell out over their fervent rotary dialing.

Having the same phone number also meant that both Dinora's and her neighbors' phones would ring at the same time. While I often picked up the neighbors' calls, Dinora always seemed to know whom the phone was ringing for. She'd stare at it as it let out its shrill, urgent cry and then she'd say, "*No, es para* Marianela."

Today, I arrived downstairs a minute too late and found Nitza staring angrily at the telephone on her nightstand.

"*Se rompió,*" she said. "Again. And this time it cut me off right in the middle of a conversation with Rey."

The pay phone at the end of the street was broken too. So as a last resort, I knocked on the door of Dinora's neighbor Gertrudes, who had one of those coveted phone connections that worked more often than it didn't. This was such a rarity that Gertrudes had been able to turn her prize phone line into a *negocio*, charging her less-privileged neighbors one peso per phone call.

Gertrudes's phone was my least favorite option, because it was in her dining room, and although no one in her family seemed to mind my conversations interrupting the middle of their dinner discussions, I always felt awkward. But not to worry—Gertrudes's phone wasn't working today, either.

"Why don't you come to the movies with me and Liudmila?" Amy asked when I returned home, dejected. "It's opening night for a new Pedro Almodóvar film, and we're meeting at Cine Yara in half an hour. There's that whole wall of pay phones outside. One of them has to work."

Unfortunately, not one of them did. I wondered whether the phones at Alfredo's work were even functioning, and then I further frustrated myself by thinking about how, in the time all this had taken, I could have already walked the two miles to Alfredo's work to talk to him in person. I debated doing so now and forgoing the movie, which didn't start for almost an hour anyway. Movie times in Cuba were rarely posted anywhere outside the ticket booths, so filmgoers showed up when it was convenient for them. They arrived prepared to rush the ticket line if the show was just starting, or to dillydally outside the theater for upward of an hour if the flick had already begun. Another frequently employed option was to watch the movie piecemeal, entering in the middle and then, since no one was ever kicked out after paying for a ticket, staying on for the next showing to see how it had started. Once I understood the routine, I had ceased to be bothered by it and had even at times enjoyed the spontaneity it offered. But tonight I felt my patience dwindling.

I walked over to the movie line to tell Amy and Liudmila of my change of plans, but just before I reached them, I saw Alfredo coming from the opposite direction and heading straight toward me.

For a beat, we both stared at each other, too shocked to say anything. Then, with a smile that was a mixture of nervousness and excitement, Alfredo finally broke the silence.

"What luck!" he said, smiling. "I was just going to stop by your house again. I wasn't feeling well, so I left work early. I was going to catch the bus, but it was so crowded I decided to walk instead, and I saw Amy and Liud-mila, so I came over to say 'Hi.'"

I nodded.

"When I stopped by Dinora's earlier," Alfredo continued, "I had been thinking we could talk."

"Okay," I said, motioning to Amy and Liudmila to go ahead without me. "But let's go somewhere else."

We walked away from the crowds and down to the corner of 21st and L Streets, where we stood alone and uncertain of what to do next. Unlike my last attempt at breaking up, which had clearly caught Alfredo off guard, I could tell by his hesitancy now that he was well aware of the tension.

Finally I spoke, unleashing all of my suppressed anger from the night before as I recounted how Alfredo had destroyed our relationship by choos-ing to view me as an American rather than as an individual. I yelled at him in bad Spanish and he just nodded, not correcting me.

"Instead of trusting me and really listening to what I had to say," I told him, "you spent your time searching for my ulterior motives."

"You're right," Alfredo said when I stopped to catch my breath. "I left work early today because I had this pain in my chest. I thought you were go-ing to say you'd had it with me this time. When I lay in bed trying to fall asleep last night, I realized that I have been very immature with you."

"What made you realize that?" I asked, unconvinced.

"I was replaying everything in my head and I heard your words, and I saw how I hadn't really listened, because I only wanted to be right," Alfredo said. "But now I have a proposal for you. If you give me another chance, I will stop arguing with you and always trying to change your mind. Really, all I want now is to enjoy the little time we have left together."

"And do you still think it's something personal that I didn't want to live with your family? Do you still not believe me about my feeling vulnerable without my own space?" I asked.

"I believe you," Alfredo said. "And I have some advice. I think you need to find a way to let yourself be vulnerable sometimes, to take a risk and try new things even if at first the thought of them might make you feel uncomfortable."

"Okay," I said. "I can try, but I refuse to spend my last week and a half here arguing with you."

"It's different this time," Alfredo said. "All the other times we've made up, we just talked about whatever was going on in that moment, not the reasons behind it. Now I know that I need to stop judging you as an American."

"That's right," I said.

"And you need to stop judging me as a Cuban," Alfredo added.

"As a Cuban?" I asked, surprised. "What do you mean?"

"I mean as *un latino machista*. Do you remember what you said to me that first night we kissed, when we were standing in the line at Coppelia and I said I was going to see about bribing the policeman to get in quicker?"

"I said, 'Okay.' I didn't know what was going on."

"No," Alfredo said smiling. "You said something else first. I told you not to talk to anyone while I was gone, meaning don't tell them where I went or what I was doing, but you interpreted it as some sort of *machista* command."

"What did I say?" I asked, a faint recollection of the scene forming in my head.

"You said, 'I'll talk to whomever I want to,'" Alfredo said, laughing so hard he almost lost his balance.

I laughed too, but then suddenly, Alfredo stopped. "So, what do you say?" he asked. "Can we try again?"

"Okay," I said. "Okay, but just . . ."

"Just what?"

"Just . . . be good now," I said, all my more specific, articulate words used up, all my anger spent.

Alfredo laughed again. "Alright," he said. "And now, if you want, I'd like to invite you out for a drink. That's actually why I stopped by before. If you had been awake, I would've called in sick to work so we could've talked and gotten a mojito somewhere, because in the afternoon, a lot of bars sell drinks in pesos."

"And now, in the evening?"

"Well, let's see," Alfredo said, taking my hand as he started walking down the street. "Maybe we can still find something. It's just that after six, the tourists come out, and the bars start selling all their drinks in dollars."

I made a grunt of disbelief, but as we moved from one smoky, dimly lit bar to the next, with a simple shake of their heads each bartender confirmed Alfredo's story. After our fifth attempt, Alfredo turned to me and shrugged his shoulders despairingly.

"Maybe we should just head home before you turn into an orange squash," I said, attempting humor, although I didn't know the Spanish word for "pumpkin" or even whether such a vegetable existed in Cuba.

"An orange squash?" Alfredo repeated blankly.

"Like Cinderella," I said. "And how she had to be home by midnight."

"I'm sorry," Alfredo said, "but I don't know what you're talking about." He rested his head atop my shoulder as if too worn out for further conversation.

"It's okay," I said, feeling my own exhaustion as Alfredo's breath whispered softly against my neck. "It doesn't really matter anyway."

17

Departures and Returns

The week before my scheduled departure from Cuba, I bought a round-trip ticket to Cancún so that I could extend my visa by leaving the country.

At eight-thirty on a Saturday morning, with nothing but my wallet, passport, and nearly expired student visa, I stood in the shade of a chipped Spanish archway on Infanta and waved down a taxi to take me to the José Martí International Airport. Within an hour and a half, I was on the airplane, and within another two hours, I was waiting in the immigration line at the Cancún International Airport.

After having my passport stamped by a short, stocky Mexican immigration officer, I continued down the airport corridor and turned left when I spotted a duty-free shop around the corner. I pulled out of my pocket a crumpled piece of paper, a free-market shopping list that had an item for everyone I knew in Havana, and then some. Dinora said she'd love some almond-scented liquid soap, and Liudmila had requested an English–Spanish dictionary. I wanted to buy some tampons for myself, and Alfredo had asked for a pair of sandals. His sister needed vitamins, his grandmother aspirin, and some guy I'd met on Infanta while I was waiting for my taxi had asked if I could bring him a Coca-Cola.

For a moment now, as I gazed through the store's large front windows at the multitude of goods that lay on the other side, I felt dizzy from the excess, once familiar but now so foreign, and almost obscene. Spanking-new best-selling books and thick, crisp newspapers in every language lined the walls, while glossy postcards and kitschy key chains with minisombreros attached filled in the middle of the store. A rainbow array of gums and candy bars of varying sizes lined the checkout counter. I wanted to buy everything and disperse it to strangers waiting in the endless *bodega* lines of Havana. I wanted to turn around and run away.

I glanced up at an overhead clock and, with a sense of relief, realized that there was time only for the latter option. My plane back to Havana was leaving in just forty-five minutes. When I bought my round-trip ticket to Cancún, I had arranged it so I'd have as little time as possible there, not wanting to break the dream of Cuba.

Now I rushed over to the gate, handed my ticket to the steward, and settled into my seat for the return flight. As I waited for the plane to begin its dizzying runway rush, I thought about something Alfredo had said to me when I told him I was going to stay on for a fourth and final month, having to return in early June for a writers' workshop.

"I want you to stay for me, but I don't want you to stay *just* for me," he'd said.

I'd nodded. "I've been thinking about that too."

"I think you should use this month to write some stories, to contact some editors before you go home," Alfredo said. "And when you fly back here from Cancún, you should imagine you're coming to Cuba for the first time. You should think of it as a new start."

Then, perhaps to add to the fantasy, Alfredo had offered to feign illness at work so he could leave early and meet me at the airport.

"I've never been in an airport before," he said. "It'll be fun, like you've come back to visit and I'm waiting for you."

"That's sweet," I said, "but my flight might be late, and then you could be stuck waiting for hours."

"I don't mind," Alfredo said, undeterred, but I too remained firm.

"I'll just call you when I get back to Dinora's," I said casually, although Alfredo's suggestion had caused me to catch my breath. It offered up too vivid and concrete an image of us in a setting that would ultimately only carry memories of separation.

I returned to Havana at 4:30 and saw Amy, who was leaving the house as I was approaching. She was flying home the next morning, and all week I'd been trying to imagine what my life would be like without her in Cuba, in this surreal socialist world that we'd plotted our way through together, two lone Americans in the supposed enemy's terrain.

"How do you feel about leaving?" I asked Amy as we stood under the sliver of shade beneath Dinora's balcony.

"I feel a little scared," she said.

"Of what?"

"Of falling back into the American lifestyle, of forgetting what it's like here," she said. "It's not that I was unhappy at home, but I've been so happy here."

"I understand," I said, giving her a hug. "I'll be scared when I go back too."

Amy stood silent and motionless for a beat before asking, "Do you want to come with me to get some food for my *despedida*?"

For Amy's goodbye party, we had planned an American dinner for our Cuban friends, who were always questioning us about our country's culinary traditions. In Cuba, there was only Cuban food and a dish of fried rice with chicken bits, which was passed off as Chinese. When I described my favorite meals back home—gnocchi and burritos and veggie pad thai—Cubans protested that none of them were American.

"Don't you have a national dish?" Dinora had asked me once.

All I'd been able to come up with at the time were hamburgers and hot-dogs. Later, when Liudmila asked me, I added meatloaf. And when Alfredo's family reiterated the question, I expanded my list to include McDonald's, to which everyone nodded approvingly.

With the exception of Antarctica, Cuba was the only place in the world without a McDonald's. While this was reason enough for me to fall in love with the island, Cubans viewed the golden arches as yet another icon of the embargo, and consequently they longed for the Happy Meals and prepackaged, microwaveable apple pies they had been denied.

Those who left the country were always quick to send back reports on McDonald's, which, since Cubans had difficulty wrapping their tongues around Irish surnames, they pronounced "Madonna's." Those who had never left Cuba had to content themselves by counting, like children collecting baseball cards, how many of their friends or family members had visited the ubiquitous yet elusive hamburger haven.

"My grandfather ate at one in Russia, and my uncle has been to one in Germany . . . and a friend of mine who moved to Toronto last year, the first thing he did was go to Madonna's," Alfredo had proudly told me once.

For Amy's *despedida* dinner, I told Alfredo that we'd be having a good old American classic—macaroni and cheese. But the first *chopping* we went to was out of both items, and the second one had only cheese, so we modified our meal to spaghetti with cheese sauce.

Soon after sunset, as we were in the middle of chopping mangoes for a fruit salad, the electricity went out.

"What timing," Liudmila said with a sigh. She had come over early to help with the preparations, and soon after her arrival, she announced that she'd accompany Amy on her taxi ride to the airport at four in the morning.

"I'll go ask Dinora for some candles," I said, but when I went downstairs, I found only Abuela swaying slowly in her rocking chair next to the neighborhood nurse, who now stopped by daily to make sure she didn't have a relapse.

"Dinora had a headache," Abuela said. "She went to the hospital to get an injection."

Dinora had suffered headaches since I'd met her, but this was the second time in the three weeks since I'd returned from traveling that she'd gone for an injection.

"Is she going to be okay?" I asked. "Does anyone know what's wrong with her?"

"Probably stress," the nurse said. *"La situación."*

"Well, when she gets back, tell her to come upstairs for the *despedida*," I said to Abuela. "She can bring you down some food."

"They're making an American meal for us," Abuela told her nurse. "La Gorda is returning to her homeland."

In my absence, Amy and Liudmila had found a candle and lit it in the middle of the kitchen. Its glow was dim, barely highlighting the little mountains of food we'd spread across the kitchen counter, and soon we gave up on trying to decipher one fruit from the next. We chopped indiscriminately in the dark, mistaking avocados for guavas, oranges for limes, rum for water.

Perhaps it was this final equivocation that caused the hours to run together, but this seemed like the longest blackout I'd experienced in Cuba. At nine, when our guests began arriving for our scheduled nine-thirty dinner, the lights were still out. By ten, everyone, excited by the abundance of food, had taken on a plate of their own to prepare. My friend Pepe boiled milk and sugar for flan, and his cousin Mercedes arranged an avocado, tomato, and cucumber salad. Liudmila mixed up the fruits in a glass bowl for *un coctel de fruta*. Alfredo made tamal appetizers with freshly ground *masa* he'd picked up at the farmers market on his way over. And Amy's friend Alexis played bartender, chopping up *hierba buena* leaves for mojitos.

We didn't sit down to eat until eleven, by which time Abuela had gone to sleep and Luis was out patrolling the neighborhood on his late-night CDR shift. Dinora made her final trip upstairs at ten-thirty and asked us to wake her when Amy left.

The seven of us who stuck it out crammed ourselves around the small kitchen table for the feast, the boom box blasting Los Van Van's "Havana City." Conversation, which at first zigzagged across the table, soon retreated to closer corners, people tiring of shouting out their every word.

After dinner, with still no sign of the electricity returning, we all climbed the narrow kitchen-side staircase up to the roof and sat on the cement shelf lining the edge, gazing at the stars and watching the moon swim between the clouds until the early morning hours.

At 3:30 AM, everyone said their goodbyes until only Alfredo, Liudmila, and I were left to help Amy with her luggage. I woke Dinora, and she joined us on the balcony to watch for the taxi while her gauzy blue nightgown rustled in the soft early morning breeze.

When the taxi came, Amy bent down to heave her bulging backpack onto her shoulders, and Alfredo rushed over to take it from her.

"No, no, I'm fine," Amy said, nearly losing her balance. I laughed, seeing my own fierce independence mimicked in her motions.

Dinora stepped forward then, her voice all business.

"*Vaya chica.* Let Alfredo get it. He may be skinny," she said, "but he's still a man, and that's what men are for."

We all laughed this time, and then Alfredo carried the backpack down, and Liudmila scooted into the taxi.

"Oh, my God, I almost forgot," Amy said as she leaned in to hug me goodbye. "My money, your money."

She reached into her pocket and handed me a fistful of wadded bills, the last four hundred dollars of her travel money, which, combined with my remaining hundred and fifty, would have to last for my final four weeks, unless I could find an unofficial Cuba courier to bring me more.

"I'll send you a check when I get home," I called out as Amy got into the taxi.

Alfredo went over to the window for a final goodbye kiss, and Dinora was right behind him, her arms outstretched.

And then Amy was gone, the taxi making a sharp left onto Soledad, leaving behind only a sooty puff of diesel.

When we turned to go back into the house, Alfredo halted at the door as if some invisible barrier prevented him from entering. I waved Dinora ahead.

"We'll be up soon," I told her.

"What's wrong?" I asked Alfredo as we stood in the predawn silence of Centro Habana.

"I just feel like it's going to make me sad to go back inside and see all of Amy's stuff gone," he said. "It'll make me think about you leaving."

I reached out to hold his hand. "Where do you want to go?"

"Do you want to sleep at my mother's?"

"Will she mind?" I asked. "Won't she be asleep?"

Alfredo laughed. "It's okay. I live there too. I have a key."

We took a scenic detour to his house, walking along the Malecón while faint ship lights flickered in the distance and waves collapsed softly against the coral outline of the sea. The air was still warm and heavy, with none of the invigorating chill that characterized early morning walks in the U.S.

"We haven't really talked about what we'll do when you leave," Alfredo said as we turned inland onto Hospital Street. "I know the telephone is expensive, but maybe we could schedule a time and talk every two weeks, even if it's just for ten minutes."

"That's a good idea," I said, although it made me feel a little sick to think of our full-time relationship dissolving into a few minutes of static-filled conversation each month. "Maybe I can get a good long-distance deal," I added, "and we can talk more often."

Since U.S. phone cards didn't work in Cuba, I really had no idea what the rate would be for phone calls from the U.S. With the Cuban phone card I'd used during my first month, it had cost me nearly five dollars per minute to call the U.S.

At Dinora's, I often signaled my parents by calling collect from the house phone, since there were no direct residential service connections to the U.S. After refusing the charges, my parents would immediately call Dinora's house, but often they wouldn't be able to get through for several hours. Once I didn't hear back for two days. When we did connect, our voices were gravelly and delayed.

Soon after I moved into Dinora's, I had met an American who was visiting her Cuban boyfriend of the past two years. They spoke on the phone when they were apart, and the woman told me that it wasn't the time limitations or the cost or the bad connection that made her conversations difficult but rather the gulf between her and her boyfriend's lives.

"Once I was hurrying home from work during rush hour to call him at the time we'd arranged, and this crazy man, talking on his cell phone and not paying attention to anything, ran a red and almost hit me," she said. "But you know the really crazy thing? My heart was beating so fast, but instead of thinking about how I could've died, all I kept thinking was, 'How can I explain this to Orestes? Rush hour? Cell phones?' It's not Spanish or English but the language of my life here that I don't know how to translate."

As Alfredo and I continued down Hospital Street, it dawned on me that I had never seen his mother's house before, had never met his mother, had never even ventured this far into the heart of Centro Habana.

Without the tourist draw of the University of Havana's imposing Roman columns and Callejón de Hamel's colorful Sunday morning rumba drum circles, there were none of the blue-and-white *casa particular* signs so prevalent on the doors in Dinora's neck of the neighborhood. Here, there were only the gritty, gray streets and, despite the urban setting, a faint scent of farmyard animals.

"This is it," Alfredo said as we stopped at 68 Hospital Street, just past the intersection of Salud Street. By now it was 4:00 AM.

Alfredo opened an unlocked front door, tall and paneled like Dinora's but without the well-lit, polished marble steps behind it.

"Be careful," Alfredo said, taking my hand in the darkness of the staircase, "some of the steps are chipped."

Ascending the jagged stairs, I remembered our trip to the *posada particular* and felt a similar sense of jittery anticipation. The feeling only increased as we walked onto flat land via a narrow balcony, which, in the darkness, felt like a plank walk above an invisible sea.

We passed two doors on our right, and then, as Alfredo fumbled with his key to unlock the door at the end of the balcony, I looked up and saw that we were under the open sky, a cluster of stars glittering above us.

"This used to be a mansion before the Revolution," Alfredo whispered while the lock clicked open. "But now it's a *ciudadela*. Instead of there being just one family here, there are five families, each one living in what used to be just a room for the rich people who owned the mansion."

Inside his mother's house, a sliver of fluorescent light stared out at us from behind another closed door.

"Oh, my mother must be in the bathroom," Alfredo said. "Good, you can meet her."

I swallowed, and the clicking sound of my tongue seemed to echo throughout the silent house. A toilet flushed, the light switched off, and a woman stumbled into the shadows cast by the moonlight seeping in through the open door. Alfredo flipped on an overhead light, revealing a worn green love seat, a card table, a TV sitting atop a step stool, and his mother, rubbing her eyes. She was a robust woman, taller and darker-skinned than Alfredo.

"You scared me," she said to Alfredo, not seeming at all startled by my presence. "I thought you were at Lea's house. Good timing, though. I just got in. You know, it was Soyla's birthday, and I've been at her party all night."

"My neighbor downstairs," Alfredo told me and then said to his mother, "We're going to stay here tonight."

"Oh, sure," his mother said, and without any introductions or explanations, she waved us in, patting the love seat for me to sit down. Then, just like the woman in the *posada particular*, she set about preparing our bed.

"Let me go grab the sheet from the clothesline," she said. "I just did the laundry this morning."

She walked into a pink tiled kitchen and pulled a sheet from a rope strung out across a back wall.

"Alfredito," she ordered when she returned, "go downstairs and see if Soyla has a pillow."

Without a moment of hesitation, Alfredo headed back outside, leaving me and his mother alone in the living room. Not knowing what else to do, I stood up and offered her the love seat.

"No, no, *mi reina*," my queen, she said. "I'm just going to make the bed and then get to sleep. I hope I don't have nightmares, though. I watched The Movie tonight and it was just terrible."

I nodded sympathetically but refrained from asking which movie she was talking about. After two months of living in a Cuban house, I now knew that The Movie, as everyone called it, referred to whichever crappy American horror or action flick the government selected to show every Saturday night on channel 6, one of its two stations. Although most people watched The Movie too halfheartedly to even note its title, they still welcomed it as a break from the Save Elián roundtables that dominated the airwaves every other night of the week.

"Well, it couldn't have been as bad as The Movie last week," I said. I hadn't actually seen it, but I felt the need to say something.

"Oh, yes," Alfredo's mother said, sighing. "You're certainly right about that."

Alfredo returned with a pillow and two gooey coconut sweets wrapped in wax paper.

"Breakfast," he announced proudly. "Or do you want yours now? Are you hungry? Or thirsty?"

"Maybe just a little thirsty," I said.

Alfredo opened the refrigerator, which contained only the dried-out remnants of an uncovered tomato-and-onion salad and a pitcher half full of water.

"Oh, but it wasn't boiled," Alfredo said as he began pouring the water into a mug. "Maybe you shouldn't have it. I drink it all the time, but since you're used to bottled water from the *chopping*, maybe you shouldn't."

"Yeah," I said. "That's fine. I'm actually more tired than thirsty."

"*Ve a dormir, muchacha,*" Go to sleep, said Alfredo's mother, who had been standing in the living room, watching us. "It's practically morning already." She retreated into a darkened, doorless room, and then I heard the soft movements of her settling into bed.

"My room's up there," Alfredo said, pointing to a small balcony loft above the TV. I followed him up a wobbly ladder to a space roughly twice the size of the twin bed that was squished up against the back wall. A pile of folded underwear, T-shirts, and pants lay on the floor next to a pair of flip-flops. Beneath a jagged-edged wall mirror was a dresser with an alarm clock, a desk light, a fan, deodorant, Alfredo's razor and shaving cream, and a wooden palm tree figurine inset on an oval of wood.

The straw hat Alfredo had received from his *guajiro* friends in Santiago hung on the back wall beside a polished piece of driftwood we'd found on the beach that day. A weary, beat-up stuffed gorilla guarded the bottom of Alfredo's bed, and at the top, in place of a pillow, was a Spanish–English dictionary I'd lent Alfredo, as well as my book *Two in the Wild*, which contained a travel story I had written.

"This is it," Alfredo said, sitting next to the gorilla. "This is everything I own." Alfredo's tone, at once familiar and also so very distant, surprised me at first, because it seemed devoid of emotion. There was no hint of pride or embarrassment, anger or despair or even sarcasm. In the ensuing silence, I realized that, just as the color black is actually the presence of all colors, resignation is also the accumulation, disguised as negation, of all emotions. It is the aftermath of expectation.

"When I took drumming classes, I used to practice what I learned on this bed," Alfredo said, tapping out a silent rhythm on the sagging mattress.

I sat down next to Alfredo and picked up the little palm tree island from his dresser.

"Is this Cuba?" I asked.

"I don't know," Alfredo said. "Someone gave it to me a long time ago. Do you like it?"

"Sure."

"Here," he said, closing my hand around the delicate twig of a tree. "It's yours."

"Oh, no," I said, quickly unfolding my fingers. "No, it's yours. I can't take it."

"But I want to give it to you," Alfredo said. "Like a gift."

"Okay," I said, touching the side of his face with my free hand. "Thank you."

I realized that I was whispering, afraid of waking Alfredo's mother.

"It's so quiet here," I said. "It seems quieter than it's ever been at Dinora's."

"That's because we're not usually up at five in the morning at Dinora's," Alfredo said, laughing. "And also, there's no water pump here."

At Dinora's house, at one-thirty every morning, an alarm would go off in her bedroom, and then I'd hear the sleepy footsteps of her or Luis trudging over to the water tank to switch on the sputtering pump. Its metallic groan would echo throughout the house as it siphoned off the next day's water supply from an underground reserve.

In the U.S., where my house water arrived silently and without any effort on my part, I'd never paid much attention to the amount I used. But at Dinora's, there had been times when an extra boarder took an extra shower and the water simply stopped running. Then Luis would fiddle with the pump, often to no avail until the allotted early morning retrieval hour, when the water flowed faster and more freely. Knowing how difficult it was to get water even with a pump, I wondered how Alfredo managed to get it without one.

"Every day I take a bucket and fill it at a fountain downstairs, and then I come back up and pour it in there," Alfredo explained, pointing to a four-foot-long tank attached to a corner of the living room wall below us. "I keep doing that until there's enough for the next day."

"Does everyone in the *ciudadela* have to do that?"

"Some people have motors like Dinora, *pero no es fácil*," it's not easy, Alfredo said. "First you have to invent some *negocio* to get sixty dollars for the motor, and then once you have it, you have to go to the Oficina de Acueductos, the Aqueduct Office, and get on a list for them to come out and break the street so they can connect a tube to your pump. But there are so many people on the list that you have to bribe the aqueduct people, give them seventy, maybe seventy-five dollars so you don't have to wait a year for them to get to you."

"So if you can't come up with the money, you just do what you do and lug it up in a bucket every day?"

"Or you find another way. Maybe you try to get in good with the government by telling the police about a neighbor who's bribed the aqueduct people. Or maybe you make your own motor from an old Russian fan that probably never worked very well to begin with. Or, like my mother," Alfredo added, lowering his voice, "you wait around, hoping things will change."

I leaned over to embrace Alfredo, and when we pulled apart, he said, "Maybe we could talk about something different now." I nodded, and he kissed me, smiled, and added, "Or maybe we don't have to talk at all." And again, I nodded, but soon, as we became entangled in each other, I realized I couldn't quite escape from our conversation or these newfound details of Alfredo's life. I couldn't stop thinking about the near-empty refrigerator and the palm tree figurine, the shaky fan whose head I worried might snap off and fly across the room at any moment during the night, the holey bottom bed sheet his mother had just washed, the missing top one.

"I'm sorry," I said, pulling away from Alfredo. "I just feel a little strange tonight."

"What's wrong?" he asked. "Did I do something?"

"No, it's just, I think I'm a little worn out, you know." I searched for the words to explain without spreading my sadness and opted instead for a half-truth. "It's just been a long day—going to Mexico and Amy's *despedida* and talking about my leaving."

"Oh, don't be sad, *mi amor*," Alfredo said. "You have to think about the good things. Now, at least, we have another month together, just you and me."

I nodded.

"Close your eyes, and don't think anymore about leaving," Alfredo continued. He patted at our single, borrowed pillow, motioning for me to lie down. "Think about how beautiful it is to have someone, somewhere in the world who really loves you and know," he said, smoothing back my hair with his fingertips, "that even when you're gone, I'll still be that person for you."

18

Hasta Siempre

That night in Alfredo's mother's house I dreamt of another house, one I'd never seen before but which nonetheless felt like home. I dreamt of a vegetable garden in the mountains of Northern California, of a small cabin with a room where I could do my writing and one where Alfredo could practice his drumming on actual drums.

I dreamt of us building a snowman atop the icy peak of Mt. Shasta, swimming in the warm, deep blue of Lake Tahoe, biking up Mt. Tamalpais for a Sunday pancake breakfast at the West Point Inn. I dreamt of Alfredo working at a Latin American cultural center during the day and of the two of us sitting at a knotty wood table in the evening as I gave him English lessons by a crackling fireplace.

My wish for Alfredo to come back to the U.S. with me seemed too complicated to really fathom, with so many variables at play and political roadblocks to be cleared. I decided to let these thoughts settle in a bit more, and mentioned nothing to Alfredo as we silently ate our coconut treats beneath a green pinstriped sundress and a pair of black underwear hanging on the clothesline in his mother's kitchen.

I carried my dream around with me all day, from Alfredo's mother's house to the sweaty streets of Havana to the *chopping* on San Lázaro, where in the checkout line, I ran into Rebecca, an American I'd met during my time at Hotel El Bosque.

Rebecca had come to Cuba with a two-week dance program, and I distinctly remembered watching her board a bus to the airport in mid-February. Yet here she was again, more than two and a half months later, buying rum and toilet paper with her salsa instructor boyfriend, Ledián. Theirs had been one of the Hotel El Bosque poolside affairs, and since Rebecca's departure, I had seen Ledián twice more, once at a party, and once at an art opening. Both times he had been flirting with a different foreign salsa student.

"I didn't know you were back," I said to Rebecca now. "When did you get here?"

"Just yesterday." Rebecca smiled as she placed her arm around Ledián's shoulder. "Do you remember my boyfriend Ledián?"

"We've bumped into each other a few times," I said, and Ledián smiled at me, not the slightest hint of guilt on his face.

"Even though I only have a week, it still feels so good to be back," Rebecca said dreamily. "I actually came for three days in March. I was just too lovesick to stay away. But what are you doing here still? I thought you were just going to stay for one more month."

I laughed. "Me too, but then each time I planned to leave I just started to feel like I wasn't ready to return."

"It sounds like you might have a case of lovesickness yourself," Rebecca said slyly. "Am I right?"

"Yeah, I have a boyfriend. But now I have to leave at the beginning of June."

"Are you going to come back?" Rebecca asked.

"I don't know. Really, I wish my boyfriend could come visit me in the U.S."

Briefly, I considered telling Rebecca about my dream, but something about the moment—perhaps the presence of Ledián, or the casualness of our encounter, or any other number of variables conspiring to destroy the sanctity of my dream—made me reconsider.

"You could always get married," Rebecca responded so quickly and matter-of-factly that it startled me. "I have two friends from my program who met Cubans, and now they're doing their papers to get married."

"Oh, no," I said. "I think it's a little too quick for me."

"Well, anyway, one of my friends' weddings is in July," Rebecca said, squeezing Ledián's shoulder, "so that's a good excuse for me to come back."

I smiled. Ledián shifted his weight between his feet, back and forth like a child trying not to pee. For a beat, no one said anything, and then Rebecca asked, "Did you hear that Lorraine is pregnant?"

"Who?"

"Oh, she was at Hotel El Bosque too, and she was dating her drumming instructor. But he was a good twenty years younger than her, and I don't think she really wanted any more children. I don't think she even thought she could still get pregnant, so she's kind of freaking out right now."

"That sounds difficult."

"Pues," Rebecca said, giggling nervously, *"así es el amor."* Such is love.

Walking down San Lázaro on my way back to Dinora's, I sighed, relieved that I hadn't shared my dream with Rebecca, and I planned to continue guarding it for a few more days before telling Alfredo. But when I met up with him in the evening for a walk along the Malecón and he asked, seemingly out of the blue, "Do you think you'll come back to Cuba?" I felt such a rush of emotion, and my heartbeat sped up so much, that for a moment, I felt incapable of speech. And then, once I caught my breath, I felt incapable of holding anything back. I recounted my entire dream, ending with, "I want you to come home with me, to see my world."

"I would love to see your world, but I don't know how," Alfredo said as he looked down from our post atop a salt-eaten portion of the Malecón. I followed his gaze over the black night waves of the Caribbean, and I felt a sense of déjà vu so strong it seemed to erase all other memories, as if I'd spent my entire life sitting on this seawall with Alfredo, trying to explain my reality to him. Trying to describe my life in a country so close to and so foreign from his own that, despite my many attempts at translation, I could never come across the right words.

"You know," Alfredo said slowly, "there is one way I could see your world."

"How?"

"We could get married." He looked straight at me as he spoke, anxiously awaiting my response.

"Oh, Alfredo," I said, my mind immediately flashing back to Rebecca's stories. "That's very flattering, but how could we get married without you even knowing what you thought of life in my country? Without us knowing how we would be together there?"

"But otherwise, how will we ever know?" Alfredo asked. "There's no other way for me to go there, and getting married could just be a way for us to test out our relationship in your world."

I tried to appear calm for my response, but my tensed facial muscles gave me away before I could speak.

"Think about it this way," Alfredo said, his voice even and calming. "If we're happy in your world, great, then we're already married, and if we're not, then we can just get a divorce and I'll come back here."

Alfredo smiled, proud of his plan, but I just shook my head, biding time until I could find my words.

"Alfredo," I finally said, "in the U.S., divorces cost money, and lawyers get involved, and it's not easy and, besides . . . I don't want to get married like that, with so many unknowns, looking for an out."

"I only mentioned divorce because you seemed unsure," Alfredo said. "You know that as far as I'm concerned, there are no unknowns, and I don't need an out. You," he said, pausing dramatically, "are the woman I've been waiting for."

"That's very sweet," I said, laughing. "And although I haven't been waiting for a man, you're not so bad either."

We both laughed, and then Alfredo, his voice soft and hopeful, asked, "So?"

"So life isn't that easy in the U.S.," I said. "And you don't speak English, and I don't even have a job there."

"I can learn English. I'm capable of doing whatever I need to to make money. I can do construction. I can be a janitor."

I ran my hand across Alfredo's smooth, moist cheek, the air still full of heat and humidity well past sunset.

"I'm not questioning that you would do everything you could, but people usually wait until they're a little more settled to get married, and even then it can be difficult," I said. "Not having money will put all that much more stress on our relationship. You know how everyone in Cuba always says this is the only country where you don't have to work and you still get fed?"

"Yeah . . ."

"Well, it's true. It's not like that in the U.S."

"Okay, Lea, so maybe you have to work harder there, but I can't imagine that life in the U.S. is as difficult as it is in Cuba," Alfredo said, shaking his head, unable to reconcile the challenging world I was describing to him with the stories he'd grown up hearing, stories of the easy life in the U.S.

Alfredo lived in a world where Miami exiles sent back hundred-dollar bills and photos of themselves standing in front of glistening new Japanese cars and miniature houses built solely to store these automobiles. Those who sent back nothing were considered selfish and simply dismissed as *descarados,* disgraces. No one considered the possibility that perhaps, for some, life in the Promised Land had been more of a struggle than a success story.

"Maybe life in the U.S. isn't difficult in the same way it is in Cuba," I said. "But it's still difficult. It's more complex." I wanted to tell Alfredo about mailboxes and insurance bills, and how rent money just disappeared at the end of each month rather than accumulating toward the cost of your house. But instead, I just shook my head, near tears from the effort of trying so hard, so often, to explain the routine details of daily existence in the U.S.

"To be honest with you, I don't understand," Alfredo said. "Maybe it's because I've never left Cuba and there are no immigrants here, so I can't even imagine what it would be like to be away from my culture. But still . . ." Alfredo left his sentence unfinished and scooted over closer to me, so that we sat with our foreheads nearly touching while we straddled the Malecón as if we were riding a giant seahorse.

"You know, you never answered my original question," Alfredo said. "I know that you're a writer and you need to go back for your workshop, but if you are happy with me but not ready to marry me, why not come back to Cuba afterward?"

"When?"

"Whenever you want. Maybe in August or September. Go back to your world in June. And if you can't take me in full, take the parts of me that you know, that you can imagine, that you've written about," Alfredo said. "Sometimes you just have to be creative, like a Cuban."

"Think about me while you're in the U.S.," he continued slowly, pausing after each sentence, as if unsure of what might come out of his mouth next. "We'll find a way to keep in touch, and maybe you could work for a little bit and save up some money and talk to editors to see if you can get them to buy a Cuba story. And then you could come back, even for just a week or two, and you could compare your life with and without me. We could take things slower, the way you like. Think about our relationship over time."

I started to protest but realized there was nothing to dispute in Alfredo's plan. There was no reason why I couldn't return for a short visit after my workshop and, compared with the prospect of marriage, a return trip sounded suddenly simple.

"That sounds good," I said, wrapping my arms around Alfredo's neck.

Alfredo smiled, pleased with our compromise. "And now at least I don't have to say goodbye when you leave next month, because it won't really be a goodbye."

"Right, just a short separation."

"Have you heard of *'Hasta la Victoria Siempre'?*" Alfredo asked.

"Of course."

"Hasta la Victoria Siempre," Until Victory Always, was painted on walls throughout Havana, commemorating the closing words of Che Guevara's goodbye letter to Fidel in 1965, when he resigned from his position as head of the National Bank, leaving the island whose independence he'd fought for so he could organize revolutions elsewhere.

"When you leave, instead of saying, *'Hasta luego,'* I'll say, *'Hasta siempre,'*" Alfredo said smiling. "Just like El Che."

I laughed, envisioning our goodbye as a new revolutionary slogan, our relationship as a revolutionary act in its own right.

19

Apprentice
to a Housewife

After deciding to return to Cuba, I was finally able to stop thinking about departure, and I found myself in Havana in a way I'd never been before. For the first time since my arrival, there were no more panicked rushes to extend my ticket, no more clandestine meetings in hotel hallways to claim money brought by friends of friends in the U.S. There was no more questioning of the rightness of my relationship with Alfredo, as the ultimate decision about our future was now postponed for at least three more months, until my return trip.

With none of these previous stresses to occupy my mind and my time, and with no more Spanish classes left for me to take at the university, I felt at a loss as to what to do with myself for my remaining month in Havana.

To make up for having earlier abandoned my Cuban women article, which had grown out of control, with too many poignant stories I couldn't bear to cut, I compiled a list of more focused stories that I could research and write before I left Cuba. I interviewed Pablo Menéndez, a jazz musician from Oakland who came to visit Cuba when he was fourteen and, thirty-three years later, was still here, playing guitar in a fusion band.

I spent one evening shadowing a friend of Dinora's, who moonlighted as a freelance barber, earning more with this *negocio* than she did with her job as a technical engineer at a tobacco factory.

And at a baseball game at El Estadio Latinoamericano, I interviewed Armandito El Tintorero, a senior citizen who dry-cleaned and ironed clothing at a *tintorería* during the day and, for the past thirty-five years, had been leading the fans' chants at night. He had a reserved seat in the stadium and had been flown to Baltimore when the Havana team played there in 1999.

After I completed my stories, I opened an email account at the University of Havana, pretending I was still a student there. For five dollars, I received access to a computer that had nothing but an email connection—no Internet access and no word processing. I would bring a book and sit sweating in the university library for upward of two hours until one of the four computers became available. Then I would query as many editors in the U.S. as I could until, inevitably, the electricity went out or the email line grew so long that I began to feel guilty.

I sold the story about the musician to a paper in Oakland, and I spent many hours handwriting the article atop my crisp white bed sheets, beneath the soft hiss of a fluorescent light strip, whose flickering always made me feel as if I were in a discotheque.

One Saturday, seeking a break from my writing and the strobe light of my bedroom, I decided to head outside to read a novel in a park. While I had many fond memories of relaxing in the parks of other cities I'd traveled in, I had not yet attempted to do so in Havana. Most of Centro Habana's common areas were unattractive cement diamonds, best suited for playing baseball and sweating beneath the scorching sun.

Desiring a space with more green than gray, I thought of a quad on the university's south side, where leafy *jagüey* trees canopied over a scattering of ankle-high signposts, which demanded PROTEGE LA NATURALEZA, Protect Nature, and AMA LAS MATAS, Love the Plants.

I walked down San Lázaro until I got to the university, but as I began my ascent up its one hundred-step *escalinata*, sweat streaming down my forehead, a guard walked down to meet me.

"I'm sorry but the university's closed today," he said. He was an older man, and as he spoke, he feebly patted at his leg to call back a small brown dog that had stood at his side but now moved away, nervously eyeing me.

"*No pasa nada*, Pluto," the guard said, continuing his coaxing until Pluto stopped walking, although he made no motion to return to his former post. Few in Cuba had heard of Disney, but many of its characters had still somehow worked their way into the language. While dogs were commonly named Pluto, fashion-mongering humans were called "Mickeys" after the *ratoncito* who dressed so sharply.

"Pluto's very shy," the guard told me. "I found him on the street, and he was afraid of me too at first, so don't take it personally."

"Oh, no," I said, shaking my head and stretching my hand out toward Pluto, hoping to earn points with his owner and, by extension, entrance to the university grounds. But the guard would not be swayed.

"I'm sorry," he repeated when I asked if I could just sit under a tree. "No one's allowed to walk across campus when we're closed. Those are the rules, but don't ask me why."

I laughed, and the guard did too, his tanned face wrinkling up like a maze of miniature rivers.

"I'm Miguel," he said. "What's your name? Where are you from?"

When I told him I was from the U.S., Miguel's eyes widened, and he clasped his hands together excitedly.

"Well then, you can call me Michael," he said in heavily accented English. "I lived in New York City for seven years before the Revolution and two years after it."

"Why did you go to New York?" I asked, surprised. "I've never met anyone who left Cuba before the Revolution, or even anyone who came back after living abroad."

"My family left along with many others because Batista was a terrible man," Miguel said matter-of-factly. "And we returned, along with many others, because your country was fighting ours, and this is our homeland."

I nodded solemnly, embarrassed.

"But don't take it personally," Miguel said again. "You're here. That says something." He paused for a minute before adding, "I hope you come by the university again. Pluto and I are always here, guarding these steps."

Miguel lifted his arms up to the cloudless sky and then let them flop down to encompass the wide, empty mass of the *escalinata*. There was something so poignant and at the same time futile about his gesture that it reminded me of that fine line between patience and passivity, a line that so many on the island tiptoed across every day. I wondered but couldn't bring myself to ask Miguel if his life in Cuba had ended up to be what he'd hoped for when he returned.

"Well, I think I need to go indoors now," I said. "I feel like I'm melting out here, but I'm sure I'll see you again before I leave. I'll be here for three more weeks."

"That's all?" Miguel asked. "Why not stay longer? There's Carnaval in July."

"No, I have to go home in June," I said. "But I'll be back in the fall."

"Ah, so you'll come back too," Miguel said, pleased. "Then you'll know two people who've returned."

After my brief, failed search for shade, I began spending my afternoons inside with Dinora. As giddy as a little girl whose best friend has just moved next door, Dinora immediately set about creating a plan for our playtime. Her first suggestion was that we create a language and literature *intercambio*, exchange. Dinora gave me a collection of Chekhov short stories in Spanish, and I gave her an English-language book, *Dreaming in Cuban*. We even set a time for our first meeting, where we would discuss what we'd read.

"So there'll be more to my life, so I'll feel less like a housewife," Dinora said.

But despite our lofty literary intentions, I ended up spending most of my time with Dinora helping her with her many mundane but still pressing domestic tasks—those she claimed to detest so much yet did so well.

Dinora was meticulous with her housework: always scrubbing at the miniscule food specks left on the dishes I washed; always dusting, even though each new gust of seaside wind brought in a fresh batch of debris through the always-open louvered blinds.

"If this is what I am right now, then I will be the best housewife I can be," Dinora told me when I questioned her about her enthusiasm. "It's good to know how to do a little of everything," she continued. "Then whatever turns life takes, even if they catch you off guard, you can always adapt. That way you're never vulnerable."

And with that declaration, like a college professor summarizing the class goals on the first day, Dinora set about teaching me how to clean better, how to be more ordered in my life, and how, in essence, to live as resourcefully as a Cuban.

First, Dinora taught me how to make pineapple juice *a la cubana*. "This way, it's like two pineapples in one," she said as she delicately sliced off the prickly skin so as not to lose too much flesh. Setting aside the naked pineapple torso, she filled a bowl with water and submerged the jagged scraps of skin in it. After a day in the refrigerator, the skin was tossed out, all its sweetness leeched into the surrounding water, now Cuban pineapple juice.

To save money on cooking oil, Dinora advised me to keep the oil from my olive jars and to classify and preserve in appropriate bottles the different types of oil (from omelets, or vegetables, or rice and beans) left over in the frying pan from the previous night's dinner. She showed me how to salvage a mound of moldy potatoes, which I was on my way to dump.

Dinora washed off the potatoes and then chopped and chopped until she found a white, mold-free heart in each one. What at first seemed like a menial outcome, in the end yielded two heaping platefuls of thick, crispy french fries.

In the evenings, I tested out my newly acquired domestic skills on Alfredo, and he taught me some of his own. We made *pepinos encultivos* by slicing cucumbers, submerging them in hot vinegar water, and then chilling them in the refrigerator overnight. It was such a simple, obvious process that I was embarrassed to admit that, until I ate the crisp, savory pickles, I hadn't known what we were preparing, accustomed as I was to the prepackaged, grocery-store variety.

Alfredo showed me how to make tamales too, and when it came time to tie them up in their compact corn-husk coverings and we realized we had no twine, he took a brief survey of the house and returned with a pair of scissors and my all-purpose sarong. During the course of my travels in Cuba—as well as during my travels five years earlier, in Central America, where I had bought it—I had used the sarong as a skirt, a tapestry, a bed sheet, an impromptu picnic blanket, and a quick-dry towel. But Alfredo's proposed alteration was more permanent than any I had ever considered.

"Can I cut this off?" he asked, motioning to the sarong's fringe.

I ran my hand over the red and black trim, and then, putting aside my sentimentality, gave a silent nod of consent. Together we tied up the tamales, a time-consuming task, with me wrapping our makeshift twine around the length and width of each tamal as Alfredo strategically placed his index finger to secure my knots.

As we lay in bed, exhausted and full following our tamal feast, Alfredo turned to me, a contented look in his eyes, and said, "You know, I was thinking when we were cooking together that I like this life with you more than when we were traveling. It just feels . . . more real."

I smiled, understanding perfectly. After Amy left, Alfredo had moved into the room with me, bringing his clothes and toothbrush and razor. Now, instead of calling to say he'd be coming by after work, he just came.

Instead of feeling like an American tourist who invited her Cuban boyfriend over for the night, I began to feel like we were an actual couple living together. And even the routine, domestic details of our life took on a certain charm, a sweetness that I never before would have associated with such ordinary tasks as buying groceries or making meals.

For breakfast we had toast, cooked campfire-style over the stovetop flame, since there was no toaster and the oven didn't work. We disguised the charred taste by slathering our toast with pungent black-market cheese Alfredo brought home whenever he was paid. And then we disguised the cheese's stink by coating it with honey from a bottle that resided in a saucer-sized moat of water, which Alfredo had set up to keep away the ants.

We made elaborate fruit cups of mango and guava and plantain and pineapple, and while Alfredo washed our dishes afterward, I dried. When Dinora praised me for putting more effort into my plate cleaning, I told her it was Alfredo, and she smiled.

"You've found yourself a good boyfriend," she said.

The day before I left Cuba, after several hours of surprisingly sad goodbyes despite the fact that everyone knew I would be returning in a few months, Alfredo and I ran into Alfredo's friend Gerardo. All of us had been caught in the bottleneck of a Save Elián march.

"*¡Socio!*" Gerardo called out. To reach us, he had to push his way past the crowds, who were waving flags and chanting "*¡Viva la Revolución!*"

"*¡Estabas perdido!*" he said, tackling Alfredo in a bear hug. "Where have you been?"

Although I hadn't seen Gerardo since my first week in Havana, when he had brought Alfredo to meet my friend Heather and me at Hotel El Bosque, he had been kept alive in my memory by Alfredo's frequent reminiscing. Walking through the city with Alfredo, there was always some park or crumbling house that triggered a memory of his childhood with Gerardo.

"I haven't seen you around the neighborhood in ages," Gerardo said.

"Well," Alfredo said smiling. "I've been staying with Lea in Centro Habana."

Gerardo looked at me, and a flash of recognition sparked in his eyes.

"So you're still here?" he asked. "After all this time. You're practically a *cubana* now."

I laughed. "It hasn't been *that* long."

"Well, we met at the beginning of February, so let's see," Gerardo said, counting on his fingers. "March, April, May, and today is the third of June. I'd say you've been here for a while. Don't let the lack of seasons fool you."

After we said goodbye to Gerardo, I walked Alfredo to work and then made my way back home. It had been exceptionally humid all day, and now I could see the sky darkening and could almost feel raindrops in the air, an invisible presence taking shape. I lingered as I walked up Animas, excited to see my first storm in Cuba. I hung outside the house for a while, talking to the man next door, whom I'd never seen without a cigar in his mouth, and watching a game of street baseball, waiting. But even though Gerardo had dubbed me a *cubana*, I knew I didn't have that type of patience, and soon I went inside.

I sat on my bed, planning to read, but instead I quickly drifted off to sleep, awakening first to the crackle of thunder and then to Luis telling me to shut the windows. I stared out across the rooftops of Havana, at this city I'd come to know so well. Although I doubted it would come out, I snapped a shot of the skyline separated by the dusty white slats of my louvered blinds.

I went back to sleep and then woke a third time, not because of the thunder or a voice, but because of an intense, silent stare I could feel through the back of my head. I rolled over, opened my eyes, and saw Dinora standing in my doorway, looking down at me. In that split second of my movement, before Dinora could shift her glance, I saw something in her eyes that startled me. It was a dreaminess, a soft yet fixed gaze, like that of a mother studying a child who she has watched grow up, who she knows is slipping away.

"I didn't mean to wake you," Dinora said as I sat up. "I just wanted to make sure you had shut the windows. But please, go back to sleep. *Duerme, mi hija.*" Sleep, my daughter.

20

※ ❦ ※

Imagining Cuba

For my first few days back in the United States, everything was intensified, and I walked through my once familiar world like a stranger, an anthropologist taking notes on a foreign culture.

The U.S. was so utterly and fantastically different from Cuba that I encountered very little in my then-reality here that reminded me of my recent past there. And with so few points of reference from which to make comparisons, without even a hint of jetlag from the mere three-hour time difference, I found myself, within a week, comfortably settled back into the life I had abandoned four months earlier.

I returned to my old job at a local bookstore, where I sold and discussed literature to the backdrop of a Buena Vista Social Club CD, which some customer would request we play at least once a day. Magazine covers plastered with Elián's face surrounded me. Neither of these media icons quite described my experience in Cuba, although for the majority of the people who asked me about it, these two subjects covered the extent of their questions.

When Elián was finally sent back to Cuba at the end of June, I showed a coworker an article I'd read stating that the U.S. government had spent nearly two million dollars on the case.

"Just think how many Cubans that could feed," my coworker said.

"Or," I added, recalling how many homeless people I'd seen earlier that day on Van Ness Avenue, "how many Americans."

On my days off, just as I had done before Cuba, I went on long runs in the mountains, or met up with a friend for dinner, or caught a film at an arts theater. Or, during those times when I felt overwhelmed by the sheer scope and pace of life in the U.S., I simply lay down and read on my sprawling, queen-sized futon, which was bigger than any bed I'd shared with Alfredo in Cuba.

Oddly, even though I'd never known him in this landscape, Alfredo's absence echoed everywhere. It wasn't that anything I saw made me think of him but rather that everything I saw or smelled or heard made me wonder how Alfredo might react. Would he be appalled or amazed by kitchens in the U.S., with their cookie jars and unlimited dairy products, their freezers full of meat, and their cat-food bowls filled not with scraps from last night's dinner but with salmon suppers and feline breath mints? Would he do his little dance of excitement walking across the Golden Gate Bridge for the first time? Would he want to go backpacking with me in the Point Reyes National Seashore on New Year's Eve?

Every question I had ever asked myself in Cuba about what Alfredo might think of life in my world seemed to feed off itself now, splintering, reforming, and multiplying into different generations of unanswerable questions. Still, I asked myself anyway, and attempted, with mixed results, to share the details of my life with Alfredo during our scratchy, twice-a-month phone conversations.

Unfortunately, after Alfredo would pick up the phone on the first ring and ask, "¿Hola? ¿Mi amor?" the phone would often partially shut down, refusing to relay my voice to him, despite my increasingly loud and desperate cries of, "¡Estoy aquí, mi amor!"

"¿Hola? ¿Mi amor?" Alfredo would repeat every few seconds until, sick as it made me feel, I finally hung up, cutting him off mid-*amor*.

Then I would start all over, dialing up my eleven-digit calling-card number, my ten-digit pin code, the three-digit international code, the two-digit country code, the one-digit city code, and the six-digit phone number to Alfredo's grandmother's house. My calling card, like my even more expensive international phone service, was the only one I could find that allowed calls to Cuba—albeit at a rate that was double that of calling neighboring Haiti, four times that of dialing Kazakhstan, and ten times more expensive than connecting with Japan. The few places that cost more to call than Cuba were war zones like Afghanistan and Rwanda, or places I'd never heard of, like Tokelau and Diego Garcia.

When I did finally get through to Alfredo, I would sit at attention in my bed as if the slightest slouch or inadvertent movement might cause something in our connection to click, pulling closed that imaginary curtain that allowed me access to Cuba.

"Lea!" I could hear the smile in Alfredo's voice, almost feel the gentle warmth of the embrace that would have followed had we been able to meet in person. "How are you?" Alfredo would ask in English, his voice high-pitched and almost unrecognizable. Soon after I left Cuba, he had started taking classes, and now he threw in English phrases whenever he could, his favorites being, "Oh my God!" and "Are you my neighbor?"

"Maybe when you return, we can speak in English," he told me. "And then some day I can read your writings."

"I'd like that," I said, smiling into the receiver.

I was touched by Alfredo's desire to read my stories, but I knew that he would need more than good English to understand the meaning of my writing, just as I now needed more than good Spanish to explain the nuances of my life in the U.S.

Yet we struggled along together through this new setting, somehow surpassing roadblocks that we had stumbled upon in Havana. On the telephone, Alfredo never sighed with exasperation and declared, "You Americans," and I never accused him of speaking in a *machista* way. At nearly one dollar per minute, I knew that if we got into an argument on the phone, we'd never have the time to arrive at a resolution. So I had to let go of my long-held, newly acknowledged belief that we could not grow as a couple without our arguments.

We had to edit down our conversations, to strip spare our insecurities and make poetry out of prose, grasping onto words and tones of voice so we could replay our conversations in our minds during the long, intervening weeks of silence. We had to abandon our prior pettiness in favor of real listening.

Alfredo set the tone, taking mental notes on all that I'd told him during our prior conversation and following up on details of my life that even I'd forgotten about. He would ask about friends of mine he didn't know, and he would ask about jobs of mine he couldn't fathom.

"Did the editor like your book review?" Alfredo asked me during one call, even though I knew, from questions he'd asked me during a previous conversation, that he had never read a book review and couldn't quite grasp the point of it.

"Why wouldn't you just read the book if you wanted to know what it was about?" he'd asked.

"Well, a book review isn't really a report of what a book is about," I said. "It's more a critique of whether it's good or not, so you don't waste your time reading bad books."

"But what if the person who wrote it thinks it's bad, but you like that type of writing?"

"Well, you get to know the critics," I said. "So you know which ones have the same tastes as you."

"So, you read reviews to save time, but then you have to spend time studying the critics so you know what to read?" Alfredo persisted, at which point I gave up, laughing at the absurdity of it all.

Sometimes it went like this, and at first I enjoyed the challenge of explaining everything. The search for the perfect word reminded me of writing. The constant reexamination of the routine made my world new.

Other times I grew tired of the seemingly interminable cultural translations that, in the end, never really translated anyway. I wavered back and forth between feeling okay and feeling distraught about the ways in which our relationship roles had changed during this transition from close contact to long distance.

In person, in Havana, Alfredo had always played the persuer, the persistent—sometimes verging on desperate—one. In the beginning, he had memorized my phone number before I'd even asked for his. He had reached for my hand first while walking home from our Coppelia date, and he had initiated our first kiss outside Hotel El Bosque that night. When I gave him my breakup letter, Alfredo had argued against it, and during our subsequent disagreements, he had often been the first to make amends. He had been the first to say, "I love you," and the first to cry when I'd left.

Liudmila had come over for dinner the night before my departure, and afterward the two of them had joined me in the bedroom as I sat on the floor packing.

"Lea," Liudmila said, interrupting my nervous ramble about my flight and my parents and friends back home. "Look."

I turned around to find Alfredo lying belly down on the bed, his head drooping over the edge. My first thought was that he had fallen asleep, since it was after two in the morning, but as I moved closer, planning to startle him by wrapping my arms around him, I realized that his eyes, while downcast, were fully open and glossy with tears.

Alfredo never cried on the phone, although I sometimes felt like I might, worn out by the enormous weight of my new role as the persistent one who was single-handedly responsible for maintaining the lines of communication in our relationship. I always had to call Alfredo, since Cubans could only call the U.S. collect, and at a rate that was significantly higher than what I paid to call Cuba.

In a sense, these were the same old roles Alfredo and I had been trapped in in Cuba. The money, the power, was still in my hands, although now there was an added dimension to this power, which was no longer simply economic but also emotional. Now I had to risk vulnerability by pursuing our relationship in a way I never had in Cuba. When we talked about the future, I felt this same sense of inequality; once more, it was all up to me.

"When will you be coming back?" Alfredo asked during a conversation in mid-July. "When can I see you again?"

"I want to save up a little more money," I said. "I was thinking of the end of September."

"Oh," Alfredo said, his voice subdued. "That means we'll be apart for nearly as long as we've been together."

"I know," I said. Searching for a positive side to my delay, I thought of our birthdays, which were both coming up in October.

"We can celebrate together," I said.

"Okay," Alfredo said, partially appeased. "I guess we just have to be patient and . . ."

"Creative, like a Cuban," I said, offering up the refrain, which had concluded so many of our conversations on the island.

"Yes," Alfredo said as my phone card beeped and a recorded voice announced that our time was nearly up. "We can pretend we're still together. We can dream of each other at night."

While it made me breathless to hear Alfredo's voice on the telephone, it was our emails that set the stage for our calls, that were the constant of our communication.

In the beginning we wrote every day. Alfredo would stop by the University of Havana to use my old account in the mornings before work. Reading his emails, I would try to imagine him sitting in the sticky university library, pecking away at the chunky, yellowed keyboard. I recalled the baffled, awestruck expression on his face as I had, before leaving Cuba, tried to teach him how to use Shift and Enter and other function keys, a skill I now realized he hadn't quite mastered.

Some days Alfredo's emails would arrive in all capitals, like an extended shout.

"MY LOVE," he'd write. "I DON'T KNOW WHAT'S GOING ON WITH THIS COMPUTER!"

Other days there would be no email at all, the streets surrounding the university blocked off for a Save Elián/Anti-U.S. Imperialism march.

And then there were the occasions when I would receive, in lowercase letters, a two-line email reading, "I wrote you a long letter but then there was a blackout, and I lost it all, and now everyone's waiting for me to get off. And *la pesada* is giving me dirty looks."

From my emailing time in Cuba, I had had my fair share of run-ins with *la pesada,* the jerky woman, whose job it was to silently monitor the computer use. Although there was no official time limit for emailing, about half an hour after someone sat down, *la pesada* would begin to circle around her victim's computer, casting a telling glare.

I could easily imagine that *la pesada* would not be a big fan of Alfredo and his ten-word-per-minute typing rate. And, sure enough, as the weeks passed, Alfredo began mentioning her more frequently, once even writing that she had asked for his receipt for the email account.

The following day, I received another email, which read, "Lea, if only you knew the happiness I feel after reading your emails when I sit down to write, *'Hola, mi amor.'*" I scrolled down my screen, thinking maybe Alfredo had hit Enter one too many times, but there was nothing more.

Knowing better, I tried to convince myself that the electricity in the library had just gone out again. But then came the email I'd been dreading.

"I'm sorry, *mi amor,*" it began. "*La pesada's* boss is here now, and he said I have just a few minutes to write you this last email. He said that since you paid for the email account, you're the only one who can use it, and even if I had the money, I couldn't open an account, because I'm not a student here. It makes me angry, *pero ya tú sabes. Es Cuba.*"

But I also knew from my time in Cuba that there was always an alternate way. I had only to wait three days for another email, although this time it came from an address I wasn't familiar with and was written by a man I didn't know. In awkwardly formal English, it read, "Alfredito asked me to announce to you that he will soon be scripting an email to you. In the future, please respond to this direction. Sincerely, Ernesto."

Soon I learned that Ernesto, or El Corrupto, as Alfredo referred to him on the phone (because he was a fifty-five-year-old dating one of Alfredo's twenty-five-year-old friends), had managed to rig up an Internet connection from his home in Miramar.

When he received my emails, El Corrupto would print them and call Alfredo for him to pick them up. In turn, Alfredo would handwrite his responses and give them to El Corrupto to be typed and sent back to me.

At first I censored my emails, embarrassed by the thought of some corrupt stranger, whom I might have to meet on my next trip, reading about the depth of my feelings for Alfredo. But if Alfredo had any similar concerns about the possibility of El Corrupto snooping, he didn't let it interfere with the candidness of his emails, which only grew more intimate as he tried out his emerging English.

One day he wrote of my approaching return: "I'll be waiting for you with my arms wide open and my heart on my hands," reminding me of one of those disturbing Frida Kahlo paintings where internal organs floated freely around the body they belonged to.

Another time, in what I was sure must have been a typo of El Corrupto's, Alfredo wrote, "I am so tired now because I worked all day and then wanked for many kilometers through Havana."

After I finished laughing, I thought about how much Alfredo's learning English scared me. What if I didn't like who he would become in English? What if I discovered that all the witty things he said to me in Spanish were just translated clichés, which sounded somehow more profound with foreign words? What if, with two shared languages, I realized that the passion was born out of our differences, not our commonalities?

Often I felt like I was just imagining Cuba, like Alfredo was a character I'd created; our relationship a story I'd made up; my stay on the island no more than a fairytale, a short, sweet dream I'd had once upon a time.

Even looking at my Cuba photos did little to dispel this feeling. One of my photos of Alfredo had been sent to me by Heather, the American woman on my program who'd introduced me to Alfredo.

"It's not great," she wrote. "But still, I thought it might mean something to you."

A stranger had taken the photo on the first night I met Alfredo, as we sat on the Malecón. I framed one side of the photo while Heather outlined the opposite end, with Alfredo and his friend Gerardo in the middle. Somehow the camera shutter hadn't completely opened, so the only part of Heather that was visible was her legs. One of my eyes and a portion of my forehead were missing, and Gerardo was just a torso. Alfredo was here in full, but he was wearing all black, and only the whites of his eyes were visible, glowing eerily in the night sky, his face a shadow receding into the darkness.

Never before had my memories quite so literally faded this quickly. And never before had they lingered on in so many ways. In their absence, I kept Alfredo and Cuba alive through my stories and articles and letters to the editor.

Once I got beyond my irritation with only being asked about Elián González and began talking about what was really going on in Cuba, I realized that the public's lack of knowledge, just like my own before I'd gone to Cuba, was not a symptom of indifference. It was a direct result of the embargo's censorship of all things Cuban. In reality, people were hungry to learn about life on the island and eager to share the small details they knew about Cuba.

Soon after publishing my first Cuba article—about renting and riding my clunky Flying Pigeon through Havana—a reader called to tell me that he had been biking in Cuba too.

"I think we might even have been there at the same time," he said excitedly. "I was just so happy to find your article, because whenever I try to tell people here about what it was like, I have trouble finding the words."

Then there was the night I returned home to find this message on my answering machine: "Hi, my name is William," said an unfamiliar voice, "and when I was randomly walking down Calle 64 in Havana the other day, I ran into your friend Liudmila, who got very excited when I told her I was from California. She invited me into her house and introduced me to her grandmother and showed me some articles written by her California friend, and I recognized your name from a Cuba story I'd read before coming here. And it ends up, I live near San Francisco too, so I'd love to meet you and give you a letter from Liudmila."

When I called William back, expecting to make plans to meet at a central location, he instead invited me over to have dinner with his family, a gesture that reminded me more of Cuba than anything else had since my return.

In my mailbox, I regularly received letters from my Cuban friends, although all were sent secondhand from people passing through Cuba on their way to places I'd never been—Boulder or Miami or Quebec—since Cubans had little faith in the follow-through of their country's mail system.

In a letter postmarked from New York, Dinora told me that she was going to start teaching part-time at the university again in September. "So when you come back," she wrote, "you'll be staying with a professor rather than a housewife." At the end of her letter, Dinora wrote, "It sounds like Alfredo's doing well. He called to wish Luis a happy Father's Day last month."

"So you actually called Dinora's house?" I asked Alfredo on the phone. "Does that mean that you're feeling better about them?"

"Yes," he said. "And you know, Dinora answered the phone, and we had a good talk. She said she had misjudged me at first because of my hair."

"Your hair?"

"You know, because it's so crazy, and it's what all the Rastas wear," Alfredo said.

"Hmm," I said, "well, I'm glad you both feel better around each other now."

Then we were off discussing the plans for my return trip again, how I'd arrive in early October and we'd spend the first three weeks in Havana, the next several days in the central Cuban city of Trinidad, and my final few days back in Havana.

Until October, I bided my time by sending Alfredo bits of my life—articles I'd written that he could study with his English teacher, photos of the mountains near my house. My packages were delivered by an extensive network of unofficial Cuba couriers, whose names I got from Global Exchange, the local nonprofit with which I'd gone to Cuba.

Sometimes, via a customer buying a book on Cuba, I would find a courier on my own. But here I had to be careful, approaching my potential messengers in the softest and most casual manner possible.

"Oh, planning a trip to Cuba?" I'd ask as nonchalantly as if inquiring about whether they thought it might rain that afternoon.

A familiar, furtive glance would follow; an unspoken question of "Is this person safe?" would ripple across their forehead; and then the connection would be made.

I employed this technique well and frequently enough that about every two weeks I was able to find someone going to Cuba. If it wasn't someone I met myself, it was the friend or boss or dog walker of someone's brother I'd met who was going.

"Don't you think it's strange that before you went you hardly knew anyone who'd been to Cuba, and now that you've returned, everyone you meet is somehow connected?" a friend of mine asked.

I didn't think it was strange at all. I had returned from a world most Americans had heard of but not many had ventured to visit. Those of us who had been to Cuba, like members of clandestine clubs and subcultures around the world, looked out for each other, maintaining our underground networking system, guarding it like the lifeline it was.

With the help of our Cuba couriers, Alfredo and I began our international gift exchange. I sent him Timberland sandals, sunglasses, a Spanish–English dictionary, and an album filled with photos of us.

Alfredo sent me a bilingual magazine detailing the history of the Cuban Revolution and a postcard of La Gran Piedra, the rock mountain we'd climbed in Santiago. He sent me outdated, out-of-order letters that had never made it into email, but his most touching present was a matte, black-and-white photo, curled and yellowed around the once-white framed edges. In the photo, a miniature Alfredo stood on a tile floor in front of a TV, a ceramic duck by his feet, his arms still chubby with baby fat, his hair short, and his ears sticking out. He wore shiny white shoes and dark corduroy pants with a matching paisley vest over a striped button-down shirt. His oversized smile reminded me of the Cheshire cat.

"I was only four when this was taken," he wrote in his accompanying letter. "But look, I was already in love with you."

I sent Alfredo back a photo of myself at age four, pudgy and pouting about some injustice that had been done to me in the instant before the shutter blinked.

The one thing I was careful not to send Alfredo was money. It wasn't that I didn't trust my Cuba couriers. I didn't trust the ways in which money might transform our relationship. I remembered all too well the Hotel El Bosque poolside affairs, since many of the Americans involved in them called me regularly to compare relationship notes. Always, I felt proud to report that Alfredo didn't ask for money like the poolside partners who often requested, and were granted, a few hundred or a thousand dollars for some urgent expenses they'd incurred since their lovers had left.

Rather than money, I offered to send Alfredo an extra-large duffel bag.

"I can line it with down feathers for comfort, and all you have to do, when my coworker Susan comes down next week, is to curl up in it when she leaves," I emailed him. "She's a good friend, and she owes me a few favors. She'll check you in at the baggage counter, and then in a few hours, we'll be together again. No marriage, no papers, no politics."

"*¡Ay, mi amor!*" Alfredo wrote back. "If this were possible, then you could write your best story yet."

When Susan went to Cuba, instead of the extra-large duffel bag I gave her fiancé visa papers for Alfredo to sign. This visitation option, which I'd learned about through a friend of a courier who was applying for the same visa with her Cuban boyfriend, would allow Alfredo to come visit me for three months. At the end of this ninety-day trial period, we could either get married or, if we still weren't ready for such a huge commitment, Alfredo could simply return to Cuba.

It seemed like the ideal option, other than such minor details as Alfredo's not having permission to work for those three months and my not having a private apartment where we could have our own space. I also worried that even if we agreed to view the visa as simply a visit—with no strings attached, and with the added benefit that if things were so great that we couldn't bear to separate, we could simply get married—it would never be quite that simple. I worried that the weight of the word "fiancé" would place undue pressure on our relationship, causing everything, especially our moments of discord, to take on a greater significance. And fiancé visa or no, the future of our relationship, as residents of two countries pitted against each other in an everlasting Cold War, was already flawed with so many odds stacked against it that it made me dizzy to contemplate them.

Still, when I thought about the daunting alternative of getting married on my next visit to Cuba so that Alfredo could come to the U.S., my worries about the fiancé visa seemed small in comparison. And when I told Alfredo about the fiancé visa, he responded with pure, uncomplicated excitement.

"So when do you think I can come out?" he asked.

"Well, the whole process is supposed to take about nine months, but ..."

"That's it? Just nine months? That's nothing." Alfredo paused to calculate, adding excitedly, "So by May, I could be out there with you in your world."

"Maybe," I said, "but more likely, you wouldn't be able to come out until next fall, so I could save up money."

"Money?" Alfredo asked, as though the thought hadn't crossed his mind. "Well, I can ask my dad for money for the visa." Alfredo's father had moved to the U.S. just before I had left Cuba, and within a month, both he and his wife had found work in Miami.

"He doesn't have much now, but I know he'll want to help us," Alfredo continued, adding, "I'm sure he's doing fine with the Cuban Adjustment Act."

Passed in 1966, the Cuban Adjustment Act guaranteed Cuban exiles more benefits than any other ethnic group in the U.S., including native-born citizens. In the early years following the Cuban Revolution, Cuban exiles who fled to the U.S. were allowed to attend private schools for free, to indefinitely default on their college loans, and to take out business loans at rates well beneath those offered to anyone else. Historically, while Haitians who have arrived in the U.S. on inner tubes have routinely been sent home despite their pleas of political persecution, Cubans, thanks to the Cuban Adjustment Act, have needed only to set foot on U.S. soil to be granted permanent resident status and collect benefits. As Fidel once put it, "If a Mexican goes to the U.S. illegally, he's expelled. If a Cuban enters illegally, he's given a house."

In the case of Alfredo's father, for his first six months, he and his family received three hundred dollars in food stamps each month, free medical care, free bus tickets, and five hundred dollars in cash.

"That's nice of you to offer to ask your father for help," I said to Alfredo. "But really, I'll be okay. I just need time."

I wanted to tell Alfredo that I probably had enough money in my savings to support both of us for three months, but I knew that would only further complicate the situation. Then I would have to explain that when I told

Alfredo he couldn't come out until the fall because I didn't have the money, I wasn't speaking literally, as someone in Cuba might have been. I would have to clarify that what I'd meant was that I wasn't willing to use up my entire savings. I would have to explain once more the need to always have something stashed away—a foreign concept in Cuba's socialist society. In the process of all this cultural translation, I would undoubtedly feel stingy, since I knew that Alfredo, if he'd had the money, would have spent it all at once, flying to the U.S. the minute his visa was approved. I knew, from the generosity I'd experienced during my time in Cuba, that when there was so little money to be had, people thought nothing of spending it all in one sitting, leaving them no worse off than they were to begin with.

On September 4, 2000, I compiled all my phone bills with Cuba calls on them, a photocopy of my plane ticket to Cuba, a letter I'd written verifying that I was single, an affidavit of support for Alfredo, a notary's signature and golden seal verifying my Spanish and English translations of our birth certificates, four pages of biographical forms, several photos of Alfredo and me together and alone, and a check for ninety-five dollars. I crammed all this into an oversized envelope, which I addressed to an INS office in a town I'd never heard of in Southern California and, on my way to work, I dropped my package into the blue street mailbox outside the bookstore.

Although I had told a few close friends about the fiancé visa, most people, including my parents, remained unaware. I knew it wouldn't be a problem with my mother, who had fallen in love with Alfredo from one of my photos of him, declaring him to be the most beautiful man she'd ever seen. Like Alfredo, my mother was a romantic, an idealist who was quick to excite and slower to think through the practicalities of any given situation. When I'd first told her about our relationship, without worrying about any of the racial or cultural or financial or language concerns that plagued me, my mother enthusiastically cheered me on.

My father, on the other hand, was more like me. He was a realist, a pragmatist, and I could see his face fill with worry whenever I mentioned Alfredo or my plans to return to Cuba. My father dealt with his discomfort by attempting to ignore the situation altogether, and I, not really wanting to hear his concerns for fear that they might echo my own, played along. Together, we became adept at avoidance.

As I packed my bags for Cuba, I counted the days since I'd heard Alfredo's voice and realized that it had been nearly a month. During one of our last conversations, Alfredo had told me that the phone lines between Cuba and the U.S. would stop working in four days.

"What are you talking about?" I'd asked, wondering whether, like blackouts, bad phone days were also planned in Cuba.

"Oh, it usually happens once a year for a few weeks," Alfredo said matter-of-factly. "There'll be some dispute between the governments, like Cuba wants its pre-Revolution money that's in the U.S. banks, but the U.S. won't release it until Fidel steps down. Or the U.S. raises the tax that Cuba has to pay to remain connected. And then Fidel gets angry, and he'll cut the phone lines. Usually it's around the holidays, because he knows that that's when all the Miami exiles try to call their Cuban relatives."

Knowing that our time was limited, Alfredo and I talked for fifteen minutes for each of the following four days, giving our communication a much-needed continuity that had been impossible to obtain in our biweekly calls.

On the fifth day, the receiver just beeped a fast, angry busy signal in my ear, refusing to connect me with Cuba, forcing me to accept that the next time I heard Alfredo's voice would be when I saw him standing in front of me at the José Martí International Airport.

Part 2

21

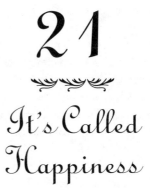

It's Called Happiness

I arrived in Cancún at the end of my twenty-sixth year and at the start of hurricane season.

Braving a flash downpour, I ran outside the Cancún International Airport to the little peach stucco building that housed Cubana de Aviación. As my foot sunk into a spongy patch of earth that filled in the gap between a missing section of sidewalk and the entrance to Cubana, I remembered my arrival in Cancún on a drizzly morning nearly eight months earlier. Like a movie flashback, I saw myself standing in the same spot, the same mud seeping through the same slats of my same sandals as a wave of anticipation and anxiety washed over me. Slowly, as the other members of my program arrived with their own worries and expectations for the coming month, I'd felt my apprehension fade. Surrounded by the buzz of our nervous energy, we had huddled together under the roof's tiny overhang, trying to stay dry while we waited for someone to come unlock Cubana's front door.

Today the office was open when I walked in at 7 AM, but the ticket agent's detached response to my request for a ticket did little to calm my edginess.

"Come back tomorrow or maybe the next day," she said nonchalantly before beginning to sort a pile of papers on her desk.

"*¿Por qué?*" I asked. It was strange to be speaking once more in person-to-person Spanish, and I wondered whether I'd understood the agent correctly.

"We haven't had any flights leaving for three days now," she said. "This always happens in hurricane season. It's just too dangerous."

"But what about all these other planes?" I asked, turning my head in the direction of the runway, where I had just witnessed several planes taking off.

"Those are new planes," the agent said. "Not old Russian ones like ours."

"Oh, right," I said, recalling that even under the best of circumstances, Cubana planes had a troubled reputation. I remembered Dinora telling me how she worried each time Luis or Nitza flew, always recalling the airline's 1989 crash near Havana in which 126 people had died. On my last Cubana flight, everyone had clapped when our plane touched down on the runway.

Pushing aside her papers for a moment, the agent pointed to a pile of backpacks and suitcases in the corner of the office.

"You can leave your luggage there for the night," she said.

I turned twenty-seven while wandering the overtouristed streets of Cancún, dodging the vendors who called out to me in Spanglish, "*Un sombrero, se-ñorita. For you, very buen precio. Muy cheap.*"

When my disrupted red-eye sleep from the night before caught up with me, I retreated to the hotel for an overdue nap. And there, in the crisp, air-conditioned silence of my room, I slept an intermittent sleep, full of disturbing dreams not just about my arrival in Havana, but also about my departure from the U.S.

On my first trip to Cuba, I'd fit everything I'd needed into my trusty old camping backpack. But for this visit, to accommodate all the presents I'd brought for people, I'd bought a fancy, fashionable wheeled suitcase. Despite its supposedly comfort-enhancing pullout handle, I had calluses on both hands after wheeling it from the airport entrance to the check-in terminal, where the agent had promptly informed me that my suitcase was fifty pounds overweight.

"It's ninety-five, and the maximum is forty-five," he'd said as I'd stared in disbelief at the digital scale. Gripping the suitcase handle with my callused hands, I moved off to the side of the check-in to sit down and see what I could bear to part with.

My suitcase contained multivitamins and ibuprofen for Alfredo's grandmother, toilet paper, an assortment of energy bars and dehydrated bean soups, twine for impromptu laundry lines, automatic laundry detergent for Dinora, bedsheets for Liudmila, and running shoes for Alfredo.

Among my less-essential items, I had a bottle of California red wine, a box of macaroni and cheese, and a half-dozen apples, which were expensive imported delicacies in Cuba. I also had a mix tape of the music I listened to in the U.S., as well as photos of my running trail, of my dogs, and of my parents and friends. I had a copy of the newspaper I used to write for, even though I doubted Alfredo would be able to understand anything in it.

I doubted too that Alfredo would understand the words to the music I listened to. And I had a feeling that he might balk at the idea of eating pasta out of a box that included a dusty, prepackaged, pseudo-cheese sauce. But after months of trying to explain and imagine whether Alfredo could fit in to my life in the U.S., I just needed to show him some tangible evidence of this other world I inhabited.

At the San Francisco International Airport, I spent half an hour weeding out my weightiest gifts and several more minutes trying, without success, to convince other departing travelers to take them. The airline attendants also refused, and one even directed me to a trash can, explaining that in the newly opened terminal I was departing from, there were not even storage lockers I could rent. Unwilling to throw out my presents, I abandoned them in a dark corner of the airport, a shrine to the material goods that were—and would now still be—lacking in Cuba.

Two days into my Cancún layover, when the storm had blown over, I boarded the plane from Cancún to Havana. I assumed I was in the clear, having forgotten that I still had to pass the scrutiny of Cuban customs.

Just minutes after I'd retrieved my suitcase from baggage claim, a stern agent in olive military garb waved me over, ordering me to open my suitcase and carry-on backpack. One by one, the agent pulled out my remaining gifts and show-and-tell items, demanding to know their purposes and beneficiaries.

"It's to make things spicy," I said as she turned my hot-sauce bottle upside down like an hourglass, its bright red liquid sloshing around inside. "It's for a friend who likes to cook."

She eyed the Buena Vista Social Club video, which I'd brought for Alfredo, with such interest that I feared she might try to snag it for herself. She scrutinized my tampons, confiscated my apples, and questioned my perforated ribbon of two dozen Trojan condoms.

"Is this the friend that likes to cook?" she asked.

She didn't smile or even laugh, and I felt my face grow red with embarrassment.

"Uh, no, it's not," I stammered,

"Then who's it for?" She persisted. "Who exactly are your friends?"

She made me give full names and addresses, and although she didn't write anything down, she had so intimidated me that by the time she released me to meet Alfredo, I was shaky and flushed, my face sweating, my hands cold and clammy. My heart raced so fast I was certain everyone could hear its overzealous thumping. Like an accelerated case of stage fright, my throat was cotton-dry, and speech seemed a distant possibility.

I saw Alfredo before he saw me. He was stuck behind a crowd of taller people at the arrival gate and was running back and forth frantically like a fenced-in dog. Every few feet, when he found an indent, Alfredo would wedge his way into the pack and jump straight up, his eyes scanning the approaching passengers, his spiral dreadlocks, which had grown a few inches in my absence, bobbing like the hair on a jack-in-the-box.

Alfredo spotted me while I was laughing at his performance. Our eyes locked, and he laughed back. Everything else went out of focus as we walked quickly toward each other, meeting up at the end of the roped entrance chute, where, after all my rehearsals of what we might say in this long-awaited moment, we embraced silently. We held onto each other until a nearby flight attendant said something in Spanish that I didn't catch, but which made Alfredo smile and take my hand, moving us off to the side of the incoming passengers.

I stared at Alfredo for a beat. Although I had of course remembered what he looked like, I had forgotten the depth of his beauty, the earthy brown of his skin, the perfect placement of the tiny freckle on the left side of his nose, his long eyelashes, the eagerness in his eyes.

I had forgotten also about his passion for green clothing. Today he wore his favorite outfit, the same green-and-black plaid golfer's shorts and loud green Bavaria beer T-shirt that had embarrassed me on our journey to Santiago. And yet, I realized as we walked outside hand in sweaty hand, I loved him anyway.

Outside the airport, we stood comfortably silent for a moment, surveying the outskirts of Havana. It was an overcast afternoon, humid and gray, with rain hovering on the edge of several thick storm clouds.

On the road running parallel to the airport, two men pushed a beat-up blue Chevy off the asphalt and onto a grassy outcropping. Alfredo flagged down a *taxista particular,* and as we chugged our way out of the parking lot, he gave the driver directions to his father's former house.

"My cousin lives there now," Alfredo told me. "I just need to drop off an umbrella I borrowed in case it started raining when I picked you up."

He moved close to me in the back seat and draped his arm around my shoulder, enveloping me in the musky scent of cologne, something he had never worn before, and I wondered, with a mix of affection and sadness, if he'd borrowed this too.

The *taxista* waited in his car while Alfredo and I ran over to the cousin's to drop off the umbrella.

"You made it," the cousin said when he saw me. "Alfredito was afraid you'd be stuck in Cancún forever."

Alfredo laughed, embarrassed, and then the cousin asked me, "So does Cuba seem changed to you? Do you notice any differences?"

"No," I said, perplexed by the question. "Should I?"

The cousin found this so funny that he nearly snorted. "Well, it always seems exactly the same to me," he said. "But then, I've never left, so I have no perspective." He paused, sighing dramatically. "As far as I know, this is all there is."

While I had spent the past four months conjuring up recollections of Cuba and Alfredo and worrying that I would find everything irreversibly different upon my return, they had both been waiting here all along, as patient and unchanged as the surrounding sea, reflecting only the still, blue sky above.

When our taxi turned onto Animas Street, Dinora was there waiting on the balcony, waving us over as if we might have forgotten which house was hers.

"You look so healthy," Dinora gushed as she stood atop the stairs, watching me ascend. Then she sighed and added, "That must be what happens when you get to travel, to know the world around you. *¡Qué rico!*"

Smiling, she gave Alfredo and me welcome kisses and ushered us into the living room.

"*Mimi,* look at Lea. Doesn't she look healthy?" Dinora asked Abuela, who was so excited that she placed her hands on the rocking chair's armrests and attempted to stand up on her own.

I walked over to her, and she spewed out a river of muffled words, "*gordita*" being the only one that I could make out.

"No," I said, laughing. "La Gorda isn't here now. I'm Lea. Don't you remember?"

I had noticed Dinora examining me while Abuela spoke, and now she nodded her head, saying, "Yes, you're right. Lea has gotten a little *gordita*."

I looked down at myself, searching for signs of extra weight, but I couldn't find any.

"I don't think so," I said to Dinora.

"Oh, yes, you're definitely fatter," Dinora said. She turned to Alfredo. "Don't you think so?"

Alfredo smiled mischievously at me. "Maybe," he said.

Now Abuela pointed at Alfredo, bobbing her head up and down. *"Gordito. Él también es gordito,"* she taunted like a mean-spirited schoolgirl.

I waited for Dinora to correct Abuela on this last, indisputably incorrect call, Alfredo's legs as toothpickesque as ever. But once again Dinora acquiesced to Abuela's judgment.

"It's true," she said. "You both look so good, so alive, so . . ." Her voice trailed off as she searched for the word that would sum it all up, explaining our mysterious, invisible weight gain. But before Dinora could finish her sentence, Abuela interjected with another unintelligible outpouring.

"Ah, yes, of course," Dinora said, giving Abuela an affectionate shoulder squeeze. *"Es amor."*

Upstairs, I collapsed onto the familiar comfort of my Cuba bed, covered as always with a thin layer of crisp, cool white sheets. Alfredo slid across the polished tile floor and lay down between me and a vase of fresh flowers on the nightstand.

"I love this room," he said dreamily.

I glanced around us, my eyes resting on a backpack I'd sent Alfredo via my coworker. Seeing it now residing in this corner of Dinora's room was like doing a doubletake, as was looking at Alfredo's feet, dressed up in the Timberland sandals that had also spent a fair amount of time on my bedroom floor. It was as if all the goods between us, save for Alfredo's beer-guzzling golfer getup, had resided in each of our worlds. All that was needed to make this transfer sequence complete was permission for Alfredo and his beloved outfit to come to the U.S.

"I brought the backpack over with some of my stuff yesterday," Alfredo said, noticing my gaze. "I have some presents for you in there."

"Yeah? I have some for you too."

"Mine first," Alfredo said, excitedly. "I have some in the backpack and one somewhere else in this room. Do you want to play a game?" He asked his question in heavily accented English. "You have to start walking to where you think the present might be," he continued, reverting back to Spanish.

I got off the bed and kneeled down to look under it.

"Cold, very cold," he said in English.

I walked over to the closet and reached down to the cabinet underneath.

"Warm," Alfredo said, sitting up on the bed.

I stood and looked around the room. There really was nowhere else to hide anything. I walked to the other side of the room to peer into the waste-paper basket.

"Cold," Alfredo said. "Very cold."

I walked back to the closet and then in a straight line parallel to it.

"Hot, extremely hot," Alfredo said.

I looked down at the dorm-size refrigerator and reached over to open it.

"You are on fire!" Alfredo said.

The refrigerator was packed to capacity with what must have been nearly two dozen eight-ounce Ciego Montero spring water bottles, the foreigner's one-dollar-a-pop alternative to Cuba's questionable tap water. When Cubans were lucky enough to get ahold of a Ciego Montero, they preserved the plastic bottle for as long as possible, using it to chill boiled tap water, to carry black-market rum to parties, to drink beer at peso bars that didn't have enough mugs.

Because of the heat in Havana, I generally went through at least four Ciego Monteros each day, and I'd often joked to Alfredo that this drinking water was the most expensive part of my life on the island. Now, staring into the crowded interior of our tiny refrigerator, I was acutely aware that the cost of all these bottles was equivalent to two months of Alfredo's salary.

"I got them at a concert," Alfredo said, interrupting my thoughts. "They were for a group of Chilean violinists, but we had a lot left over, and everyone knew you were coming out soon, so they let me take them."

"Thank you," I said. "That's very sweet."

Alfredo smiled proudly, and we moved on to the backpack presents, his own show-and-tell collection depicting the details of his life these past four months. There was a wallet-size reprint photo of Che that Alfredo had found in the street one day and guarded for me. There was the print supplement to a recently aired TV program on Latin American literature that he had watched, and, from the July Carnaval he had described to me so vividly on the phone, there were two tiny dolls with rosy brown faces and maracas in their hands.

I gave Alfredo a Spanish-language copy of Howard Zinn's *A People's History of the United States,* a pair of running socks and Nikes, the Buena Vista Social Club video, a Bob Marley tape, a Walkman, a pair of shorts, and a bright, pressed orange California poppy.

Then, as Alfredo sat surrounded by my gifts, I noticed that, after his initial excitement, his eyes had begun to take on a glassy, distant look. I'd seen this gaze before, most frequently when I had attempted to explain the complexities of my life in the U.S., serving Alfredo a whopping dose of information overload. In this case, it was a tactile, visual overload I had presented.

I decided to hold off on my true show-and-tell items, including a story I'd written about me and Alfredo and the photos of my family. Even though they were more about sharing than giving, I was nonetheless wary of further overwhelming him.

Before I could completely abandon my part of our present exchange, there was one more gift I had to give Alfredo, because I knew that the longer I put off doing it, the more difficult it would become.

In the U.S., I had never bought underwear for a boyfriend because it had seemed trite and uninspired. But with Alfredo, whose three pairs of underwear were threadbare and ancient, things were different.

I wanted to just hand him the underwear like I'd handed him the Bob Marley tape or the Buena Vista Social Club video, no explanation needed. But cotton briefs, unlike videos and music or even silk boxers, were practical. They were a necessity and a member of that family of presents that—in their silent, accusatory manner—implied that something basic and essential was missing in the life of the giftee.

"Another present?" Alfredo asked incredulously as he watched me root around in the suitcase.

"Well, it's just a small one," I said, "nothing really special, just something useful."

I pulled back my suitcase cover to reveal the box of underwear, which, with its photo of a buff white man flexing his muscles in a pair of blue Jockeys, was almost as embarrassing as the gift itself. Alfredo opened the clear plastic box and laid out on the bed the three pairs of underwear in their gradated shades of blue.

"They're beautiful," he said without the slightest hint of embarrassment. "Did you get them at Macy's department store?"

"How did you know?" I asked, startled.

"I was just joking," Alfredo said, pulling me into his chest. "There was a dialogue about Macy's department store in those Berlitz tapes you sent me. I'd like to go there some day."

"Okay, great," I said, laughing. "What other important things have you learned from the tapes?"

"Macy's department store. How may I help you?" Alfredo mimicked in a high-pitched, clerky voice, and then, changing to a more matter-of-fact masculine voice, he said, "I enjoy scuba diving on my vacation."

"Scuba diving. Do you even know what that means?"

"No, but I do like how it sounds."

"Ay, Alfredo!"

"What?"

"You're very funny."

"And hungry," Alfredo added. "Do you want to get something to eat? I did some *negocios* this week, so it's my treat."

"Okay, *vámonos*," I said, picking up my purse from the bed and tossing the empty underwear box with Mr. Macho into the wastepaper basket, which seemed to disturb Alfredo.

"Why'd you throw out that box?" he asked.

"You want to keep it? With that silly man on the front?"

"No, it's not that." Alfredo looked down. "I was just thinking that . . . well, if someone sees it in the trash here, they might think you got me underwear because I didn't have any."

As I stood stunned by Alfredo's analysis, he pulled the box out of the trash and transferred it to my purse.

"Let's just take it with us to be safe," he said. "We can drop it in a dumpster outside."

On our route to dinner, Alfredo taught me how to do the hurricane walk. This was a variation on the summer, sun-dodging version, which involved zigzagging across the street so that you were always walking in the shade beneath a balcony and never on the *acera de los bobos*. Along this "sidewalk of the stupids," as Alfredo referred to the sun-drenched side of the street, many a dazed foreigner, mesmerized by the street life and dizzy from the streamlined Cuban diet, could be seen stumbling along in a sweaty stupor.

But during hurricane season, such shade-bearing structures as balconies were to be avoided at all cost.

"These old balconies are unsafe under ordinary conditions. But during hurricane season, you just never know when a gust of wind might hit one the wrong way, and it'll come tumbling down on top of you," Alfredo told me as we walked down the middle of 13th Street in Vedado.

Alfredo and I continued along in silence for the next few blocks until we reached our favorite dinner destination, at the corner of 17th and 8th Streets.

El Recanto was a *paladar*, which, like all such privately owned restaurants, was run out of a house. Tonight, after we rang the doorbell at the unmarked entrance, the father invited us into the living room, where he was watching the nightly *telenovela*. The daughter escorted us down the hall and through the kitchen out to the moonlit rooftop rainforest, surrounded by potted palms and inhabited by two ancient parrots that poked their heads through the bars of their shared cage to inspect us.

We ate a heaping plate of fried plantains with rice and beans, yucca soaked with garlic and orange juice, a side dish of pork for Alfredo, and an avocado and tomato salad for me.

I didn't know where the *paladares* got so much fresh food, or how El Recanto managed to sell theirs in pesos when all the others only took *fula*, charging upward of thirteen dollars for a meal. I wondered also whether El Recanto would be around long enough for us to come again.

Since our last visit, I could see that an extra table had been added, increasing the seating space to sixteen, which was four seats over the government-mandated maximum. Any day now, if an inspector chose to visit, she could fine El Recanto out of existence. Alfredo looked over at the new table, a wave of sadness settling onto his face.

"I came here once with Gerardo while you were gone," he said. "We sat at that table there, but now he's gone."

"What do you mean?" I asked. Gerardo was Alfredo's neighbor and one of his oldest and closest friends. In our own relationship, he had served as the intermediary, the friend of the friend who'd introduced us.

"He moved to Belgium last week," Alfredo said.

"Belgium? But why? How?"

"He had a girlfriend from there," Alfredo told me. "I knew that, and I'd even met her, but he didn't tell anyone that she was applying for a tourist visa for him."

"Why not?"

"You know how it is here," Alfredo said. "People are scared. They're afraid of gossipers."

"So Gerardo never mentioned anything to you about going to Belgium?"

"He left last Wednesday, and on Tuesday, he stopped by my work and invited me to a party at his house, some sort of religious ceremony for a kid in the neighborhood. I still remember him standing there on the steps of the theater," Alfredo said nostalgically. "He called out, 'We're having an Eleggua party,' and I thought at the time I might go, but then I ended up working late, and I just went home to sleep. The next day, I heard from a friend who'd been at the party that Gerardo told everyone he was leaving the next morning."

"Well, how long is a tourist visa for?"

"A month, but he won't be back," Alfredo said, shaking his head. "Gerardo always wanted out, and now he found his way. If things don't work out with his girlfriend, then he'll go somewhere else, but he won't be back. I know that for sure. And the worst thing is, I never got to say goodbye."

When we returned to Dinora's, I asked Alfredo something I'd wanted to ask ever since he started his Gerardo story.

"Have you told anyone about our fiancé visa?"

"Not yet," he said. "Because people gossip so much, I think it's best to wait until I know that it's been approved. But I can tell you that if it does go through, I won't wait until the night before I leave to tell people."

I nodded, and Alfredo moved in closer to me on the bed where we were sitting.

"Do you think the visa will be approved?" he asked.

"I don't know. The whole application process felt like make-believe. It seems so arbitrary. I don't know how the government decides who to grant visas to."

Alfredo nodded thoughtfully, and with no more insight to shed upon the subject, we spent the next few hours catching up. Alfredo told me about his sister, an independent woman who had chosen to remain single even when she became pregnant, and how she had finally given in and married her baby's father the week after she gave birth. And he described a dinner he'd had at his coworker Mamito's house, where the family dog had stood on two feet and danced when Mamito's mother played the guitar.

After Alfredo showered and returned to the bedroom, dancing around in his new underwear, I translated for him the first page of the story I'd written about us. When I read a line about our visit to the *posada particular*, he buried his face in the pillow, embarrassed. But then when he looked up, I saw that his eyes were glossy with pride.

"It's very beautiful, *mi amor*," he said. "Thank you for remembering all those details."

We laid close together for what seemed like an eternity, not speaking at all but just tracing the features of each other's faces with our fingers. And then we returned to our conversation, talking from just past sunset into the early hours of the morning, not even noticing the time pass.

"Are you tired?" Alfredo asked me when the red digital alarm clock flashed 2:10.

He curled up next to me, spoon-style, so that I could feel the constant, calming beat of his heart against my back.

"I am tired," I said. "Actually, I'm beyond tired, but I have this strange sensation that still I could keep talking for hours."

"Me too," he said. "I think it's called happiness."

22

❧❧❧❧❧

What's Changed?

On the morning after our night of happiness, I woke to a resounding thud that emanated from the back of the house and sent a plume of gray dust swirling around our bedroom window. For a second, the sky echoed with the frenzied flutter of chicken wings and the screeching of wheelbarrows in need of oil. A few muffled human voices called out to each other, and then everything went silent.

I turned to Alfredo, but, forever the sound sleeper, he lay peacefully curled up against his pillow. I pulled on my sundress from the day before and headed out to explore on my own.

A cold front had moved in, and as I stepped out onto Animas Street, I found myself in the middle of a transformed Havana, a wind-whipped, sunless city whose residents rushed about wearing layers of every item of clothing they owned.

Even though it couldn't have been much cooler than 65 degrees, women obscured their fluorescent spandex body suits beneath baggy pants and knee-length overcoats while men covered up their bare chests with multiple layers of mismatched flannel shirts. I clenched my fists around the skirt of my sundress to keep the wind from pulling it over my head.

One block down the street, I saw the source of the boom that had woken me. In a pile of chalky smoke and chipped orange tiles, the rubble of the farmers market roof stood before me, a first-hand validation, writ large, of Alfredo's fear of collapsing balconies.

I stood dazed, staring at the wreckage for several minutes until the wind got the better of me, forcing me back inside for warmth and to escape the fierce pricks of flying ceramic debris. When I returned to the house, I found Alfredo fully awake and sitting straight up in bed.

"You slept through it," I said as I sat down next to him, pulling the bedsheet around my shivering knees. "The farmers market roof came off."

"Really?" Alfredo asked. "I thought I heard something, but I think I incorporated it into my dream. And then when I woke, I imagined something even worse had happened."

"Like what?"

"I imagined," he said, leaning over to embrace me, his skin still warm with sleep, his voice still soft with the ache of absence, "that I'd dreamed your return."

Like my reunion with Alfredo, my first few days back in Havana also felt like a dream, and I passed through them in an almost timeless state. I fielded questions from unnamed street acquaintances who had noticed my absence but, it appeared, had never considered that I might have left the island.

"Are you living in another neighborhood?" they'd ask as I walked down the street. "Where's your *amiga gorda*?"

I traveled from one friend's house to the next, delivering gifts and whiling away the afternoons in rocking chairs. I participated in numerous rounds of what I'd come to think of as the "What's Changed?" game, initiated by Alfredo's cousin when we stopped by to return his umbrella my first day back.

On my previous trip, Cubans had asked me more questions about the U.S. than I had been able to answer. On my return, I found that the Cubans, as if they had forgotten where they were from, asked me only about Cuba.

Initially confused, I soon realized that, by virtue of my having left their country, Cubans now viewed me as akin to a visionary, capable of shedding light on the ever-so-subtle changes taking place on the island.

Not wanting to disappoint, I quickly began compiling a mental list of every tiny transformation I came across while meandering through Havana.

"There is the trolley," I told Liudmila, referring to a fancy new tourist bus I'd spotted along the Malecón.

"There are those decorations that weren't here before in the streets, those little lanterns made from Tropicola cans for the CDR anniversary celebration," I pointed out to my friend Pepe.

On the countless days when, as much as I strained my eyes looking for change, I found nothing, I'd revert to my old standby, which was so silly, it pained me to point it out. But I did anyway, announcing, "Well, all the Elián signs have disappeared."

A week after my arrival, the winds that had toppled the farmers market roof claimed their second casualty. It was a breezy but muggy morning when Dinora opened the balcony's French doors. A gust of wind swept in and sent the living room chandelier crashing to its death on the tile floor, scattering shards of glass everywhere.

To my surprise, rather than rushing to collect the glass, Dinora stood still, staring at the remnants of her antique centerpiece as if watching the rerun of a movie she'd seen many times before.

"First the farmers market, then this," she said, shaking her head in despair. "Havana is falling apart before my eyes."

While as dramatic as always, Dinora's most recent claim resonated with me more than her others, which had often linked a low level of shoe quality or a lack of automatic laundry detergent with the downfall of her country.

Alfredo and I walked over to Dinora from the steps where we'd been standing frozen since the crash, and I examined Dinora's weary face. Motioning for us to not get too close to the broken glass, she let out a long, loud sigh and declared, "I'll never be able to replace that chandelier. They don't make things like that in Cuba anymore."

I nodded sympathetically, and then, while I racked my mind for some words of consolation, Alfredo surprised me by speaking up.

"Don't worry Dinora," he said softly and, with an edge of excitement in his voice, added, "We have lots of extra lighting stuff at work. I'm sure I can get something, and then maybe Luis and I can invent a nice fixture for you."

Dinora smiled, and I did too, touched by Alfredo's gesture. Since my return, I had noticed a concerted effort on his part to make things work at Dinora's. He accepted more of her invitations to sit down for a coffee and chat, and he'd stopped searching for the racist undercurrents in her every utterance.

For her part, Dinora had relaxed a bit too, no longer even hinting that Alfredo might want to leave before eight in the morning so that the neighbors wouldn't report him.

Within the four months of my absence, Alfredo had gone from an early morning walk-of-shamer to the favored son of a family friend, even though no one in Dinora's family had ever met anyone in Alfredo's.

"Luis told me to tell Mielikki, in case she wanted her boyfriend to stay over, that I'm an exception because Luis and my father are old friends," Alfredo told me one day, as proudly as if there were any truth at all in this.

Mielikki was one of Dinora's new boarders, a Finnish exchange student who had moved in the day after I'd arrived. When Mielikki had come over to drop off her luggage, carried upstairs by an attractive black man whom she introduced as her Cuban boyfriend, I could see a wave of worry wash over Dinora's face.

"When she came to look at the house last week, she never mentioned that she had a boyfriend," Dinora told me anxiously after the two had left. "Did it look to you like he was planning to stay here too?"

"Probably not if she didn't mention it to you before."

"Well, I hope not, because it's just not safe to have another Cuban staying here," Dinora said. She lowered her voice and added, "It's not even safe to have as many foreigners here as we do when we're only registered for two rental rooms."

Alfredo and I were staying in the room I used to share with Amy. Mielikki was on one side of us, and on the other were two Danish women. Downstairs a Swedish woman was renting Nitza's room, and Nitza was sharing a room and a bed with Abuela. Alfredo and I shared a kitchen and a bathroom with the four foreigners, and the crowded atmosphere reminded me of dorm life.

During the day, each of us was in a different part of the city, but at some point every evening, like an impromptu international family, we all met up around the dining room table. Mielikki did her Spanish homework, and Kajsa, the Swede, sat with a dictionary in one hand and a Cuban political text in the other, taking notes for her master's dissertation on Cuba's bureaucratic structure. Anna and Vita—the Danes who were here studying film and the history of the CDRs, respectively—smoked and wrote in their journals. I read a thick volume on the life of Fidel, and Alfredo stared, amazed at the spectacle of all of us.

For Alfredo, the Scandinavians were foreigners in every sense of the word. Not only were they bigger and blonder than any *cubana* Alfredo had seen, but their native languages sounded like nothing he had ever heard.

To top it off, the Scandinavians often didn't speak at all but rather sat silently next to each other, each immersed in her own project. This sort of quiet, I'd noticed, had always made Alfredo nervous, causing him to twist his dreadlocks or beat out a rhythm on his body in a semblance of sound and movement. Alfredo came from a noisy, unreserved culture in which silence was something to be suffered when you were alone and a source of worry when surrounded by others.

Also foreign to Alfredo were the Scandinavians' independent studies pursuing a personal interest outside of the formal structure of work or school. Like the vast majority of his fellow Cubans, Alfredo spent his free time in his house with his family, in the streets with his friends, or in some in-between space searching for a *negocio,* with which he could make ends meet.

Watching him take his first tentative steps toward inclusion in the Scandinavians' world was also for me like entering a new world, where I could witness how Alfredo adapted to cultural differences. Our evenings with the Scandinavians allowed me a coveted glimpse into what Alfredo might be like in my country, ninety miles and 180 degrees to the north.

Initially, if Alfredo arrived at Dinora's after work and I was at the kitchen table with the Scandinavians, he would join me there. But if I were in the bathroom or on the rooftop collecting my laundry, he'd hide out in the bedroom, waiting for me to return to spare him the potentially embarrassing prospect of entering the kitchen alone.

I had been so irritated at having to serve as Alfredo's intermediary that it had taken everything in me to refrain from pushing him out into the hallway by himself. But then, little by little, I noticed that Alfredo, in his own way, was attempting to take part in the strange rituals of the Scandinavians. First there was the day when, soon after we walked into the kitchen, Alfredo had surveyed the scene and turned back toward the bedroom, not to retreat, but to retrieve his English notebook so he could take his place at the table and do his homework.

The next day, when I returned home from an early afternoon run along the Malecón, I found Alfredo in the kitchen talking to Kajsa and cooking up a big pot of spaghetti.

"We've been waiting for you," he told me, smiling as he added a pinch of salt to the pasta. "I'm making dinner for everyone."

And, just like that, of his own will, Alfredo joined in on the evening gatherings, which, as the night wore on and each woman finished with her solo study, moved toward a more communal reunion.

At some point, Mielikki would head out to meet her boyfriend, and soon her space would be filled by Liudmila, who alternated her visits, stopping by every other evening after her university classes and every other morning after her classes at a Japanese language school. From law to tourism to accounting, Liudmila had now decided to learn Japanese, having heard that it would help her if she wanted to go into business. Twice a week she woke at five in the morning to catch the first of her three buses to her classes on the outskirts of Havana.

After Liudmila, one or two of the Danes' tie-dyed Rastafarian friends would stop by. Because Alfredo and I never remembered their names, we privately referred to them as Rasta #1 and Rasta #2.

Rasta #1 was from Baracoa in eastern Cuba and he came bearing gifts of homemade chocolate, harvested from the cacao trees near his family's house. Rasta #2 brought beeswax and dreaded a lock of Vita's hair one night.

Each evening, I watched Alfredo become more comfortable with the Scandinavians until, instead of growing silent as he'd done in the beginning when someone broached a topic he was unfamiliar with, Alfredo now abandoned his embarrassment and began asking his own questions, both informed and otherwise.

When Mielikki talked about volunteering at a maternity ward in China, Alfredo asked her if it was true that parents didn't want female children. And when Kajsa recounted the year she'd spent studying in Kenya, Alfredo asked her if she had seen any lions in the streets of Nairobi.

The Scandinavians had plenty of questions of their own for Alfredo, and it made me happy to see him in this role, to watch the pride dance around his eyes as he fielded queries about school and family and the customs of his culture.

But it wasn't until the evening, when Liudmila asked Alfredo whether he'd cast his mandatory vote in the National Assembly elections that day, that I witnessed Alfredo completely burst out of his shell.

"No, I haven't voted yet," Alfredo said, matter-of-factly. "And I don't have any intention of doing so."

"Alfredo!" Liudmila exclaimed. "And what will you do when the CDR comes to your house asking why you haven't voted?"

"I'll tell them I was at work. I'll tell them I was busy," Alfredo said, some of his cool nonchalance dissolving into irritation.

"Well, you're very brave," Liudmila said. "I would never not vote."

"Why not?" asked Kajsa, who immediately after Alfredo's declaration of defiance had pulled out her notebook to record this personal side of the political process.

"Because voting is our duty as Cubans," Liudmila said.

Alfredo snorted his dissent, and as the Scandinavians looked on, eager for his rebuttal, I found myself silently cheering for him, just as I did when Kajsa laughed at his jokes, or when Anna or Vita smiled at the same moments in his conversation as I did.

Kajsa poised her pen as Alfredo spoke his first words, declaring, "If it's our Cuban duty to vote, then how come we can't vote for the most important delegate of all? How come we've never had those presidential elections that Fidel promised forty years ago?"

In response, Liudmila looked thoughtfully down at her water glass. As always, even though she'd arrived just as we'd been preparing dinner, she'd refused all offers of food or drink except water. And now, before she had a chance to speak, Kajsa looked up from her notebook, where she'd been furiously scribbling away, and asked Alfredo, "So you're not afraid of getting in trouble for not voting?"

"I haven't voted in years," Alfredo said. "And my thinking has always been that, first of all, until there are presidential elections, nothing is going to change anyway. And, second of all, why would the CDR officials bother me? I'm not some delinquent who doesn't work and hangs out in the street all day like a *jinetero*. If they did try to make me vote, I'd just go in and close the curtain, and mess up my ballot," Alfredo continued. "People do that all the time."

Liudmila looked up now, clearly dismayed by this sacrilegious talk.

"Have you ever been made to vote?" I asked Alfredo.

"No," he said. "Last time I didn't vote, the CDR came by my house when I wasn't there, and they told my mother to tell me to vote when I got home, but I didn't."

"And was your mother upset?" Anna asked.

"Oh, she was upset alright," Alfredo said, laughing. "She was yelling at me that I was an antisocial counterrevolutionary, just like my father. And I went into my bedroom and put on some Carlos Varela music to try to get away from her. And then the next day, when she came home from work, she said, 'You know, some people at work were saying that Carlos Varela's lyrics are counterrevolutionary.'"

For Liudmila's sake, I hadn't planned to join in on Alfredo's parodying of his mother's revolutionary sensibility, but now I couldn't help myself from laughing, imagining a Cuban mothers' committee created to rate albums for their counterrevolutionary content.

By one-thirty, I realized that Liudmila and I were alternating yawns. After I returned from walking her to the door, my eyes watery with sleep and my head dizzy with all the conversation and sweet Cuban wine we drank, I announced that I was going to turn in too. I expected Alfredo to follow, as he always did, but instead he gave me a goodnight kiss and said, "I'll join you soon."

Once in the bedroom, I was tempted to sneak back out and eavesdrop from the hallway to hear how Alfredo might conduct the conversation without me there as a buffer of familiarity, of safety. But then I thought better of it and, embarrassed by my own nosiness, I forced myself to lie down in bed and close my eyes.

I was in the middle of a deep sleep when I felt Alfredo slip into the bed beside me. As I flipped over to face him, I caught a glimpse of my alarm clock's red digital face flashing 4:00.

"Have you been talking all this time?" I asked.

Alfredo nodded, a satisfied smile on his face.

"We talked about everything," he said. "Not just politics and life in Cuba, but philosophy and culture, and even relationships too. Did you know that Kajsa had a black boyfriend when she lived in Kenya?"

Without giving me a chance to respond, Alfredo held up the photo album I'd given him of our first four months together and launched excitedly into his next story.

"I showed them the photos of us traveling," he said, "and they said they would like to go on a weekend trip with us sometime."

"I'm proud that you stayed up," I said, running my hand across Alfredo's face.

He kissed my fingers as they crossed his lips, and then he took my hand in his.

"You know," he said, laughing a small, self-conscious laugh. "I always listened to the Scandinavians talk to you, and now it seems silly, but I thought they were always just nice to me because I was your boyfriend."

"Why would you think that?"

"It doesn't bother me," Alfredo said. "But it's like Cubans are always interested in you because you're a foreigner, an American, and other foreigners are interested in you because you're all in the same boat here. But tonight, I felt special."

I stared at Alfredo, startled by his line of thinking, which, in all my musings about his shyness with the Scandinavians, I'd never considered.

"Tonight I felt like I was interesting," Alfredo continued. "Like I was valued for being who I am, for being Cuban."

"And why wouldn't you think that foreigners would be interested in you because you're Cuban?" I asked. "That's why they've come here. To learn about people like you."

"I used to feel like that, but I don't remember when anymore," Alfredo said. "Maybe when I still voted. Maybe before everything began being catered to the tourists and I started wondering what my place was here. Maybe," he concluded, reminding me of his cousin and everyone else's pressing question to me, "it was before I started wondering how everything changed so quickly."

23

❧❧❧❧

What Would a Capitalist Do?

Little by little on this trip, an illness had been creeping into my body. Originally, I had dismissed my dizziness and occasional nausea as an exaggerated hunger pain. But then one afternoon, too lightheaded to stand, I collapsed into bed, only getting up later to pop Imodium AD tablets and, while I waited for them to take effect, to run to the bathroom.

Had this been my first visit to the island, I might have attributed this sudden attack to a Cuban variety of Montezuma's Revenge, but even on my first trip, I hadn't had any health problems. This time around, I had become pickier with what I ate, avoiding my previous staple, Havana's greasy street pizzas, which, while they had once sustained me and at times even entertained me via the friends I made while waiting in long lines, now made me sick to my stomach. The street pizzas had been interesting initially in the same way that a country is when you're just passing through; in the way that a person is when you're still in the first throes of attraction; in that stage when the difficulties, with a little tweaking of the outlook angle, can easily be construed as adventures. Often, though, with the passage of time and the on-set of permanence—or at least short-term stability—the sense of adventure fades, revealing only the tried, tiresome reality of struggle.

While I felt that my relationship with Alfredo had managed to escape this fatal pattern because longevity had imparted depth and absence had fostered patience, my connection with Cuba seemed more complex this trip. For as much as the island still fascinated and inspired me, I also knew that my love-turned-hate relationship with the street pizzas was indicative of my growing exhaustion with the struggle to find not even healthy but just edible food that would fill me up.

I remembered being hungry on my first trip, but the hunger I was experiencing now was more intense, as if it was not just about the moment but was rather a composite of hungers past. This hunger moved beyond my stomach, lodging itself in my head in the form of an unrelenting ache so that it remained with me always, a constant memory of absent nourishment.

Just as I had never before experienced this sort of lingering hunger, I had also never been so violently and steadily sick. Ironically, the onset of my illness coincided with an unexplained disappearance of all the toilet paper in the *chopping*. So, as Cubans had been doing for more than a decade now, I finally learned to use the national newspaper, *Granma*.

And, as bedridden people everywhere had been doing since the beginning of time, I received my visitors from my captive post, lying patiently as they paraded in and pontificated on the myriad causes of and cures for my unnamed sickness. But unlike the medical musings of my laymen friends back home, I found my current companions' diagnoses all the more bearable because of their very interesting, very Cuban take on health and medicine, which was a mix of medical misnomer, hearsay, and Santería superstition.

Dinora suggested that I had become sick from showering too soon after I ate, thereby robbing my body of its requisite amount of motionless digestion time. Alfredo took this theory several steps further, reprimanding me for having read in bed after a late meal the previous night.

"You know, he's right, Lea," Liudmila had joined in. "You shouldn't read so soon after eating."

"But I don't move around when I read," I protested.

"Reading is mental motion," Liudmila had replied matter-of-factly, while Alfredo nodded somberly.

"But in the U.S., people often read after eating," I countered again, pausing for the kicker. "And while they eat breakfast, many people even read the morning paper."

"*Escucha eso,*" Listen to this, Alfredo said, raising his eyebrows at Liudmila.

Although I refused to give up reading after meals, since it remained one of the few diversions I could still partake in from the bed, I did compromise and agree to take my evening showers before dinner.

For more advice, Alfredo consulted his grandmother, who asked whether I'd been outside in the *madrugada,* the early morning hours before dawn, when, according to the Santería religion, Echus, a devilish spirit, was rumored to roam the streets. Alfredo's grandmother recommended that, to draw the good spirits to me, I bathe with perfume, *mariposa* flowers, and *cascarilla,* miniature meringues made entirely from ground-up eggshells.

I didn't try to come up with treatments of my own, because in contrast to everyone else's opinions, I felt the cause of my illness was something totally out of my control and that the cure, by extension, was beyond my ability to find. I thought the source was something in the air or, more specifically, the air itself.

Two weeks into my return, the government had begun an intensive fumigation campaign to combat a reported case of dengue fever. Now, at least once a day, platoons of miniature tanks descended upon Centro Habana, thundering through the streets and spewing out toxic black clouds of fumigation.

Before I became bedridden, I would help Dinora secure the house at the first sighting of a distant cannonball cloud, shutting the balcony and all the louvered blinds in preparation for the invasion. On the day after I got sick, when the fumigators came into the house to carry out their dirty work and Dinora came running up to my room, shouting, "*¡Al balcón, al balcón!*" I hobbled out of bed and rushed downstairs to huddle on the balcony with her and the Danes and Abuela. We stood with the closed door pushing up against our backs as we watched the cloud of chemicals settle below us, and we listened to the hiss of the clouds being released into the living quarters behind us.

The worst, though, was an afternoon before my illness, when I was out in the street with Liudmila and I felt the earth shake beneath my feet. I heard the fumigation boom of the tank and tasted the suffocating, metallic powder of the filmy black chemicals before I saw them. I started coughing immediately, and Liudmila took my hand and ran with me to a parallel street out of the direct line of the spraying.

When my coughing fit subsided, she patted my back and said, matter-of-factly, "There, now you know for next time. When you hear the explosion, just duck down another street and you're safe."

I tried to explain that the atmosphere was one entity, that just because I was not doubled over with respiratory problems in that moment did not mean that the tank's chemicals were not still infiltrating my body and infecting it in unforeseeable yet nonetheless significant and detrimental ways. I tried to tell Liudmila and others about DDT and endocrine disorders, but my concerns fell on deaf ears.

"The government is in charge of fumigating," Dinora told me. "Why would they use something that wasn't safe for us?"

It was such a reasonable question that I could come up with no response except to say that I wouldn't have trusted my leaders in the same situation. But I knew that this statement would have little relevance to someone whose consistently high expectations of her government were matched only by her constant complaints about it and her uneven yet recurrent faith in its ability to take care of her.

"Would your government use toxic chemicals to fumigate?" Dinora asked as we sat on my bed on the first hot afternoon since my return.

"It probably wouldn't be the government doing the spraying," I said. "In the U.S., there are a lot of private companies that fumigate houses, and often it's not for many years or maybe even many generations later that it's discovered that the people who were exposed to these chemicals were affected."

"And then what happens?" Dinora asked, her eyes wide with intrigue.

"Then, if it can be proven that the company's chemicals were at fault, someone will sue them, and they'll have to pay a lot of money."

"But why wouldn't they just test their products before using them?" Dinora asked, perplexed.

"I'm sure they do," I said. "But probably the most important tests are expensive, and if it takes generations to track the effects, maybe the companies don't want to wait that long before releasing each new product. Maybe," I added, "they don't run those tests because there's no one in the government making them do it."

Dinora remained silent, shaking her head while her lips curled up in something resembling a laugh.

"You surprise me," she said finally. "All this thought behind someone spraying to get rid of insects. You know, I believe what you say, but it's just that I have never thought in that way. In Cuba, we don't question so much. I don't think we know how to think like that, how to be so . . ." Dinora paused as she searched for the right word. "Cynical."

"I don't know if it's so much cynicism," I said. "I think it's more just about being critical, about thinking critically."

"I'd call it thinking capitalistically," Dinora said, finally releasing her laugh.

"What do you mean?" I asked, taken aback by her flippant tone.

"I'm not saying it's a bad thing," Dinora responded quickly. "It's just so obviously the way of thinking of someone who comes from a country where the government doesn't protect them. And maybe we wouldn't be so vulnerable to change, maybe it would even help us, if we thought a little more like that." Dinora scooted in closer to me on the bed, lowering her voice to add, "Maybe you could even teach me this."

"Teach you what? How I think?" I asked.

Dinora nodded eagerly. "Do you think you could?" she asked.

"But how?" I asked.

"Well, you could just explain things to me as different situations arise."

As I considered how exactly I might do this, Dinora stood up and announced, as if suddenly embarrassed by her proposal, "*Bueno, solamente fue una idea.*" Well, it was only an idea. Before I could respond, Dinora made her way to the door.

I could have called after her, but in truth I felt relieved that she had so abruptly ended our conversation. I had become so accustomed to being Dinora's student, to playing her apprentice in housework and in maneuvering the myriad other details of daily Cuban life, that I felt unprepared for her suggested role reversal, especially when, after her letter to me in the U.S., I had imagined that during this trip she would be even more in teacher mode.

When Dinora had written me that she would be returning to the university to teach Russian, I'd pictured her standing in front of a classroom of captivated students, rattling off the day's lesson plan in rapid-fire Russian. Yet when I had returned to Cuba and found Dinora waiting for me on her balcony, there had been something about the way she'd jumped up to greet me, so hungry for companionship and with such a sense of weariness in her eyes, that I knew immediately that she was living the same life she had been when I'd left four months earlier.

The next day, Dinora had revealed to me that she had paid her doctor to write a note declaring her unfit to teach but qualified for disability and, in a year, when she would be eligible for it, retirement pay.

"Dinora!" I'd said, shocked by her confession, even though after so much time in Cuba, I knew I shouldn't be. The week before Amy left in May, Liudmila, on the recommendation of her mother, had offered to visit her doctor so she could get some time off school to spend with Amy.

And, also during my last trip, Alfredo had bought a five-dollar urinary tract infection, which enabled him to miss a busy two weeks of work to go to Santiago.

"A urinary tract infection?" I'd asked him afterward. "How did you come up with that?"

"It was the doctor's idea," Alfredo said. "I'd been thinking about hepatitis A, but he said that would be more complex. He said if you want a disease like that, you have to start acting sick a few days before you get your note. Also, a urinary tract infection was a lot cheaper than hepatitis."

"How much does it cost to have hepatitis?" I asked, trying not to laugh.

"I don't know," Alfredo said. "He just told me that a urinary tract infection was cheaper, but I know people who've paid more than fifty dollars for their notes. It depends, too, on how long you need to be sick for, and where you work, and why it is you need to be sick."

I stared at Alfredo, fascinated by the intricacies of this *negocio*.

"If you work in tourism or if your family's coming to visit from Miami," he continued, "then you'll have to pay a lot more, because the doctors will assume you have money."

When Alfredo had worn his *guajiro* hat from Santiago to work, I'd asked whether anyone had questioned how he'd managed to procure this when he was supposed to be sick in bed with a urinary tract infection.

"Oh, no," Alfredo had responded, unconcerned. "Everyone knew that we were going to Santiago. That doctor's note was just a formality."

When I asked Dinora which disease she had bought to permanently relieve her from work, she cleared her throat and said, "I told the doctor to put down that I was mentally unstable."

"Are you serious?" I asked. "Why would you choose to be labeled mentally unstable for the rest of your life rather than teaching Russian for one more year?"

Dinora glanced down at the floor, embarrassed. "Really, I got so anxious at the thought of teaching again that I began to feel a little like I was going crazy," she said. "I started thinking, 'What if I don't have it anymore? What if after being holed up in this house with so little social interaction for so many years, I no longer have the ability to engage the students?'"

"And then, you know how my mother is," she said suddenly. "My brother was going to watch her while I was at class, but when I came home, I knew she'd be like she always is, demanding my attention and time. I wouldn't have been able to get any school work done, so really it's all for the best."

After this first and last mention of Dinora's thwarted teaching career, our conversations, as usual, continued to touch upon many different topics, from food to friendship, but they had a different rhythm to them this trip, an unspoken urgency that I hadn't recalled being there before. At their core, all our discussions circled around what Dinora had so eagerly enlisted me to explain earlier—the capitalist way of thought. During our third day of bedside chats, Dinora revealed to me the reason for her abiding interest.

"Last night Nitza finally told me what I've suspected for a while now," she said as she set down a trembling bowl of *potaje* on my nightstand. She stood silently for a moment, staring down at the black bean soup as she clasped her hands in an attempt to steady them.

"Please don't tell anyone," she said, taking a deep breath before announcing, "Nitza has filed papers to move to Argentina."

"To move?" I asked. "You mean like, to live? Forever?"

Dinora nodded. "She's tired of the life here," she said, her voice more empathetic than angry. "She's too old to be sharing a bed with her grandmother, *pobrecita*. She wants independence, which I understand because I never had it either. I never had the opportunity to live alone. Look at me, all my married life living with my mother. All Nitza really wants is some sovereignty in her life. She wants to experience life in the capitalist world. And who can really blame her?"

"So you're okay with her going to Argentina?" I asked.

"*¡Ni después de muerta!*" Over my dead body! Dinora responded quickly, slapping her hand against the bed. "After all I've done for her, my only child, I won't have her abandoning me here."

"Did you tell her this?" I asked.

"Yes, I did," Dinora said, releasing a short, sharp laugh. "But she still wants to go."

"What are you going to do?"

Dinora laughed again. "Hope that her request is denied."

"And when will Nitza find out?"

"Thankfully, it'll be a while," Dinora said. "It's a long process, and I don't even know what it involves, but probably it will be at least a year, maybe even more, so I'm worrying prematurely. And really, I didn't mean to bother you with all this. It's just that sometimes I feel like you're the only one who takes the time to listen to me, the only one who truly understands me."

I nodded solemnly, simultaneously flattered and saddened by Dinora's praise and the lack it implied.

"When you went back to your country, I was so sad," Dinora continued. "With Luis and Nitza always off traveling, I had only Abuela to talk to."

"What about the Scandinavians?" I asked.

"Oh, well, the Danes have always been very sweet to me," Dinora said.

"But they usually have their Rasta friends over and, well, you know how they are. Not exactly the type of people you want to share personal problems with." Dinora wrinkled up her forehead in distaste.

"What do you mean?"

"Well, I don't know them very well, but I just don't like them. They're just . . . not very educated," she said. "Have you ever seen them when they come into the house?"

I shook my head.

"Well, they ask if Anna and Vita are here and if I say yes, they get so excited that they practically run up the steps like animals, just like this," Dinora said. She crouched down to the floor and scrambled across my room like an ape, alternating between all fours and a weird, three-legged trot with one arm raised as if reaching up to the sky for a falling banana. Despite the comic quality of Dinora's performance, I still somehow couldn't bring myself to laugh.

"I've never noticed that," I said.

"Oh, well, you're lucky," Dinora said. "When you were gone, it was basically just them and the Danes around the house. And that Swede, Kajsa, well, I just think she's very demanding, if you know what I mean."

During the two weeks I had known Kajsa, we had become fast friends and such close confidantes that I'd come to consider her an alternate Amy. But knowing how delicate Dinora was, I could also see how she would mistake Kajsa's trademark assertiveness for a personal affront.

"When Kajsa came to look at the room for rent," Dinora continued, "I told her it was fifteen dollars, and she told me she'd just seen a room down the street that was almost identical, and that it was only ten dollars."

"So?" I asked. "That is possible, isn't it?"

"Possible, but not likely. Fifteen dollars is the going rate, and besides," Dinora said, pausing dramatically, "this is the only *casa particular* along this stretch of Animas Street."

"Well, maybe she didn't literally mean this street," I said. "Maybe she just meant nearby."

"No," Dinora said, shaking her head emphatically. "She meant this street, and I know because I called her on her lie. I told her, 'I can give it to you for ten, but all you had to do was ask. You didn't have to make up a story,' and she looked at me like I had a head growing out of my armpit. But," Dinora added triumphantly, "she didn't deny that she'd lied."

"But that's normal," I said, confused by Dinora's outrage. "Where I live, people do that all the time when they want to get a better deal."

Dinora stared out the bedroom window, taking in what I'd told her. Then, suddenly, she turned back to me, her face aglow with the first blush of a bold new thought.

"Tell me, Lea," Dinora said excitedly. "If Kajsa can lie to me about having looked at another house just to get me to lower my price, then if I can find someone who's willing to pay more, can I kick her out?"

I almost laughed. "No, you can't."

"No? Why not?" Dinora asked, perplexed.

"You already told her she could stay. You already agreed to the lower price," I said. "You can't just go back on all that now. It doesn't work that way."

"Then how does it work?" Dinora asked eagerly, sitting down on the chair next to me. "Lea, please. Tell me. What would a capitalist do?"

"Oh, Dinora," I said, shaking my head. "I'm not really a very good capitalist. I don't know what to tell you."

Dinora stared at me intently, silently willing me to answer.

"Well, I don't think there's much more you can do now, but maybe a capitalist wouldn't agree so easily to lower the price next time," I said. "Maybe a capitalist wouldn't have bargained at all. Probably, if you'd just held firm, Kajsa would have agreed to your price."

"Ah, yes," Dinora said, pleased. "See, you do know, Lea. You shouldn't be so hard on yourself."

I laughed. "Thanks, I'm glad I could help."

"Well," Dinora said, standing up. "I think I'm going to go lie down for a bit. Maybe it's all this stress, but I feel a headache coming on." She smiled weakly and then shrugged her shoulders as she turned toward the stairs. From my bed, I watched her descend step by step until she was no longer visible and there remained only the soft padding of her footfalls growing fainter.

24

Other Types of Wealth

On my first day of feeling better, I trudged over to Alfredo's grandparents' house with a backpack of gifts so full that I worried that I had once again overdone it, proving that, along with my capitalist know-how, I was also a first-class consumer.

As if to spotlight my excesses, the early evening sun beat relentlessly onto my backpack. It sent rivulets of sweat down the black evening gown I had unwisely donned for my hike so that Alfredo and I could go directly to a wedding party after our dinner with his grandparents.

More sensibly dressed, less-encumbered Cubans walked languidly by as I approached the asphalt desert of the Plaza de la Revolución. Already, I could imagine the glazed-over expression, which, like a carbon copy of Alfredo's reaction to my plethora of presents for him, would settle onto his grandparents' and sister's faces when they received my offerings of coffee and tea and chocolate; T-shirts and tank tops and aspirin and fruit-scented soaps; and, for Alfredo's sister's newborn, a small, caramel-colored stuffed lion.

There was much more I'd wanted to get for the baby, but before I'd returned to Cuba, Alfredo had quickly dismissed my desire, telling me, "There'll always be someone around to hand down whatever Bruno needs and, besides, he's so young now that he doesn't really need anything yet."

True to Alfredo's word, when I met up with him at his grandmother's house, not only did the stuffed animal prove to be enough for Bruno (who, at just under three months, could do little more than drool on it), but the little lion also appeared to be more than anyone had anticipated.

"*¡Ay, qué rico!*" Alfredo's sister said, stroking a drool-free patch of the lion's fur as gently as if it were a living, breathing cub, liable to wake from a deep slumber any minute.

"*¡Qué lindo!*" exclaimed Alfredo's grandmother when it was her turn to touch the lion. "It's been a long time since I've seen such a handsome *muñequito*."

"We used to have stuffed animals in the ration shops when I was little," Alfredo's sister explained. "But all that changed during the Special Period."

Alfredo's brother-in-law nodded in thoughtful agreement. "*Muchísimas gracias*, Lea," he said.

I laughed, embarrassed by all the attention my present had yielded.

Only Alfredo's grandfather, the quiet one in the family, who always addressed me with the formal *Usted*, seemed capable of containing his excitement. He sat in his rocking chair, silently surveying the scene with an air of detached amusement.

I decided to hold off revealing the rest of my presents until after dinner, but still, much of our mealtime talk centered on the lion and Cuba's missing *muñequitos*. After I'd finished my rice and beans and tomato salad, and everyone else had had several helpings of pork, we moved on to our dessert of chilled papaya cubes. And from here the conversation branched out into a discussion of everything—including cigarettes and clothing—that had disappeared from the ration shops since their long-gone glory days.

At the end of our meal, Alfredo's brother-in-law stood up, pushed in his chair, gave a round of goodbye kisses, and headed for the door, turning around at the last minute to call out to Alfredo's sister, "I'll be by tomorrow night."

"Where is he going?" I asked.

"Home," Alfredo's sister said with a brusque laugh that made me feel silly for having asked.

In the kitchen, as we cleared away the dinner dishes, Alfredo explained that his brother-in-law lived with his family in a one-room house in Vedado.

"There's no room for my sister there," Alfredo said. He laughed wryly and added, "And my grandmother says there's no room for him here."

"Couldn't she make room, I mean, especially since they're married now?" I asked, confused. I had seen Alfredo's sister's room, and it seemed to me that there was plenty of space for two people. "Does your grandmother not like your brother-in-law?"

"Not really," Alfredo said. "She thinks he's lazy and a loudmouth."

"And that's the end of it?" I asked, surprised that Alfredo's sister, who could be quite outspoken herself, would let something like this go without a fight. "Why don't they just get their own place?"

"Because they don't have any money."

"But I thought the government gave people houses. Couldn't they apply for one?"

"Maybe, but it would take forever," Alfredo said. "And I think it would be difficult to get the government to give away a house for just two people. It's better to buy one from someone."

"Is that legal?"

"No." Alfredo said. "Of course not."

I dealt out the remainder of my gifts, with Alfredo's sister and grandmother huddling in front of me on the living room sofa and with Alfredo standing attentively at my side. Like a magician's assistant pulling rabbits out of hats, Alfredo made his own magic, transforming each gift I silently gave into a fully formed, albeit heavily accented, English word.

He did fairly well with chocolate and aspirin, but once he got through these cognates, he stumbled on soap, pronouncing it "soup." I grinned at the mistake, but his sister, who spoke fluent English, mimicked a game-show buzzer going off at a wrong answer.

"Alfredo has been so diligent about studying his English. He must really be in love with the language," she said to no one in particular and then, winking at me, added, "or maybe it's just Lea."

I looked at Alfredo, who smiled shyly back at me.

After his sister and grandmother had had their fill of sniffing the fruit-scented soaps, Alfredo asked me to describe for them, as I'd done before for him, the dozens of different soaps sold in the U.S. His grandmother and sister exchanged a wistful glance, reminding me of the eagerness in Dinora's eyes whenever we discussed capitalist goods. But when I searched Alfredo's grandfather's face, again I found only a calm, distant look, devoid of longing.

As I wondered what enabled Alfredo's grandfather to remain so detached while surrounded by everyone else's excitement, I recalled Alfredo once telling me that his grandfather was the most revolutionary member of his family. And I also remembered, on another occasion, watching his grandfather excuse himself in the middle of a conversation so that he could attend a neighborhood CDR meeting.

Just as Alfredo's grandmother wouldn't let her grandson-in-law live in her house because she didn't like his personality, Alfredo's grandfather had denied the same privilege, but for political reasons, to their *contrarevolucionario* son-in-law, Alfredo's father, after he attempted to flee to the U.S. in 1980.

Now, after the initial soap euphoria had subsided, Alfredo's grandfather finally spoke.

"You know," he said slowly, as if at the end of a long sermon that had been going on in his head. "There are other types of wealth than the material. There is cultural wealth, and emotional, and spiritual, and intellectual."

When we stood to say our goodbyes, Alfredo's grandmother scolded me for not having stopped by sooner.

"Don't wait another two weeks before your next visit," she ordered me.

"I won't," I said.

"Will you even be here in another two weeks?" she asked hesitantly.

"Yes," I said, "but not for much longer. I'm only staying for a month this time."

"Such a short trip," Alfredo's grandmother said sadly. "You should stay longer, go travel and explore another part of the island like you did before."

"We're going to," Alfredo said. "Didn't I tell you we're going to go to Trinidad for Lea's last week?"

"No, you didn't," his grandmother said, sadly shaking her head as if this omission of information, combined with my belated visit to her house and premature departure from Cuba, was just one too many a betrayal for her to bear. She pulled Alfredo in close to her, and said to me, "You just shouldn't leave Cuba. You know when you left before, Alfredo cried all the time and didn't eat for three days."

I turned to Alfredo, shocked by this revelation. But instead of commenting on his grandmother's charge, Alfredo pulled away from her, then leaned in for a quick goodbye kiss before grabbing my hand and steering me out the door with him, his grandmother calling out after us, *"No pierdan el camino."* Don't be a stranger."

"Alfredo," I said as we started walking down Panorama Street. "Is that true about your not eating?"

Alfredo shook his head. "My grandmother always says things like that," he said. "She exaggerates everything."

"She does?" I asked, never having heard this particular complaint from Alfredo before. "How so?"

"Like saying I didn't eat for three days," he said matter-of-factly.

I eyed Alfredo suspiciously, and for a beat he stared back at me, holding his ground. In the distance, the 9:00 *cañonazo* cannon blast reenactment thundered through the sky.

"Really," Alfredo said, a tentative smile forming on his lips. "It was more like two and a half days. I had dinner that third night."

We both burst into broad grins, the tension broken.

"You know what I wish?" Alfredo asked. "I wish we could freeze this moment, that it could always be nine o'clock on this night, and we could always be standing here together."

"That's a nice wish," I said, resting my head against Alfredo's shoulder and watching the pockets of stars glitter above me. "Maybe the fiancé visa will come through, and then we won't have to freeze time to be together."

I felt strange mentioning the visa, which we hadn't discussed since my first night back, when Alfredo told me that his friend Gerardo had secretly left for Belgium on a tourist visa. I knew that Alfredo wanted to keep quiet about our fiancé visa until we heard something back from the bureaucrats who were in charge of granting us the opportunity to test out our relationship in the U.S. Like his grandfather's behavior, Alfredo's silence was also motivated by politics, although in his case this meant a fear of the *fidelista* response.

Alfredo felt confident that his family would understand that our decision to apply for the fiancé visa had been motivated by love and not politics, but he was afraid that if he spoke too soon, someone who didn't see things this way might find out. And this person might speak to another person of similar sensibilities, setting off a domino effect that could result in Alfredo being declared a *contrarevolucionario* and, in turn, losing his job.

Still, on more than one occasion, I'd been tempted to say something, most recently to Alfredo's grandmother, and most frequently to Dinora. I recalled now how, soon after my return to Cuba, Dinora had pulled me aside and asked if I'd found a boyfriend in the U.S.

"A boyfriend?" I had repeated. "Do you really think I'd go through all the trouble of getting back here to see Alfredo if I was already involved with someone else in the U.S.?"

"*Pues, uno nunca sabe,*" One never knows, Dinora said, shrugging her shoulders innocently. "But anyway, that's good news. That means it must be true love. Now, all you have to do is hurry up and marry Alfredo."

Alfredo and I walked to his coworker's wedding party in the dark, the streets of the more residential Nuevo Vedado quieter than those in Centro Habana.

"Why didn't we go to the wedding ceremony?" I asked as we stepped cautiously between potholes.

"Oh, the ceremony," Alfredo said, sounding surprised. "Well, I guess we could have gone. Usually only those who feel they're obligated to go, like the family, attend the ceremony. I've heard they're really boring, just a lawyer at the Palacio de los Matrimonios dictating the vows."

"You've never been to one?" I asked. "What about when your sister got married?"

"No one really went to that," Alfredo said. "They just wanted it to be the two of them. Don't people ever do that in the U.S.?"

"Sometimes," I said. "But usually weddings are a really big deal. People prepare for them for a year in advance, maybe more."

"Why?"

"They have to decide who they're going to invite, where the wedding will be held, where the reception will be, how to decorate the dinner tables, and who will sit where. And then they have to save up money to pay for it all."

"Oh, my God!" Alfredo said in English. "What a complicated life."

Like every other Cuban social function I'd attended, the music at Soyla and Argeo's party was so loud that just entering the living room felt like stepping into another dimension. It was a world consisting solely of sound and movement, where language existed only if it could be sung, and people spun by too quickly to be identified.

Alfredo and I edged our way past a circle of salsa dancers over to a back table with munchies, where we each took a cardboard deli-style takeout box, prepacked with a slab of frosting-heavy cake. I followed Alfredo's example as he picked through the remaining refreshments and deposited a handful of popcorn in his box. I passed on the *ensalada fría,* a salad with macaroni, pineapple, mayonnaise, and bits of ham. There were several cans of Tropicola, but the rum bottles were all empty.

I looked around for a place where we could sit to eat and talk. But unlike parties back home, where conversations were struck up in every corner of a house—from the line outside the bathroom to the overcrowded living room sofa—here there was neither a space to sit nor a place quiet enough to carry on a conversation. Unlike wedding receptions in the U.S., there was no table overflowing with presents.

"You give a present if you can," Alfredo said. "So most people don't, except for the couple's family. They all try to put together a little money."

"Man, they've got the worst of both worlds," I said, laughing. "They have to sit through the ceremony, and then they have to give money too."

Alfredo smiled at my joke and we stepped out onto the balcony, balancing our boxes on our palms, the oil from the frosting seeping through the cardboard and staining it a muddy gray-brown.

He pointed to the living room wall where a sepia-toned photo of a ballerina hung, only a triangle of her silhouette visible from behind the half-open front door.

"Soyla's a dancer," Alfredo said. "This is her mother's house."

"Will she and her husband live together here?" I asked.

"Probably," Alfredo said. "It looks like there's enough room."

"Will they go on a honeymoon?" I asked. "Do people do that here?"

"Of course. Everyone gets two nights at a hotel, but not any hotel." Alfredo paused, thinking. "I'm pretty sure you can't stay at Habana Libre. You have to pick one from the list."

"What list?"

"When you buy your marriage certificate, you get a list. You pay twelve dollars in pesos, and then the government gives you a hotel room and rum and several cases of beer and this cake," Alfredo said, dramatically dropping the final crumb of his into his mouth. "This is the official Cuban wedding cake that you'll see at every wedding you attend."

Before I could move it out of his line of vision, Alfredo looked down at my box with its slice that I'd been poking at and reshaping with my fork for the past several minutes.

"Don't you like it?" he asked.

"It's just a little too sweet for me."

"*¡Ay, a mí me encanta!*" I love it, Alfredo said. "It's very popular here." Lowering his voice, he added, "Sometimes Cubans get married just for the cake."

"What?"

"Well, really for the whole package—the cake and the alcohol and the honeymoon room," Alfredo said. "The government gives them to newlyweds for so much less money than anyone else could buy them for, so people get married, and then they sell everything for a profit, and then, a few days or a few weeks later, they get divorced."

"Really?" I asked, amazed by this underworld of Cuban coupling. I won-dered if Alfredo's calm when he had previously proposed that we get mar-ried and just divorce if things didn't work out had been informed by this very pragmatic and casual attitude toward matrimony.

"Is it common to marry like this?" I asked. "*¿Como un negocio?*"

"It was more common during the Special Period," Alfredo said. "But it still happens. There's even a Los Van Van song about it where they sing, '*La gente se está casando para vender la cerveza.*" People are getting married to sell the beer.

"Do you think the government is aware that this is going on?"

"I'm sure they are, but what can they do? Tell you that you have to stay married for a year before you get your cake?"

When we reentered the party, I spotted one of Alfredo's coworkers scanning the dance floor with the symphony's camcorder, and the thought of having my clumsy salsa moves so formally recorded was nearly enough to make me walk back out. Fortunately, another of Alfredo's coworkers motioned for him to dance with her and, relieved to be off the hook, I quickly nodded for him to go ahead.

As Alfredo spun around, I caught his eye and motioned that I was step-ping outside. I walked onto the balcony and then down the steps into the front yard, where I saw Roman, one of Alfredo's fellow light technicians, leaning against a thick-trunked *jagüey* tree. We talked about upcoming con-certs at the symphony, about his mother's health, about his Mexican girl-friend, and then we walked back into the house together.

To my surprise, the party had transformed itself in our absence. The front door, which had been trembling from the vibrations of the stereo when I'd left, was now still. The air felt several degrees cooler than it had been before, and the flashing fluorescent lights overhead had been replaced with a half dozen candles laid out in a circle in the center of the living room floor. Inside the circle, a couple, who I assumed were the bride and groom in street clothes, danced a fast-paced salsa to "La Vida Es un Car-naval," performed live by an outer circle of impromptu musicians. About a dozen members of the party composed the chorus, while one of Alfredo's coworkers beat out the rhythm on the wicker underside of an overturned chair, and Alfredo stood tapping out the time with a spoon on the back of a frying pan.

I stood, awed by the beauty of the moment and amazed by the way this spontaneous version of the song so closely resembled the original. With a wave of his frying pan, Alfredo motioned for me to come over, and the chorus circle parted to absorb me.

I felt like I had entered into the middle of something magical, and soon I found myself singing along without any of my usual self-consciousness about being off-key. But after just one round of the chorus, a light from a beaded bamboo chandelier flickered on and flooded across the room. And then, almost simultaneously, the fluorescent lights returned, and the stereo blared back on, and everyone clapped as though this, rather than the a cappella musical performance, had been the real showstopper.

"*Fue un apagón,*" It was a blackout, Alfredo said, reading the confusion on my face.

I watched as the newlyweds stepped outside of their candlelit circle and the groom switched off a miniature flashlight that adorned his belt loop, where a cell phone or pager might have hung in the U.S. Within minutes, everyone was dancing again, the quiet spell of the blackout quickly forgotten.

When the newlyweds headed outside for their getaway, I stood on the street with the symphony staff to watch. Like a master of ceremonies, a friend who had lent Soyla and Argeo a fancy cherry-red Chevy for the occasion presented the key through the driver's side window. Argeo turned the ignition while everyone poised their hands for applause. But after an initial rumble, the engine choked and then died. The air echoed with disappointed cries of "*¡Pinga!*" and "*¡Coño!*" followed by a flurry of other angrily yelled out private parts.

Alfredo ran over to help the owner of the car and several other men inspect the engine. Each amateur mechanic took a turn at poking around under the hood, but after about fifteen minutes, Alfredo returned to me, shaking his head.

"It's not going to start," he said. "They'll have to walk."

"Do you think we should go out to a main street and get them a taxi?" I asked.

Alfredo shook his head once more. "Look, they're already on their way," he said, pointing as the bride kissed her mother goodbye and then joined hands with her new husband, followed by a procession of cheering guests.

I thought about the simplicity of this wedding reception without a band, without presents, without a bar of endless drinks for the guests, without tables to sit down and eat at, and, for a while, without electricity.

"*Me encanta mi vida aquí,*" I love my life here, Alfredo said, looking into the distance thoughtfully as the newlyweds and their entourage disappeared around a corner. "It's peaceful in my country, and I have a good job and good friends. The only thing that's missing," he said as casually as an afterthought, "is that I don't have any money."

I smiled at Alfredo's sentiments, silently wondering about this other life—my capitalist life—that I was inviting him to join me in. I worried that perhaps I should have brought something more significant than macaroni and cheese and scented soap to prepare him for the transition. And then I worried that, like a trip to the moon, there was no real way to prepare Alfredo for life in the U.S. No way to preserve the sincerity and simplicity that I so loved about him, which, in many ways, existed because of his lack of experience with my world and its other, very different types of wealth.

25

❧❧❧❧

Como Ser Negro y No Morir en el Intento

The day before Alfredo and I left for our Trinidad trip, Dinora's Finnish boarder announced that she would be moving out.

Of the Scandinavians, Mielikki was the one I knew the least, because she was always out with her Cuban boyfriend, Onelio. So it was through a secondhand account that I learned she was leaving.

"She said she found a better deal—a bigger room, closer to the university, for the same price," Dinora told me, shrugging her shoulders and releasing an exaggerated sigh as we sat in the living room, waiting out the midday heat. Minus the space helmets, we were like old ladies in a beauty salon, each of us positioned beneath a private fan, our heads angled to receive the maximum breeze.

"I know that was probably my cue to lower the rent," Dinora continued. "But I didn't feel like playing that capitalist game again, so I just said, 'Okay, I guess you should go then.'"

I knew that Dinora and Kajsa, the Swedish boarder who'd originally offended with her failed attempt to negotiate by bluffing, had since made up. But now I could see that even though Dinora had not spoken of the incident again, she was still far from forgetting it.

In the case of Mielikki, who had paid her weekly rent without complaint since she'd arrived a month ago, I sensed that something other than money was at issue here. And sure enough, when I passed by Mielikki's room on the way to mine and poked my head in to ask about her sudden departure, she confirmed my suspicion with a simple snort.

"So she told you just that it was a bigger place closer to the university?" Mielikki asked incredulously as she stuffed a pair of jeans into her backpack. "I told her the main reason was because Onelio could stay over at my new place, but you know, people hear what they want to."

"I know it's different with Alfredo because he's a family friend," Mielikki added, reminding me of the lie that Luis had invented for me. "But from the first day, Onelio's never been comfortable here," Mielikki said. She looked up from her packing and paused dramatically before concluding, "He feels like Dinora and Luis look at him funny because he's black."

As Mielikki said this, I felt my heart skip a beat, and I stood speechless, taking in the gravity of her words and the way in which they echoed Alfredo's earlier criticism of Dinora.

"And do you know what pisses me off the most?" Mielikki continued, squaring her hands on her hips like an angry child as I shook my head in response. "She keeps trying to win me over to her side, trying to get me to find a nice white Cuban boy."

"What?" I almost asked if Mielikki was sure she hadn't misunderstood, but then, for once, instead of defending Dinora, I decided to just remain quiet and listen.

"Haven't you noticed how Dinora's always inviting that Johan boy over?" Mielikki asked. "I'm sure you've seen him, the Party Puppet."

I laughed, recalling immediately the dirty blond–haired boy whom I'd never formally been introduced to but whom I'd seen several times before sitting at our kitchen table with Anna and Vita, espousing the many freedoms Cubans had been granted under Fidel's rule.

"But I thought he was Anna and Vita's friend," I said now, confused.

"It looks that way, doesn't it?" Mielikki asked. "But really what happened is that when Dinora realized I wasn't going to break up with Onelio for Johan, she moved on to Anna and Vita to try to replace their Rasta friends with Johan. And they're just too nice to say anything."

I wanted to doubt Mielikki's stories. But instead, I found a series of disturbing memories of my life at Dinora's flooding my thoughts. There was Alfredo's first visit, when Luis had asked him to leave early, and Dinora's later request that once Alfredo had supposedly won their trust and been granted permission to spend the night, he leave before the neighbors woke up. There was the panic that had crossed Dinora's face when she'd seen Mielikki's black boyfriend helping her move in, and, most offensive of all, there was the dramatization of how the Rastas climbed the stairs like monkeys.

As if Mielikki had read my mind, she now interrupted my silent reverie to announce, "Yeah, Anna and Vita are pretty nice, but if you asked them, I bet they'd say they're getting tired of Dinora's racism too."

I nodded solemnly, and then, after we'd said our goodbyes, I followed Mielikki's lead and went next door. As I questioned Anna and Vita about their experiences with Dinora, I felt like a lawyer collecting evidence for a harassment suit—a traitor to this woman who housed and often fed me; who loved me like a daughter and offered me wise, motherly advice; who confided in me like a friend and shared with me her most guarded secrets.

Anna and Vita told me that, from the start, they had noticed Dinora's odd behavior around their Rasta friends.

"She's made them give her their ID cards every time they come over," Vita said.

"And what does she do with them?" I asked, startled by this image of Dinora demanding ID for admittance into her house, like a domestic bouncer.

In response to my question, Vita simply shrugged her shoulders. "Dinora always gives them back their IDs when they leave at the end of the night," she said. "But who knows why she needs the IDs in the first place?"

"Other than as an assertion of power," Anna added.

"Do you know our Danish friend, Preben?" Vita asked.

I nodded, recalling a scraggly blond Rasta guy who had once joined us for dinner.

"When he comes over, Dinora never asks for his passport," Vita said. "And when Johan comes by, she never takes his ID."

"It's just so strange," I said. "Because although Alfredo's been upset by other things Dinora's done, she's never asked for his ID."

"Well, *that's* quite a mystery," Vita said, releasing a small laugh, to which Anna nodded knowingly and I stared blankly.

"Alfredo's been spared because he's your boyfriend," Vita explained. "And lucky you," she concluded, her voice now more sympathetic than sarcastic, "have always been Dinora's favorite."

I spent the remainder of the day following Mielikki's departure in a funk, not sure what to do with this newfound—or newly acknowledged—information.

Why, I wondered, had it taken me so long to accept these truths about Dinora? Why had it taken the accounts of three casual acquaintances to convince me of what someone I loved had told me long ago?

In part, I knew that I'd stopped listening so intently to my gut feelings in an attempt at crosscultural understanding. I had abandoned my American assumptions, which, from the start, had never applied to life in Cuba anyway.

In the U.S., I might have assumed that on a date, a man who ordered dessert with dinner did so because he was either impatient or a pig, not because he feared that the dessert wouldn't be there if he waited until he finished his meal to order it. In the U.S., I would have assumed that a twenty-four-year-old with a medical degree would be a doctor, not an airline stewardess. In the U.S., I would have assumed that someone who was racist wouldn't live in a neighborhood with blacks, or suggest that I marry my black boyfriend.

Yet, if one reason for my delayed reaction to Dinora's racism was cultural, the other, I now realized, was purely personal. The real reason why I hadn't believed Alfredo was the same reason I hadn't discussed his suspicions about Dinora with anyone. I'd feared that someone might confirm what, on several levels, I already knew but just hadn't been ready to hear yet. But now that I had been so irrefutably informed of the situation, I felt obligated to take some action.

"Maybe you and Alfredo and I should move out and get a place together," Kajsa suggested when I asked her advice. We were walking down D Street toward the symphony to meet Alfredo for a concert that I had been looking forward to all week, but now I felt so distracted that I didn't know how I'd be able to concentrate on the music.

"Are you having problems with Dinora too?" I asked. Kajsa rarely brought home Cuban friends of any color.

"I'm not having any problems with her," Kajsa said. "It's just that I know someone who's renting out a private two-bedroom house in Vedado, and I was thinking it might be nice to have a little more independence."

"But when we come back from Trinidad, I'll have less than a week left here," I said, startled by how soon this sounded. I had yet to begin the long, sad process of saying so many little, premature goodbyes to prepare my friends and myself for the big, final farewell. I hadn't even discussed with Alfredo what we would do if the fiancé visa didn't come through. Or if it did.

"I didn't realize you were leaving so soon," Kajsa said. "But then maybe that's all the more reason to move—so the two of you can enjoy your last few days together."

"Right," I said. "Well, I'll have to think about it."

As we approached the symphony, Alfredo stood on the top step of the staircase, his right hand pressed against his forehead like a visor as he scanned the crowds for us.

I waved to him and he smiled back in recognition, dropping his hand like a slow, freeform salute. We crossed the street to join Alfredo on the theater steps, where he flashed a nervous smile at me before quickly looking down at his watch.

"I have a surprise . . . something I want to do for you," he said mysteriously. "But we have to go quickly, because the concert will be starting soon."

Kajsa stood hesitantly in the lobby, unsure of whether to stay or join us.

"Ven aquí," Alfredo said, waving her over as he walked to the elevator. "You can come too."

Soon after we stepped off the elevator onto the second-floor technical offices, I realized that Alfredo's surprise was not quite so cryptic as his comments had built it up to be. Rather, it was just a round of belated introductions he initiated between his coworkers and me and Kajsa.

Even though I had been to numerous concerts at the symphony, on beach trips with the symphony, and to parties at the houses of symphony employees, I still felt like I hardly knew the majority of Alfredo's coworkers, who were mostly men.

"Don't take it personally," Alfredo told me when I'd shared my frustration with him. "It's not that they're not interested in you, because they do ask me questions about you. It's just that they see you're with me, so they feel like it's not right to approach you."

"Well, you could let them know that it's okay," I said. "I feel like most of them don't even know my name. I'm just Alfredo's *novia* to them."

"But I have told many of them your name," Alfredo protested. "Just not formally, when you were there."

"Well, maybe that's the problem," I said. "Just think how you would feel if you came to the U.S. and I took you to a party where you knew no one and no one talked to you."

At the time, Alfredo had remained silent, his brow wrinkled in thought as if this were a comparison he'd never considered, as if the concept of being at a party where not everyone was someone he'd known since childhood was beyond his ability to comprehend.

Now, as we made our way through the symphony's technical offices, Alfredo stopped to present me to everyone we passed. Unfortunately, most of his coworkers responded with bewildered expressions, wondering why they were now being introduced to this person they had already seen more than a dozen times before.

Alfredo's effort to appease me with his formal presentations meant more than I could tell him. Any attempt to explain would involve revealing the carefully guarded mental checklist I had been carrying around with me since I had returned to Cuba.

After returning to the U.S., I had begun compiling all my concerns about Alfredo—about who he was and who he wasn't, about how he might adjust and who he might become in my world. Back in Cuba, I found myself silently testing him at every turn. Alfredo might be asking me about the weather or what we'd be doing in this moment in California, and I would be asking myself how he might react to Ethiopian food. Or driving on a six-lane freeway. Or being the only black person at a party.

Following Alfredo's overdue introductions, I felt relieved to be able to cross off one of my worries about his adaptability, made moot by his willingness to break out of what felt comfortable and natural to him, even at the risk of appearing strange to those around him.

By the time we left the symphony offices and walked into the actual performance theater, nearly all the seats were taken, the air filled with the chatter of anticipation.

"Are Frank Delgado's performances usually this crowded?" Kajsa asked Alfredo.

"I don't know. This is my first one," he said. "Actually, I've never even heard his songs before."

"Really?" I asked. Alfredo had been excited about this concert all week. "So why did you recommend it so highly?"

Alfredo smiled. "Because it has to be good," he said. "His songs are *censuradas*."

"How so?" I asked.

"You won't find his CDs in any music store in Cuba," Alfredo said. "Even though he uses beautiful words to do it, he still sings about Cuba's problems, about the unfulfilled promises of the Revolution—and the government doesn't want this getting out."

"Then how have all these people heard of him?" I asked.

"Well, just because he's censored doesn't mean he stops playing. He probably plays for his friends, and they probably tape his songs, and then those tapes get circulated and copied."

"But you've never heard his songs," Kajsa pointed out. "This isn't how you've heard about him."

Alfredo shook his head. "No, I know who he is because there have been other times that he was supposed to play here but then, always at the last minute, his concert was canceled."

"And how is it that he's getting to perform here tonight?" I asked.
"Bueno," Alfredo said, smiling, finally out of explanations. *"Es Cuba."*

When the curtain went up, a white man dressed all in black stepped out onto the stage to uproarious applause. He coughed several times, said, *"Gracias,"* and sat down on a wooden chair center stage, cradling his guitar in his lap and strumming the opening chords to his first scandalous song.

Immediately, I understood what Alfredo had said about the beauty of Frank Delgado's words, which flowed with a poetic sweetness, a haunting mixture of love and sadness, of national pride and nostalgia, the underlying sense of outrage wrapped in wit.

In a song about tourism on the peninsular beach of Varadero—once a Cuban vacation destination and now off-limits to locals—Frank Delgado lamented, "The last time I walked through this land, it was still my friend Cuba . . . I didn't need a passport . . . I don't remember when the peninsula was taken from my hands or even whether anyone asked my opinion."

He sang about the Cubans who had died fighting for Angolan independence, about the Taliban and feminism and Simone de Beauvoir, who had been friends with Fidel. He sang about the song "Guantanamera" and Elián González and *jineteros* and Hemingway. He sang about a Milan Kundera book he'd hidden, a dream of living in the country and growing squash. In several different songs, he sang of the irrelevancy of Marxist literature in his life, of Lenin, Che Guevara, *el bombo,* and ripped *guayaberas*—the gauzy, four-pocketed cotton shirts symbolizing Cuban masculinity.

His concert was a mini-lesson in the history of postrevolutionary Cuba, and I felt like I could stay and listen to his wise, mournful voice forever. To my surprise, I understood nearly every word Frank Delgado sang. I even got the jokes, like when he sarcastically said, "I'd like to thank the Cuban TV for all the coverage it's given me."

With each brazen declaration, I was afraid that someone might rush the stage and shut down the show. But there was only applause and the soft sway of the audience, the occasional lighter raised in solidarity.

I was so caught up in the lyrical rhythm of Frank Delgado's words that

I often didn't notice that he had gone a cappella until he began playing his guitar again. I completely forgot my previous worries about Mielikki's departure and its implications until the end of the concert, when Frank Delgado introduced one of his final songs, "Como Ser Negro y No Morir en El Intento," How to Be Black and Not Die in the Intent.

He dedicated it to the black writer Alberto Guerra, and he introduced it with a joke:

> A black friend says to his white friend, "White friend, when I'm born, I'm black. When I'm growing, I'm black. When I'm in the sun, I'm black. When I'm cold, I'm black. When I'm surprised, I'm black. When I'm sick, I'm black. When I die, I'm black. When you're born, you're pink. When you're growing, you're white. When you're in the sun, you're red. When you're cold, you're purple. When you're surprised, you're yellow. When you're sick, you're green. When you die, you're gray. And despite all this, you have the nerve to call me a man of color."

Frank Delgado sang of black policemen who behaved like whites, stopping Alberto Guerra in the street to ask for his ID and then harassing him about why, if he were a member of UNEAC, the writers' union, he was carrying a bag of vegetables instead of books. He sang of another policeman asking Alberto why he was walking in the upscale neighborhood of Miramar if he lived in middle-class Vedado. And, taking poetic license with his subject, he sang of a third who stopped Alberto late one night, making him miss the bus he was running to catch to ask, "Didn't you know that after midnight, blacks can't run in Parque Central?"

Alfredo and the rest of the audience responded to each affront with a round of knowing laughter, which I had difficulty participating in. At the end of the concert, I stood with everyone as they clapped for an ovation, and I wished for a song explaining how to be friends with a racist and not be complicit in the act.

26

Invented Identities, Imagined Lives

On the bus to Trinidad, after a restless night replaying the words of Frank Delgado's final song in my sleep, I decided to grant myself the gift of avoidance. For the time being, I would hold off on telling Alfredo about Dinora, the news still too new, too raw and delicate to be voiced yet.

When we arrived in Trinidad at dusk, we were greeted by no less than two dozen *casa particular* owners. Like picketers at a strike, each one carried a sign advertising an abode, and everyone simultaneously shouted their rates as we stepped off the bus.

"Come with me, okay?" one especially aggressive woman demanded as she reached out to grab Alfredo's arm.

"A house just for the two of you," someone somewhere else in the crowd shouted.

"Listen," Alfredo shouted back. He let out a small laugh, embarrassed by all the attention. "We can't make a decision when everyone's yelling at once."

A heavyset black woman jumped in front.

"Get off them," she shouted at the crowd. "Leave them alone. You're like wild dogs, all of you."

She raised her arms to block anyone from moving closer, but hands still poked out from every direction, like basketball players blocking a pass. Finally, we gave in to the momentum. A voice called out, "Eight dollars," and a corresponding hand pulled at Alfredo and Alfredo pulled at me, and suddenly, with a snapping sensation, we were free. The owner of the hand that pulled us out was named Leosmani, and he quickly apologized for the chaos.

"Really, we're good people," he said. "These are just tough times in Trinidad."

"They're tough times in Havana too," Alfredo said.

I wasn't certain, but I thought I caught a snicker at the tail end of Alfredo's statement. Like most Cubans, Alfredo was well aware of the contradictory modern history of Trinidad. The nearby Sierra del Escambray mountains had been an embarrassment to the Revolution, as they were a hotbed of CIA-backed *contrarevolucionario* activity in the early 1960s. But since Trinidad had been declared a UNESCO World Heritage Site in 1988, the quaint colonial town, with its red-tiled roofs and ornate wrought-iron grillwork, had been forgiven its earlier digressions. Trinidad had become the darling of the Cuban government, basking in its attentions and money while other sites of architectural significance, such as the crumbling Centro Habana mansion where Alfredo and his mother and four other families lived, remained largely neglected.

Leosmani led us down a sleepy cobblestone side street of pastel houses before stopping at a two-story lavender apartment, which he shared with his mother.

Inside, he took us to a spotless, windowless bedroom. After he left us alone, I collapsed onto the bed, but then, just as quickly, jumped back up, as its springs jutted into my back like miniature swords.

"If we're not going to be comfortable here, we shouldn't stay," Alfredo said as he tested out the mattress, each bounce of his accompanied by a corresponding creak.

I found Leosmani in the kitchen with his mother, chopping sweet potatoes for dinner.

"On second thought, I think we're going to look around a little more," I said.

Leosmani looked at me, perplexed.

"I need a firmer bed," I said. "This one is too springy."

"You won't find a better bed anywhere," Leosmani said indignantly. "This one's practically new."

"Listen," Alfredo said, trying to make peace. "We'll just look around. We might be back."

"There might be someone else here then," Leosmani said, and then suddenly, he asked, "Are you two married?"

"No, why?" Alfredo asked.

"Well, I doubt you're going to find any other place then," Leosmani said. "I was going to tell you that. We're the only place in Trinidad that'll take foreigner–Cuban couples without marriage papers. Most people are afraid of the fines. The government's testing this out in all the touristy areas outside Havana. Probably within a year, it'll be like this everywhere."

"Well, we've been to Santiago, and the first place we tried let us stay without asking if we were married," I said, attempting to call Leosmani's bluff.

"Right," he responded, not missing a beat. "And this is your first place in Trinidad."

Eleven houses, twenty-some blocks, two hours, and one *apagón* later, so disoriented that we no longer knew how to get back to Leosmani's house for that now luxurious-sounding springy bed, we finally found a woman who agreed to take us without papers.

The *casa particular,* which we viewed by candlelight, was comfortable, with a spacious upstairs flat all to ourselves, but, our host told us, there was one condition to our stay. If anyone asked where Alfredo was from, he would have to lie.

"If people think you're both foreigners, there won't be a problem," our host continued. "Say you're from Panama, the Dominican Republic, wherever. Just whatever you do, don't let on that you're Cuban."

"What about Puerto Rican?" Alfredo asked me as we settled into our new bedroom. "Does that sound believable?"

I nodded, thinking, as I often did, how everything between us would be easier if I were from somewhere else. If I were from anywhere else, I wouldn't have to fly through a third country to visit Alfredo. We wouldn't have to apply for a fiancé visa for him to visit me.

"Can I be Puerto Rican too?" I asked.

"Oh, that's good," Alfredo said, smiling. "So now, if anyone asks, we'll be *la pareja puertorriqueña*."

We linked arms and walked back outside with our new nationalities, a Puerto Rican couple out for an evening stroll along the cobbled streets of a foreign city.

The first person we tested our identities out on, on our first morning in Trinidad, so thoroughly fell for them that he began questioning us about every aspect of our make-believe homeland.

"I've heard it's a pretty island. Is that true?" our new acquaintance asked. He was an elderly, leather-skinned *guajiro* who told us he made the two-hour trip to Trinidad every afternoon to sell his crops. As he leaned excitedly in toward us, awaiting our response, I could smell his parched scent of sun and hay and dusty, country roads.

"Puerto Rico is very beautiful," Alfredo said, getting into his new role. "It looks a lot like Cuba."

"*Yo lo sabía.*" I knew it, the old man said, slapping his hand against his knee. "We Cubans have always felt an affinity with your people. You know, we have the same flag as you do, just with the colors reversed, and we have this saying that Cuba and Puerto Rico are two wings of the same bird."

"We say that in Puerto Rico too," Alfredo said.

"And what part are you from?" the man asked.

Here Alfredo drew a blank and quickly turned to me, relinquishing his star role for the sake of the show.

"A big city," I said, stalling to think. "San Juan."

"Ah, the capital," the man said, delighted. "And what do you two do there?"

"I'm a music student at the university," Alfredo said. "And Lea teaches writing there."

"That sounds like a nice life," the man said as I gave Alfredo's hand a sharp tug to indicate that we should say our goodbyes before we got caught in our lies.

"Well, I won't keep you all day," the man added, noticing my unease. "Let me just say that I hope you enjoy your time here, and I hope that maybe some day your country can also be free of the U.S." With this, the old man raised his arms into the air and declared, "The only way is through armed revolution. Someone's got to teach those bastards that they can't control the whole world."

Once we were a safe distance down the street, Alfredo hunched over and raised his arms like the *guajiro*. Laughing, he shouted, *"¡Que viva la Revolución!"*

I laughed too, but silently I couldn't help wondering what this man would have said had he known the truth of our identities, of my identity. I wondered too if maybe behind all the friendly Cubans I'd met elsewhere who'd been quick to tell me they knew the difference between my government and my people, there had not also lurked at least a little of this man's anger. Or maybe this sense of national pride and outrage was intensified in Trinidad because of the U.S.-backed, counterrevolutionary history of its surrounding mountains.

I mulled this over during our days in Trinidad, while Alfredo spent his obsessing about another aspect of the town's history, his discovery of which was set off by something as simple as the structure of the streets.

Trinidad's cobblestone streets were as painful to walk on as they were pretty to look at. Their raised stones formed something more akin to a dry riverbed than a pedestrian thoroughfare. When we tired of constantly tripping and catching each other, Alfredo and I retreated to the narrow sidewalk.

"I wonder when these streets were made," Alfredo said. "I wonder if they were made by slaves."

In the Museo Histórico, Alfredo found entire exhibits devoted to the history of slavery in Cuba, including stocks for holding his African ancestors. In Trinidad, slaves harvested sugarcane and, as Alfredo had suspected, built the cobblestone streets. As Alfredo read the exhibit plaques, I saw some of his earlier excitement at being in Trinidad seep out of his eyes.

Other than the proindependence *guajiro*, no one else we met in Trinidad bought our Puerto Rican personas. A man who rented us bikes to go to the beach suggested we both claim to be Cuban.

"Tourists aren't allowed to rent bikes," he told us. "The government wants them to rent motorcycles from the hotels."

"So if people question us about the bike, we say we're Cuban, and if they want to know where we're staying, we say we're Puerto Rican?" I asked.

The man laughed. "Or maybe just bike fast," he said. "So no one has a chance to ask."

Biking fast was good advice, because right after we passed the last house on the block, I felt a gust of wind followed by a loud *thwap*, and I turned to see the remnants of a tile roof come tumbling to the ground. As an older woman nearby motioned for us to move ahead, perhaps fearful of another collapse, I looked on, awed by the routine ease with which people rearranged themselves and began clearing away the wreckage, reworking the landscape without a word.

On our final day in Trinidad, we left the town's slave-built cobblestone streets, climbing into the heart of the Sierra del Escambray.

Unfortunately, I missed the scenery for most of our ascent, because our driver, fearful of being fined for transporting a tourist in his *taxi particular*, had demanded I duck down in the back seat lest a roaming police officer spot my smudged foreign figure from afar.

When I got the okay to sit up, we were at the entrance to Topes de Collante National Park, where birdsong blended with the rush of a nearby waterfall, and the scent of pine and eucalyptus filled the air.

We spent the afternoon hiking through the woods, tickling *dormideras*, Venus flytraps, and swinging across small creeks on jungle vines. We climbed two hundred feet up a wall of moss-covered rocks to the upper pool of Salto de Caburni, the first waterfall Alfredo had ever seen.

"*¡Qué fuerte!*" he exclaimed as the thundering cascades pounded down around us.

Back at the bottom, as Alfredo dove into the fall's chilly green pool, I stood shivering at the thought. Along an overgrown trail downhill from the waterfall, we came across a tree with berries as deep red as mistletoe. Alfredo reached up to pick a handful and held them out to me, smiling as proudly as if he had grown them himself.

"A present for your mother," he announced.

I had once told Alfredo that I thought my interest in the outdoors came from my mother, who regularly collected rocks and leaves and interesting insect specimens. Now, though, I didn't know quite what to make of Alfredo's selection.

"That's nice," I finally said after carefully examining the hard, oval-shaped berry. "What is it?"

"It's coffee. Didn't you say your mother has coffee every morning?"

"Really? But aren't coffee beans brown?"

"Well, once they're processed. But first they have to be dried, and then the husks taken off. Then they have to be roasted and ground," Alfredo said. "But I can show you how to do that. It'll be very natural, just like you like things."

We stuffed handfuls of slick, ruby coffee beans into our pockets, but as mine filled to capacity, I had a sudden, worrisome thought.

"Is this legal?" I asked. "To be taking this many, I mean."

"It's not legal to be taking any," Alfredo said matter-of-factly. "Coffee beans belong to the government."

"Right," I said, laughing. "Of course."

We finished our picking and then continued on deeper into the woods until we came to a flat, unforested stretch of land, a plateau of honey brown spreading out to the horizon. There was a small farmhouse with a chicken coop and then, on the other side of the field where the grassland reunited with the trees, an abandoned ramshackle cabin. One of its plywood walls was near collapse, and as we walked closer, I could see that the top half of its front door had somehow fallen off and was now covered with an intricate weave of cobwebs.

Alfredo and I sat down on the wobbly planks of the front porch, jumping up quickly as a board creaked threateningly beneath us.

"*¡Candela!*" Alfredo said, taking a few steps back to survey the cabin. "Can you imagine if this were our house?"

"Well, we'd have to do a lot of renovation," I said laughing.

I pointed to the wall that needed to be torn down, and then Alfredo said we could put a window where the missing half door was. I recommended a tile roof, and Alfredo proposed a second-story writer's room for me.

"And there could be a fireplace in the living room," I said. "So on cold evenings we could pull up our rocking chairs and read by its light."

Alfredo sighed contentedly, and we continued on with our game of house. We moved from one structural adjustment to the next, from inside to outside, until, midway through Alfredo's description of what we might grow in our garden, he stopped and, as if suddenly lost, asked, "So, where is this house?"

"What do you mean?"

"I know this is all pretend," Alfredo said. "But I started to feel like we were talking about something real, and it just made me wonder, is this our life in the U.S.? Our life if the fiancé visa comes through?"

The way Alfredo lowered his voice for the last part of his question reminded me of how skillful we'd both been at avoiding this issue, as if to speak of the pending visa would be akin to placing an obstacle along its already tenuous path to approval.

But of course, albeit indirectly, I had been thinking about the visa now. The cabin I'd imagined, just like the one I'd dreamt of on my first trip to Cuba, was firmly planted in Northern California.

"I *was* thinking of our life in the U.S.," I told Alfredo. "Were you?"

"Yes. Maybe. I don't know," Alfredo said all in one breath. "I think I was, until we got to the outdoors and then I realized I didn't know what that would look like in the U.S. or what would grow there."

"Well, it depends," I said, searching for the simplest way to explain the complexities of my world. "It depends on where we live, on how we live. On the choices we make about all these things."

"Choices?" Alfredo asked, looking momentarily lost again.

"Yes," I said. "There are a lot of choices to make in the U.S. Remember how I told you about the dozens of different types of soaps?"

Alfredo nodded.

"Well, it's kind of like that for everything. For the type of car you want, or bike or running shoes. A garden would depend on where we lived. In the country and even the suburbs, there's room for gardens in your yard, but if I were in a city, I'd try to have a rooftop garden. And then there are decisions about what type of city or where in the country you'd live—in the mountains or the desert or by a river or the ocean . . ."

"Those are all choices?" Alfredo interrupted. "Say we lived in San Francisco, but I was too cold, so we decided to move to Miami. Could we just do that? We wouldn't need any sort of special permission from the government?"

"No," I said, laughing. "But I don't think I want to live in Miami."

"Why not?"

"I like San Francisco. I've already lived other places, and I like where I am now."

"So we'll never live in Miami?" Alfredo asked, sounding disappointed. "Or what about Las Vegas? I've heard Las Vegas is very developed, very beautiful, with lots of lights that stay on all the time."

"No, definitely not Las Vegas," I said, feeling the familiar irritation of having to explain everything. "No one in their right mind wants to live in Las Vegas," I declared.

"But, Lea," Alfredo said. "What about all those people who live there?"

"Some of them are stuck there," I said. "They grew up there and don't know how to get out."

"But if they don't need special permission to leave, why don't they just go?"

"It's not always that easy," I said, shaking my head.

"Okay," Alfredo said, putting his hand on my knee. "Maybe I'm just not understanding, but you have to understand that I've never been to these places, so maybe I'd like to live there, not forever, but maybe for a while."

"These are things we should have been discussing all along," I said. Seeing an opportunity to throw out one of the mental checklist questions I'd begun compiling back in the U.S., I added, "What would we do if after you learned English, you decided to go to college to study anthropology, but the school with the best program was in Tennessee, and I was working at my dream newspaper in California and I didn't want to live in Tennessee for four years? Would we have two houses and just visit each other during the year and spend the summers together? And how would we afford that? Or would we have to separate because we couldn't come to a compromise?"

Before I even saw the confused expression on Alfredo's face, I knew I wasn't being fair, but I couldn't help myself. I was tired of always carrying the weight of worrying about our future, because the reality of life in the U.S. was too much for Alfredo to grasp.

"I don't know where Tennessee is," Alfredo said after a long silence. "And I really don't know very much about anthropology, and I've never been in a relationship in the U.S."

I tilted my head to look Alfredo in the eye. As he often did when distressed, he was staring at the ground. When he did look up, although still averting his gaze, I was surprised by the red glossiness of his eyes.

"I really don't know what to tell you," he said. "I know you want more from me, but I can't give you any more. I can't imagine the situations or places you're talking about. I've never really thought much about what I want from the future. In Cuba, the future is something that happens to you, not that you choose, and most of the time, it's just like the day before." Alfredo cleared his throat before continuing. "I know how you are. I know you like to be in control of your life, but if you want to be with me in the U.S., you're going to have to find a way to be okay with not knowing every possible outcome ahead of time. You're going to have to be comfortable," he paused, finally looking me in the eye, "with uncertainty."

As we headed silently down the mountain, exhausted from our discussion and its unanswerable questions, the truth of Alfredo's words echoed in my mind. I thought about how, in comparison with all the unknowns and new challenges that awaited us in the U.S., our life in Cuba, even with its flaws and frustrations, felt comfortingly familiar.

In Cuba, if we talked about renovating a house, I would know exactly what it would look like—tile and cement floors and louvered wooden blinds with an open-air shower and French doors in the bedrooms. I would know where it would be—Havana. And I would know what we would grow in the garden—mangoes and bananas and sweet green oranges. If Alfredo decided to study anthropology, I would know where he would do so—the University of Havana.

In Cuba, I knew the answers to the questions Alfredo could not respond to about our life in the U.S. In Cuba, I knew who we were together.

In many ways, Trinidad—with its blackouts and collapsing rooftops and separate rules for Cubans and foreigners—had been like a microcosm of our previous trials in Cuba, a chorus of everything we'd stumbled over and eventually, if not overcome, at least become conversant enough with to know how to handle. It was a snapshot, a picture postcard of how far we—and I alone—had come in Cuba.

Like those people who had so swiftly rearranged themselves after the roof we biked past collapsed, I now knew how to do the hurricane walk. I knew to bring my flashlight if I went out on a Monday night when an *apagón* was scheduled. As a foreigner–Cuban couple in Havana, we had become skillful at finding *paladares* like El Recanto, where Alfredo could pay for our dinners in pesos, giving us a reprieve from the economic inequalities of our relationship. Even now, here in Trinidad, while still saddened by the situation, we had learned to work around the tourist apartheid, making a game out of changing our identities.

I thought about how long it had taken me, as a Spanish-speaker who had traveled in foreign countries before, to arrive at this place of calm in Cuba. I thought about Alfredo, who didn't speak English and had never traveled outside Cuba, and I worried about how he would adjust to life in the U.S., where the learning curve would be much greater.

While no one—except the INS—would question us about our marital status in the U.S., in many parts of the country, there would be stares and a much more overt racism than the subtle form that so upset Alfredo in Cuba. We would both be paid in dollars, but with Alfredo being a nonnative speaker without a college degree, I couldn't begin to imagine how many years it would take before our salaries would approach equality.

Given all the new inequalities I would be introducing into our relationship by bringing Alfredo to the U.S., I now wondered what I had been thinking when I'd applied for the fiancé visa, which would give us three months to make a decision about the rest of our lives. And then, of course, I knew exactly what I'd been thinking. It was that repeating, haunting dream of showing Alfredo my world. Even in my current panicked state, this vision was still with me, but now I worried that the challenges we'd have to overcome to live together in the U.S. might destroy the very core of our relationship.

With all these thoughts flooding my mind, I felt myself tensing up on our taxi ride back to town. By the time our driver dropped us off at the Trinidad bus terminal for our trip back to Havana, I was so anxious that I bought a phone card to call my mother, who didn't know about the fiancé visa, and, as casually as possible, ask about the return addresses of the mail I had received.

"I think all you've gotten since we talked last week is junk mail," my mother said when, after three tries, our phone lines finally connected. "Are you expecting something special?"

"Oh, no, not really," I said, still unwilling to reveal my secret, especially now that I was filled with so much doubt about it.

"Well, I was hoping you would call soon," my mother continued. "Because you did receive some good news this week."

"Yeah? But tell me quickly mom. This phone card doesn't have much time on it."

"I checked your answering machine messages like you asked me to, and an editor called to say he wants to use a story you wrote about you and Alfredo for a book on Cuba that he's putting together. And," my mother continued before I could respond, "he said he's leading a U.S.–Cuban writers' workshop in Havana at the beginning of January and that you should go. He said you could find out about it there at the writers' union. He said the name. Wait . . . it's some acronym. I know I have it written down here somewhere." There was a shuffling of papers followed by a loud beep, the sound of the phone card cutting off.

As I walked across the bus station to join Alfredo, I had to restrain myself from running, buoyed as I was by the editor's acceptance of my story, this formal affirmation of the real life story of Alfredo and me in Cuba. I told him the news as we boarded the bus.

"*¡Felicidades, mi amor!*" Alfredo said. "When you read it to me, I knew that one day it would be published. And that workshop sounds like an important opportunity for you. Are you going to stay on for it?"

"I'd love to," I said. "But I don't know how I could. My visa's only good for another month and then, to extend it until January, I'd have to fly to Mexico at the end of November *and* the end of December, and I can't afford that."

"Well, there has to be a way," Alfredo said, drumming his fingers on his duffel bag as he thought. "With the holidays coming up in December, probably places like *Granma International* need extra help, because foreign writers go home for vacation."

"And then you'd automatically get your visa extended if you got a temporary *pincha*," Alfredo added, using the Cuban slang for "work." "My uncle had a Canadian girlfriend who was a translator for some international wire service, and she used to go home every December. And as a foreigner, she got free housing in Cuba. It's like the best of both worlds. You're paid in dollars and you get a ration book to go to the *bodegas*. I think you even get *un carné de identidad*."

"An ID card!" I said, laughing. "Does that mean I'd get to be stopped by the police in the streets too?"

"No," Alfredo said. "But it means you're more like a Cuban. With that card, we probably wouldn't need marriage papers in Trinidad. What a difference that would've made for this trip, huh?"

"Yeah, or for our next trip," I said. And then, testing out on Alfredo a new idea that had been developing in my mind during our conversation, I added, "Maybe if I could get a job, and I liked it, and they needed someone past the holidays, then I could stay on after the workshop."

"So then we'd just stay here instead of doing the fiancé visa?" Alfredo asked, surprising me with the look of relief that crossed his face.

"Well, no, I wouldn't stay forever, but it's not like I have a job back home to return to," I said, feeling more convinced of the rightness of my plan as I explained it to Alfredo. "And we probably won't hear back about the fiancé visa for several more months. Maybe I could just stay here until we hear, and it would be easier if we went back together. If," I added, not knowing until the moment my mouth formed the words that I would say them, "we even want to go back when the time comes."

Alfredo stared at me without speaking.

"Well, what do you think?" I asked, holding my breath. "Does that make sense, or is it just too crazy?"

"I think," Alfredo said, "that I was excited to see your world, to try it out, but now I can see that there are so many important questions that I can't answer. I think this would change over time, but I can also tell you that now I'm happy here. And if you think that getting a writing job could make that be true for you too, then," he said, his lips slowly forming a smile, "I think your plan sounds like a good one."

27

❧❧❧❧❧

Leaving Dinora

We walked home from the Havana bus station in silence, although it was a different type of silence than what we'd shared on the hike down from the Sierra del Escambray. Now, for me at least, it was a quiet born not of exhaustion but of excitement and hushed anticipation.

Beyond the immediate rush of relief I felt over discarding my mental checklist of questions for Alfredo and abandoning my constant attempt to imagine the unimaginable, I was happy to have a mission, a purpose for my time in Cuba. Now, instead of viewing every situation Alfredo and I encountered as a test of our relationship's rightness in the U.S, I could put myself to the test and throw all my energy into getting a job before my visa expired in one month.

If I did get free housing with my job, perhaps Alfredo and I could live a different life in Cuba—one less marred by inequalities; one where I no longer had to use my savings to get by and, with our combined salaries and individual ration books, we could be comfortable.

My vision for this new life was a list of maybes. Maybe things could work out for us in Cuba. Maybe, with a job and a life of my own here, eventually Cuba, like the U.S., could also become my world. Maybe, with a more stable relationship with Alfredo in Cuba, I could learn to live with the uncertainty that he had referred to about our prospects in the U.S. Or better yet, maybe, after time, the need to bring Alfredo back to my first world would just fade away, disappear like a sweet, distant dream, the memory of it being enough.

I was so consumed with imagining my new, insider life in Havana that it wasn't until Alfredo and I reached Dinora's door that the one crucial detail I had overlooked dawned on me—Dinora. And Mielikki's departure. And the "Como Ser Negro" song. And most recently, Alfredo's sensitivity to the racist history of Trinidad's street construction. Now the idea of staying at Dinora's until I found a job that offered housing seemed unthinkable.

"Lea! Alfredo!" Dinora called down to us from the watchtower balcony. She waved her hands wildly in front of her face as if afraid we might not see her. "Wait, I'll get the door."

We weren't even halfway up the narrow marble steps before Dinora began gesticulating again, although her motions were slowed, her words taking center stage now.

"It's been a whirlwind here since you left," she said. "Just one thing after the other. Well, you know about Mielikki, but the day after she left, the telephone broke and I keep asking someone from ETECSA to come fix it, but no one comes. And then the hot-water heater broke three days ago, and the next day the Danes, *pobrecitas*, I think they'd just had enough so they moved out. Kajsa's sister came to visit for the week, so they went off traveling. And here I was with all these new repair expenses and no rent money coming in. *¡Candela!*" Dinora shook her wrist so that her index and middle finger slapped together. "But then, don't ask me how, I filled up the whole house again in just one day."

Tiring of shifting my weight, I put my backpack on the hall floor.

"Mainly it was coincidence," Dinora continued. "The Danes were nice enough to find a replacement, a Swiss woman they knew. And then this

Austrian couple saw the *casa particular* sign on the door, so they're here for two weeks. But I was still feeling desperate, like it was going to take so long to save enough money for the hot-water heater, so I went to the building where all the foreigners take classes at the university and, as they left, I asked if anyone needed a room. I got a Chinese guy that way, a very nice boy."

Dinora smiled, proud of her entrepreneurial savvy. "Just like a capitalist, huh?"

I nodded.

"So, I know you two probably want to unpack," Dinora said suddenly. "But, just so you're not surprised by any strangers in the bathroom, I should tell you that we also have a German guy who came last night. He'll be here for a month, and I thought, 'Well, it's getting a little crowded, but why not?' Nitza's in Argentina so we put the Chinese guy in her room and the German guy in my room."

"And where are you and Luis staying?"

"In the dining room."

"The dining room?"

"Yeah, we pushed the table over to the side, and we had an extra mattress. Really, it's not so bad. Besides, it's only temporary. I told the German guy that you were leaving at the end of the week, and then he could have your room."

After my panic about moving out, this surprise ending to Dinora's story caught me off guard. Although I tried to conceal my contentment at the way the situation had resolved itself and my satisfaction at being saved from having to bring up the "R" word with Dinora, my face must have alerted her that something was going on.

"Oh, no," Dinora said, her own facial expression quickly shifting from contentment to worry. "I just knew it. You're staying on, aren't you?"

I nodded, speechless at her insight.

"I was afraid of that," she said. "Last night I asked Luis what he thought I should do. I said, 'You know how Lea is. What if she extends her ticket again?' and he said, 'No, she said just last week that she was leaving after Trinidad.' I knew I shouldn't have listened to him. I was just so desperate because of the Danes, but I went too far. Well, I'm sure Luis isn't going to be too happy about us staying on in the dining room, but that's just what we'll have to do."

"No, please don't Dinora," I said. "That's really not necessary. We can find somewhere else to stay."

"Or," Dinora said, a thoughtful, distant look in her eyes as if she'd hardly heard me, "I don't need the German, especially if you're staying on. How much longer will you be here for?"

"Oh, I don't know. At least a month, hopefully more. I'm going to . . ."

"Well, I'll just tell him I'm sorry but actually he can't stay," Dinora interrupted. "I'll tell him . . . I know. I'll tell him that I got the date wrong, that I thought you were leaving at the end of this month, but it was actually next month."

I shook my head. I shook my whole body. "Look, I'll still come visit you," I said. "And maybe we can catch a movie or get ice cream one day. Or we could even try to do that literature *intercambio* again, but I think you should let the German stay."

"Really?" Dinora asked, perplexed. She examined my face as if I might break out into laughter at any minute, as if maybe this were a joke she just wasn't getting. "Why?"

"Well, because you already told him he could stay and . . ." I stalled for words.

"Oh, I get it," Dinora said, her smile returning. "Lea, *tú eres tan dulce*. You are so sweet, always thinking of me. I know. It's not the capitalist way, right?"

As satisfied as I was with letting Dinora believe I was thinking only of business etiquette when I turned down her offer to stay on, I still felt sad about leaving. And, like Dinora, Alfredo quickly caught on to my mood as we sat on the bed in our soon-to-be-someone-else's bedroom.

"Lea, why don't you tell Dinora to hold a room for us next month, when the German leaves?" he asked.

I took a deep breath before asking, "I didn't tell you why Mielikki left, did I?"

"No."

"Well, she said Dinora made her boyfriend uncomfortable."

I watched Alfredo's face fall. "Is that why the Danes left too? Because of their Rasta friends? Their black friends?"

"I think so," I said. "I'm sorry, Alfredo. I guess you were right all along."

Alfredo nodded without speaking.

"Do you want to just leave now? Stay at your mother's tonight and then figure out what to do?"

"What would you say to Dinora?" Alfredo asked.

"I don't know."

"We don't have to leave tonight." Alfredo said, lying back on the bed. "It's not like anything's really different now from how it was before. I know Dinora's been a good friend to you. I know she accepts me because of you. I'll be okay for a few more days, but I'd like to leave as soon as we can."

"I'll start looking first thing tomorrow," I said, grateful for such an anticlimactic conclusion.

A scratchy throat I'd been suffering for the past few days worked its way into my nasal passage our first evening back in Havana. In the morning I woke with a heavy head and a runny nose, a whisper of a voice, and a rawness not unlike sandpaper being rubbed against my throat each time I sneezed.

Alfredo prepared me a sore-throat tonic, which, save for one essential ingredient, was just like what I drank at home. Along with the warm lemon water and honey, Alfredo's concoction contained a stiff shot of rum, which he swore was the key to my cure. Before he left for work in the morning, and when he returned in the evening and once during an afternoon lunch break, Alfredo would make me one of his medicinal mixed drinks, which, when I downed its potent blend, made the searing pain of my sore throat seem minor in comparison.

As I lay listlessly in bed all day, unable to determine if the hot, feverlike dizziness I felt was the onset of infection or just inebriation, I would flip through a book I had about the Cuban media. In the back, it listed every organization's address and phone number, and I would stare dreamily at the possibilities for employment, awaiting the day when I could go out and pursue them.

If I felt well enough, after the sun dropped in the early evenings, I would venture upstairs to the *azotea* to examine the coffee beans we'd picked in Trinidad. Here, on Dinora's rooftop, we had laid them out to dry on a sheet of *Granma* and, although there was nothing to do now but wait, I tended to them with the devotion of the bored, the patience of the hopeful. I noted their change in color from ruby red to a more earthy mahogany, and I ran my fingers across their once smooth skin, now bumpy with sun blisters. I flipped them over so they would dry evenly, and I set up little brick barriers around them so the strong afternoon winds wouldn't steal away from me these delicate seedlings of my imagined rooftop garden.

In the absence of a functioning hot-water heater, I began boiling my bath-water. Although Dinora's upstairs kitchen had a four-burner stovetop, I had to boil each of my three potfuls of bathwater separately, since there was only one pot without flaky burn marks or greasy food stains. Once my water began bubbling, I poured it into a white plastic soap- and earth-scented bucket we used to buy bouquets of sweet-smelling *azucena* flowers on Aramburo and to transport our wet laundry to the rooftop clothesline. I added another pot of cold tap water and stirred with a soup ladle until the steam licking my face softened like a kiss. In the shower, I doused myself with a third of the bucket and quickly sudsed up. Then I poured the remaining water over my head, clean and content in the knowledge that every drop that went down the drain had done its job.

Unfortunately, there was no such pleasant, simple solution to the problem of the broken telephone, which, despite Dinora's increasingly shrill requests, no one ever came to fix. Several times each day, Dinora lifted the receiver, and each time it responded with the same absent dial tone, the same infuriating silence. Dinora's slam reverberated all the way up to my bedroom.

On the evenings when I was well enough to join the family for dinner, I sat at the head of the table, the back of my chair bumping up against the bottom of Dinora's and Luis's mattress, where I imagined they rested their toes at night.

At first I'd felt guilty about my continued friendship with Dinora, but it also felt unnatural to completely cut it off when, as Alfredo had pointed out, nothing had changed between him and Dinora since everyone else had moved out. In fact, when Dinora called up that dinner was ready on my second night back, not knowing that Alfredo was working nights at the symphony that week, she had set two places at the table. Sadly, I knew that, had Alfredo been home, we both would have come up with an excuse for why we couldn't accept Dinora's invitation.

On the first day that I felt well enough to venture out, having sworn off my course of hot lemon and rum water, I lathered up in my usual layer of sunscreen and walked down to the *chopping* on San Lázaro. But from a full block away, I could sense that something wasn't right. The door to the bag-check stand was shut, and there was no line in front of the store, not even a stray customer loitering about, counting his change to see if he had enough for cooking oil.

When I got to the front door of the *chopping*, a handwritten sign read CERRADO POR REPARACIONES. After I walked the ten blocks to the only other *chopping* I knew of in Centro Habana, my throat parched and sweat soaking my eyebrows, I discovered that this one was also closed for repairs. I knocked on the door to ask when it would reopen, but the lights were out, and, for as much as I pressed my nose against the tinted windows, I couldn't make out any movement inside. After several more minutes of staring plaintively into the darkness, I finally gave up, leaving only the faded smudge of my noseprint in protest.

Alfredo and I moved out of Dinora's on the 31st of October, the day on which I'd originally planned to fly home. Without even seeing it, I accepted the first *casa particular* I heard about, an illegal room in the house of a dentist couple Liudmila knew.

I didn't inquire about a telephone or a hot-water heater, knowing that their presence today didn't guarantee their functioning tomorrow, and I didn't ask Liudmila about the price of the *casa particular,* knowing we'd negotiate it when we got there. That we were leaving when we'd planned to, that my throat was healing, and that I could soon start my job search was all that mattered to me.

I kissed Dinora and Abuela in parting in the living room; Alfredo had already said his hasty goodbye and then had taken off down the stairs with our luggage.

"No pierdan el camino," Dinora called out as I started to descend the steps and Abuela stretched her neck for a final glimpse of my back. "Will you come by next week?"

"I will," I said. "I'll let you know about my job search."

"Oh, good," she said. The shakiness that had filled her voice just minutes before evened out, and a sliver of a smile formed on her face. "We can sit in the living room and talk about life," she said. "It'll be just like old times."

At the dentists' house, to keep at bay the burn I felt in my eyes when I recalled the image of Dinora standing and, as always, looking out over the balcony as I left, I busied myself with unpacking and straightening up our new room.

After everything else had been put away, I took out from the bottom of my backpack the crumpled *Granma* containing our coffee beans, carried from the mountaintops of Trinidad to the rooftop of Dinora's and now spilling onto the cool cement floor of our new house.

They reminded me of a traveling talisman, of the cowry shells that religious Cubans had a *babalawo* scatter like tea leaves across a tatami mat on the floor to predict their future. And I wondered: If these coffee beans could be read, what immediate future would they foretell for me?

28

The Real,
Real Cuba

I awoke alone my first morning in the new house. Just minutes after Alfredo
had kissed me goodbye, which he always did while I was asleep so that I shot up
startled, and then sweetly surprised, I'd drifted back to sleep. I awoke nearly two
hours later as the dentists and their daughter, Lialne, said a noisy goodbye to
each other before heading out into the early-morning bustle of Neptuno Street.

I took out my notebook, where I'd been compiling my list of job possibilities, and I stepped into my new living room, whose emptiness served as
evidence that doctors, rather than airline employees, lived here.

Here, there were no sofas with lace doilies on the armrests and no tapes-
tries with nature scenes on the walls. Here, there was only a love seat, a dining room table, and a rocking chair; the combined mass still left the room
feeling empty, like a stage set in the middle of construction.

I sat down in the rocking chair to go over my notes, and by noon, as
I turned the front doorknob to get started on this much anticipated day, I
found Alfredo on the other side, home for lunch.

"Where are you off to?" he asked, as though taken aback to find me out of bed.

"I'm going to start my job search," I said. "I'm off to find *una pincha.*"

Off the main drag of 23rd Street, the office of the Latin American wire service Prensa Latina, a blocky cement building, looked less like a newsroom than a high-security factory, a windowless prison surrounded by a mesh wire fence.

Standing in front of this very Soviet-style building, it seemed unreal to me that I, a U.S. citizen residing illegally in Cuba, could actually receive a salary from the communist government. But when I told the receptionist that I was an American journalist looking for work, she simply smiled and, sounding sincere, said, "*¡Qué interesante!*"

She picked up the receiver of her rotary phone and dialed a two-digit extension. She spoke quickly and unintelligibly into the mouthpiece, and then, as she pointed to a camouflaged door to her right, she buzzed me in.

"The editor will be waiting for you in the upstairs lobby, at the top of the stairs at the end of the hallway," she said.

The hallways in Prensa Latina were just as I had imagined they would be from the outside—long and cavernous and darker than night.

At the top of the steps, the editor—a man with a pinstriped shirt and rumpled gray hair—sat smoking. He stood up when he saw me coming and offered his free hand in greeting.

"So, you're the American," he said, smiling. "Please, have a seat."

He proceeded to tell me all about Prensa Latina—when it had been founded, how long he had been there, where the wire stories ran. He paused between each bit of information to take a drag off his cigarette, and then, in conclusion, he added, "But we don't have any openings now."

"Oh," I said, confused as to why he had agreed to meet with me. "Well, thanks for talking to me anyway."

"No problem. I always like to meet foreigners when they pass through," he said. "Let me give you my address, and we should keep in touch in case something comes up in the future."

I nodded as I handed him a blank sheet of notebook paper. When he looked up from writing his information, he smiled once more.

"I especially wanted to meet with you because I think we have someone here that you might like to talk to." He paused dramatically. "Another American."

"She works here?"

"Yes, and if there were a job opening for an English translator, she would be the person you'd talk to. Would you like to meet her? Hear her opinion on life at Prensa Latina?"

"Sure," I said, and the editor did a little parting bow before walking around the corner, returning a few minutes later with a thin, fifty-something woman who, with her butterfly-collar blouse and bell-bottomed blue jeans, looked like she'd just stepped out of a documentary on the 1970s. She too had a cigarette dangling from her mouth.

The editor rounded the corner once more, leaving us, and the American sat down next to me, her stale tobacco scent encircling both of us.

"Linda," she said as she shook my hand and, before I could offer my name, asked, "So are you going back to the U.S. soon?"

"Not if I can find a job here."

"Well, I'll make a deal with you," Linda said, releasing a hoarse smoker's laugh. "You can have my job if you can find me one in the U.S."

"What do you mean?" I asked, confused.

"I've been trying to get out of here forever," Linda explained. "But it's too expensive in the U.S. to go without a job lined up, and now I've been here so long that I've lost all my contacts there."

"Why don't you just stay here then?" I asked.

"Cuba, for me," Linda said, pausing as she searched for the right words, "has just, of late, been a really bad trip, you know?"

She tapped her cigarette ash on the floor while awaiting my response.

I nodded, not really understanding, not sure whether I wanted to ask.

"I had this guy, a Cuban I was involved with, and we got married," Linda continued. "Or at least I thought we did, but then I found out he already had another wife and two kids."

I shook my head.

"Yeah, right," Linda said. "It was really . . . just not cool. And things have just been really difficult for me ever since, so I'd like to kind of, how do you say it, blow this joint, you know?"

She closed her mouth and exhaled a snort of smoke out of her nose.

"Wow, it's been so long since I've spoken this much English at one time," she said.

"But you're an English translator, right?"

"Yeah, but that's not speaking. That's just sitting in a dark, smelly room all day with an outdated dictionary." Linda laughed again. "So listen, I want to ask you a favor," she said, leaning in closer. "If I gave you my email—I have email here, the only benefit of this job—then do you think you could send me the names of some editors you know in the U.S. and I could send my résumé to them? Anyone, really. Radio, TV. It doesn't have to be print. I'm ready for a change. You know?"

I nodded once more, understanding this time.

"Great, great," Linda said. "Thanks so much. You know, I didn't even get your name."

"Lea."

"Yeah, thanks Lea," she said, handing me a scrap of paper with her email. "And, hey," she said as I stood up to leave, "good luck with your job search."

I returned home discouraged and ready to curl up in bed for a solitary mope session, but when I unlocked the dentists' front door, I found that I had company.

By just 3:30, the whole family was home—Damaris and Manolo were squished together on the love seat, speaking in serious tones, while their pianist daughter, Lialne, sat in the rocking chair studying sheet music. As I entered, they all looked up, momentarily disoriented by the sight of me walking into their living room. The day before, Manolo had told me that having boarders was a new thing for his family.

"But, well, you know how the situation is in Cuba," he had explained.

I had nodded, understanding perfectly, just as I now understood, without any explanation, why everyone was home from work so early—to conduct their other *negocios*.

Now though, as I shut the front door behind me, whatever talk may have been going on about under-the-table jobs was quickly abandoned for the much more entertaining topic of my job search. Just the idea of it had amused the family to no end when I'd told them about it the night before.

"Work?" Manolo had laughed. "What type of work? Like a *taxista particular?* I'm sure they don't make as much as you're used to, but it's pretty good money for around here."

"Or," Lialne had added, not wanting to be left out of the fun, "she could sell cigars to tourists. That's always a solid career."

After I'd explained my situation with Alfredo, the family's sarcasm had turned into sympathy. Today, as Manolo inquired about my day, there was an earnestness in his voice.

"Did you get any leads?" he asked.

Not wanting to threaten this newfound sincerity with the ridiculous recounting of my failed attempt at employment, I simply shook my head.

"No es fácil," said Damaris, patting me gently on the back.

As a daily reprieve from job hunting, I allowed myself the mornings off to focus on revising my story about Alfredo and me.

On his message, the editor had said that I needed to cut my eight-thousand-word story in half, a daunting process that became a focus of much of my spare energy. Finding a computer where I could email the final version of my story reminded me of a treasure hunt, except that here, even upon reaching the final destination, the prize was never guaranteed.

I started my search at the University Computer Services Office, where the man at the front desk told me that he couldn't reactivate my email account without a teacher's signature verifying my enrollment. Wondering whether he had been the one to terminate my account four months ago when Alfredo had been caught using it, I continued cautiously, holding up my diskette ever so innocently.

"I just have something very important on here that I need to email today," I said.

"Try Hotel Colima, across the street," the man said, unmoved.

The woman at Hotel Colima's reception desk directed me to Habana Libre, and the man there said I should try Hotel Nacional.

Havana's luxurious landmark hotel was perched on a cliff above the Malecón and, before the Revolution, it had served as a secondary home to mafiosi like Meyer Lansky. Whenever I walked by it, the Hotel Nacional intimidated me with its history and its castlelike grandeur. Yet when I entered its majestic Moorish archway today, its lavishness felt more hopeful than imposing. And when I spoke with the doorman, he not only confirmed that there was email but told me that, in an executive suite on the top floor, there was also Internet.

I walked quickly across the mosaic floors and straight up five flights of steps, too excited to stop to look for an elevator. But once I reached the sixth floor, the woman in charge of the computers, who sat doodling on a notepad at her desk, informed me that the Internet connection had been down for the past three days.

"Hopefully it'll be working by tomorrow," she said.

I went by Alfredo's work to see if he had any suggestions, and he took a break and walked with me to the house of Ernesto, El Corrupto whose illegal Internet connection had enabled Alfredo and me to communicate after my university account was closed.

"You got here one month too late," Ernesto said when we arrived. Shrugging his shoulders, he added, "I don't know what happened, but my connection hasn't worked since I sent you Alfredito's last email."

Every few days at the dentists' house, I dangled my dirty laundry just above the surface of the small bathroom sink, attempting to wash each item without it touching the basin's petrified green toothpaste stains and black veins of scratched-off enamel. Once I'd accomplished this feat, I would begin my search for a place to hang everything (there was no rooftop clothesline at the dentists' house). After my first wash in our new quarters, I had ruled out fans and doorknobs, which left rust marks on my underwear, and wooden chairs, which seeped their caramel-colored stains into my white tank tops.

Although I had prided myself on being a resident of the "real Cuba" during the three months I lived in Dinora's *casa particular,* I could now see that I had been mistaken. Without a regular dollar income, the dentists were unable to install air-conditioning units or to hire an illegal maid to help clean the house. When they returned home from a full day of work plus several hours of carrying out *negocios,* they were too tired to do much more than collapse onto their love seat.

I tried to do my part in tidying up, but often I felt at a loss. Even the ongoing fumigation campaign could not kill the bed bugs, which nibbled at me all night so that I woke with walnut-sized welts all over my back and ankles. In our bathtub, the carcasses of less resilient cockroaches awaited us each morning.

Just entering the tiny kitchen filled me with despair. There was neither a drying rack nor a dishtowel nor counter space to spread the just-washed cookware and kitchen utensils out on, so everything was stuffed into the cabinets wet, and everything came out wet with a ripe, eggy odor that made me nauseated each time I drank from one of the glasses or ate off a plate.

Not that there was much to drink or eat these days anyway, with the *choppings* still closed. I hoarded my reserves of dried goods and limited myself to slivers of cheese, while Alfredo, like other Cubans, made do in a way that I wasn't very good at, stuffing himself with bread and consuming more oranges than I would have before imagined was humanly possible.

In addition to the diminishing food supply, the closure of the *choppings* also meant there was less soap to go around. And with Alfredo, like most cleanliness-obsessed Cubans, taking three showers each day, our last bar of generic pink Cuban soap seemed to be shrinking hourly.

"Maybe," I told Alfredo one day, attempting to mask my irritation with him and the *choppings* by making a joke, "we should start rationing the soap. You could wash one-third of your body each time you showered."

"Maybe," Alfredo responded, smiling, "you could change your last name to Castro."

On a Wednesday afternoon, following a fruitless search for translating work at *Granma* and El Instituto Superior de Artes, I discovered that the *choppings* had reopened as appliance stores.

In a glass case near the cash register, the *choppings* maintained a small stash of their previous stock in the form of some imported chocolates and several expensive perfumes and soaps. The rest of the former food markets was filled with refrigerators and stereos and hair dryers, all in U.S. dollars and all more than they would've cost in the U.S.

Yet people still flocked to the revamped *chopping*, the line outside winding around the block like a break-off from Coppelia. I couldn't imagine that everyone in Havana suddenly needed a new refrigerator and, even if they did, I didn't know how, with an average annual salary of less than a hundred and fifty dollars, they'd find the five hundred dollars to pay for it.

"What is everyone waiting in line for?" I asked Alfredo. "What are they all buying?"

"Anything they can afford of what used to be there," he said. "Because if so much of what once existed disappeared so quickly, who knows how long what remains will last?"

On my walk home, I saw a dead dog lying on its back, its feet raised stiffly in the air. A block away, several children played baseball with their makeshift bats and irregularly shaped balls, blissfully unaware of the corpse around the corner. Briefly, I considered taking another street home, but then, like a passerby at a car wreck, I felt compelled to get closer, to look for evidence of how this had happened. As I stepped around the dog—its stench like sweaty socks and rotting fruit—I saw one of its eyes, still open and staring out at me through a mass of maggots. I ran the rest of the way home.

29

*Un Socio
Me Preguntó...*

I had hoped to visit Dinora bearing good news about my job search, but instead I returned to Animas Street, followed all the way by a black cloud of fumigation, to report the symptoms for my third and most serious sickness in less than two months.

Yet unlike my first illness, I didn't believe this new one had been caused by the fumigation. And unlike the cold I'd come down with upon my return from Trinidad, my current queasiness had nothing to do with a virus floating in the air.

My present sickness, I sensed, was something internal. For the past two days, I'd felt a stinging sensation whenever I urinated, and this morning, a stream of blood had swirled around the toilet bowl. Just the sight of it made me feel faint.

As I neared Dinora's house, I could see that the balcony doors had been shut in an effort to keep the fumigation outside. Yet, when I rang the bell, Dinora still greeted me with a cough and then, sensing my unease, she asked what was wrong and I told her about my health problem.

"Is Nitza here?" I asked. "I was hoping she might know what to do."

"She's in Chile until tomorrow," Dinora said. "But maybe I can help."

Abuela mumbled something, to which Dinora nodded.

"I was just going to suggest that," she said and told me to go pee in her toilet.

When I called Dinora in for the inspection, she took one look and ordered me to go to the hospital. She offered to accompany me, but I declined, feeling that, by this point in my stay, I should be able to manage a doctor's visit on my own, and that maybe in doing so I could retrieve some of the pride I'd lost in my unsuccessful search for jobs.

Surprisingly, my trip to Hermanos Ameijeiras, the same hospital where I had visited Abuela and where Dinora went for her headache shots, ended up to be one of the easiest endeavors I'd undertaken in a while. I had imagined an expensive visit (health care was free only for Cubans), a long wait with lots of paperwork and explanations, and, after my consultation, a prescription for medication at some faraway international pharmacy with irregular hours.

Instead, the whole process, from paperwork to urine analysis, took less than an hour and cost just fifty dollars, including medication, which was delivered with my diagnosis—a urinary tract infection.

"But why? I mean, what do you think could have caused it?" I asked the doctor.

"Oh," he said, looking overwhelmed. "It could be any number of things, but the most common are unhygienic conditions and waiting too long to urinate."

I thought about the *Granma*s I had used to wipe myself when the *choppings* had been closed, and I recalled all the times I'd willed myself to wait instead of facing a scary public toilet. I remembered too that a urinary tract infection was the excuse Alfredo's doctor had given him so he could get off work to go to Santiago. But now, unlike when Alfredo had recounted his story for me, I had no laughter to suppress.

In an attempt to cheer me up, on the evening following my diagnosis, Alfredo suggested we go hear the dentists' daughter Lialne play piano at a restaurant in Habana Vieja. Manolo and Damaris offered us a ride in their 1958

Chevy, handed down from Manolo's father. Not since my Hotel El Bosque days had Alfredo and I ridden in a car to go out for the night, and momentarily, I felt my weariness of the past few days lifting over the excitement of this unexpected luxury.

But then, as had been happening with increasing frequency lately, Alfredo and I got into an argument, which not only soured my enthusiasm for the evening but also made us miss our ride.

In preparation for our big night, I had splurged on an overpriced bottle of liquid soap at the Infanta *chopping*. On the bed, I had laid out a rayon sundress with a brown and black batik flower print—my favorite item of clothing and, coincidentally, my only clean one, since I had been avoiding washing in the sink. Stepping into the shower, I had moved away from the stream of water rather than cursing it as I usually did when it suddenly changed from tepid to scorching. But when, after an ice-cold streak caught me full on and I shut off the water and jumped out of the shower to reach for the dentists' only spare towel, which Alfredo and I shared, I found that it was missing from the doorknob where we usually hung it.

I opened the door into the bedroom and discovered the towel—wadded up and still soaking wet from Alfredo's morning shower—on a bedside chair. As I picked it up, I could have sworn I smelled mold.

"How did you get it so wet?" I asked Alfredo. "Why didn't you hang it on the doorknob so it would be dry for me?"

"I thought you said that the doorknob was leaving rust marks when you hung your clothes to dry on it," Alfredo responded, sounding hurt.

"But this is just a towel," I said as I stood shivering, a puddle collecting around my feet. "Who cares about a towel?"

"But then why does it matter if it's a little wet?" Alfredo asked, confused. "Even when we hang it up, it never fully dries anyway."

"Well, still that's better than it being like a sponge," I said, sensing my voice rising as I dropped the towel back onto the chair. "This is disgusting, and now I have nothing but the clothes I was going to wear to dry myself with."

"Lea, shh," Alfredo said, placing his hand on my shoulder to calm me and handing me one of his T-shirts to dry off with.

Before I could respond, there was a knock at the door followed by the sound of Damaris clearing her throat. "Um, I don't want to rush you two," she said, an uncomfortable edge to her voice, "but I really think we should get going now. Are you ready?"

Alfredo looked hesitantly at me and I stared back angrily at him, not yet ready to end our argument. A beat passed, and then Damaris spoke again. "Maybe you should just meet us at the performance. We'll be sitting off to the side."

While Alfredo took the wet towel into the bathroom for his shower, I wondered why, even when I realized the absurdity of my complaints, even when I heard the shrillness creeping into my voice, I couldn't stop myself. It was as if once I'd decided to try to stay on in Cuba, my mental checklist of questions about whether we could survive in the U.S. had been replaced with a list of irritations about our current life, which, without my meaning for it to, often turned personal.

I remembered how, when Alfredo had started spending the night, Dinora had asked me to have him clean up the hairs that he left ringing the shower drain, and I had been so embarrassed to say anything that I'd done it myself.

Now, on top of the cockroach carcasses, Alfredo's hairs felt like an added offense, and I regularly inspected the shower after he used it, refusing him passage into the bedroom until he retrieved every last hair.

"What did you do with your hands before you had your hair like that?" I asked him one day, referring to his nervous habit of twisting and tugging at his dreadlocks, which had not only begun to drive me crazy but, I was certain, increased the number of stray shower hairs.

Alfredo looked baffled for a moment, as if unsure of whether to take me seriously. Then a small smile crossed his face, and he raised his hands, spread-fingered and palms out in front of him, before turning them inward and, with a Tarzan howl, pounding them against his chest.

When Damaris said that she and Manolo would be sitting off to the side of Lialne's show, I had been so embarrassed at being caught in my wet-towel dispute with Alfredo that I hadn't stopped to consider how strange this sounded. But as Alfredo and I approached the outdoor dining room of

Restaurante El Patio and I saw the dentists seated in flimsy folding chairs near the kitchen, off to the side of the tourist tables, I was struck by the fundamental and all-too-familiar wrongness of this setup.

Alfredo and I grabbed a couple of chairs from a stack behind the dentists, and together we watched the two shows—the practiced, polished performance of Lialne's band and the impromptu display of the tourists, who had earned front-row seats by paying for their mojitos and strawberry daiquiris with dollars. When the first intoxicating trumpet notes of "El Chan Chan" began, the tourists pushed back their tables to dance a clumsy salsa, while we, without even the space to stand and sway, drummed our hands on our thighs, keeping time.

As I continued to wander the streets of Havana, unsuccessfully searching for work with the city's alphabet of acronym-ed agencies, from ICAIC and ICAP to UNEAC and UNESCO, I began noticing new and disturbing details of daily life.

It started with the men I met in the streets, whose clever pickup lines, originally disguised as offers of language exchanges or invitations to folkloric dance performances, had now transformed into less dignified and more desperate attempts at landing not just a date but a life with a foreign woman. At a street pizza stand, an older man with a son several years my elder proposed to me.

"Marry me now, and you won't have to put up with the immaturity of men your age anymore," he said, a sliver of pseudo-cheese grease sliding down his unshaven chin. "Come home with us for dinner," he said, taking my arm. "Spend the night, and you'll see what I mean."

I wrangled myself out of the old man's grip and cast his son, who was looking at me apologetically, a sympathetic glance.

Another day, as I passed by the Napoleon Museum, near the dentists' house, a man my age called out, "I've always wanted to marry a Spanish woman."

"I'm not Spanish," I said and, hoping to avoid the tired old, "*¿Italia? ¿Argentina? ¿Inglaterra?*" guessing game, I quickly added, "I'm from the U.S."

"Oh, the U.S.," the man said, excited. "Well, then, give me some dollars."

In the days following my encounter with these forthright men, I was asked for bread by a group of kids on Callejón de Hamel, for cooking oil by a man outside the San Lázaro *chopping*, and for medicine by a mother on the Malecón who told me her son suffered an illness whose name I couldn't understand.

Late one night, as Alfredo and I walked past the the Teatro Nacional, I spotted several people lying on their backs, staring up at the sky. I wondered whether there was some special meteorological event taking place, maybe an eclipse I hadn't heard about. But when I scanned the sky, all I saw were ordinary stars.

"What do you think they're looking at?" I asked Alfredo. The people were spread out as if they'd come separately, as if each one had been assigned to monitor a specific constellation.

"Look closer," Alfredo said.

I squinted my eyes, but still I couldn't see anything more.

"These people aren't looking at anything," Alfredo continued. "They're sleeping. *No tienen casas.*"

"Are you sure?" I asked. "I've never seen any homeless before. I thought there weren't any homeless in Cuba. I don't understand."

"*Es Cuba,*" Alfredo said, with a familiar shrug of his shoulders.

Alfredo's cool detachment, his lack of surprise at this sight, made me wonder how many other homeless I'd mistaken for stargazers, how much of what I'd just been so disturbed to discover was actually new. I remembered now how, when I had told Alfredo about the dead dog I'd seen, he had appeared unfazed then too.

"Oh, I see those all the time," he'd said dismissively. "Just yesterday I walked by one on a bench on El Prado."

I tried to content myself with the thought that, even if what I was noticing had been going on before, it was mild in comparison with the social situation in other Latin American countries I'd visited. Even in U.S. cities, while I had never seen a dead dog in such plain view, there were certainly many more slimy, scary men in the streets; more panhandlers asking for money and food; and, beneath the freeways, many, many more homeless than I'd seen at the Teatro Nacional.

Still, I couldn't shake the scenes of the past few days, nor could I silence the question that reverberated in my mind. Why now, after more than five months in Cuba, was I suddenly seeing this sadder, shadier side of the island?

In answering this, I felt I was also finally, definitively able to answer the question everyone had been asking about what had changed in Cuba since my last trip. Whereas earlier on I might have dismissed, overlooked, or made excuses for the situations I had just seen, at some point during this trip, I had stopped doing so. Just like with Dinora, it had taken me a while to be able and willing to see the truth.

It wasn't that anything had really changed in Cuba, but more that all along my relationship with the island had been changing—from romantic traveler to realist resident. It had been shifting as subtly as the Caribbean seasons, a slight breeze slowly morphing into still, stagnant air.

By the middle of November, the windstorms of my arrival had died down, replaced with a heat that rivaled that of when I'd left last June. In the evenings, the clouds rolled in, offering the illusion of relief, and Alfredo and I would walk down to the Malecón, hoping to be splashed by its spray.

One night at the start of our stroll, Alfredo turned to me and asked, "Do you like Cuba?"

Having spent the past hour poring over Alfredo's English homework with him, immersed in a conversation about participle phrases and misplaced modifiers, Alfredo's current question struck me as such a non sequitur that I just stared at him for a beat.

"What do you mean?" I asked finally. This was the type of question I would expect from a new acquaintance making small talk or some *jinetero* trying to pick me up on the street, but not from my Cuban boyfriend of the past nine months. "Why are you asking me this now?"

"Lea, *no te pongas molesta,*" don't be angry, Alfredo said, sensing my irritation. "*Es que, el otro día, un socio me preguntó,* it's just that the other day a friend asked me, 'Does your girlfriend like Cuba?' and, well, I know that you came down here to learn about Cuba and originally you stayed on because you liked it and then because you liked me. And I thought," he said pausing, "you came back for both reasons, but lately I haven't been so sure anymore. And honestly, I didn't know what to tell my friend."

"What do you mean?" I asked again, searching my mind for something I'd said or done recently that could have led to Alfredo's confusion. "Is this about my soap rationing joke?" I asked, recalling how I had used Alfredo's excessive showering as a front for criticizing the abrupt, extended closure of the *choppings* and, by extension, the situation in Cuba as a whole.

"No," Alfredo said. "Well, kind of. It's about that but also about how you always complain about your bedbug bites and the fumigation and the heat and your hunger and the blackouts and . . ."

"Everyone knows how much I love Cuba," I said, cutting Alfredo off, feeling simultaneously betrayed for having shared my thoughts with him and startled by how much of the complaining that I thought I'd internalized I had actually voiced.

"I think if you asked anyone who even casually knew me in the U.S. how I felt about Cuba, they'd say I was obsessed," I said. "When I was back home, I told everyone I knew about Cuba and the Revolution. I met people who didn't know there was free health care, and I told them about that. I brought my photo album everywhere. I even read a small-print, seven-hundred-page autobiography on Fidel. And I don't mean to offend you," I continued, "but you're mistaken if you've been thinking I'm here just for you. If I didn't like Cuba, I wouldn't have extended my stay this time to look for work."

To my surprise, Alfredo smiled in response to my rant. As I looked closer, I saw that there was a smirk to his smile, as if he was pleased with my passion but still didn't quite buy the performance.

"Cubans complain too," I tried again. "Even Dinora, whose husband is CDR president. And your grandmother, with that Creemos en la Revolución sticker on her door. Even you, who say you'd fight for Cuba if the U.S. tried to invade, complain often. Why can't I complain and still love it too?"

Alfredo looked thoughtfully at a crack in the sidewalk before responding. "I think," he said, carefully enunciating his words, "it's because you're not Cuban."

"Oh, no," I said. "Not that again."

Alfredo laughed. "What I mean," he said, "is that when Cubans complain,

it's like a habit. But your complaining has this sense of urgency, this seriousness, like you think that by criticizing something you can change it.
There's this sense of possibility that makes it all the more intense, that's
completely lacking in Cuban complaining. And I think it's because you're
not from here that you can afford to be so angry. It's because," he concluded, "you know you can leave."

Despite the implication at the end of Alfredo's eloquent delineation of Cuban
complaining, I had told myself when I'd set out on my job search that I wouldn't
consider leaving until I had exhausted all possibilities. And I still had one lead
left. When I inquired about work at ICAP, the Cuban Institute of Friendship
with the Peoples, the woman I spoke with had suggested I attend ICAP's Second World Meeting of Friendship and Solidarity, a five-day conference at the
Karl Marx Theater, or Teatro Carlo Mar, as the Cubans called it.

"You'll get to meet writers and translators from all over the world," the
woman had told me. "And maybe, with a little asking around, you'll find
someone who would like a translator stationed here."

On the first day of the conference, nearly four thousand people milled
about the Miramar theater, their chatty anticipation bouncing off the walls.
I sat down next to an older, distinguished man in a suit, planning to start my
networking with him. But after an extensive pantomime session, I discovered that he spoke neither Spanish nor English but rather some language
I couldn't identify, whose letters he showed me on his conference program.
He, like other non-Spanish-speaking attendees spread throughout the theater, had his headphones on so as not to miss a moment of the interpreted
talks. As I looked across the theater, I saw that everyone sat at attention with
their Cuban Solidarity pens poised above their official conference notebooks.
At their feet were the see-through plastic briefcases we'd been given, along
with a poster and T-shirt.

This was the biggest, most professional production I'd seen in Cuba, and
as a man walked onto the stage to initiate the conference, I felt the surrounding excitement reverberate through me.

In the first hour, I learned that, of the one hundred and thirty countries in attendance, the U.S. had brought the biggest delegation. I learned that to-day was also the twenty-fifth anniversary of the Cuban-backed Angolan in-dependence. I learned that only Israel and the U.S.-owned Marshall Islands supported the U.S. embargo. And in the next two hours before lunch, I heard variations of each of these statements repeated by different delegations in different languages.

After every speaker, as a verbal accompaniment to the applause, some-one would shout out, *"¡Patria o muerte!"* or *"¡Cuba sí, bloqueo no!"*, setting off several rounds of the refrain throughout the theater.

During lunch, I began to feel claustrophobic. Even as I sat in the fresh air on a bench overlooking the Caribbean, I was still surrounded by several thousand conference cheerleaders, many of whom greeted each other with a refrain from the morning chorus.

I suffered through the afternoon session, drawing doodles during the chants and trying to absorb as much as I could of the few new bits of infor-mation sprinkled throughout the speeches. When I stood to leave at the end of the day, I noticed the man next to me had fallen asleep.

On the second morning, I made it through the conference to half an hour before lunch, when I glanced down at my notes and saw that the only new thing I had learned during the past three hours was that the U.S. spent more money per capita on cosmetics each year than any other coun-try. The last thing I heard as I exited the theater was a delegation's chant of *"¡Que viva Cuba!"*, to which the audience responded with a resounding, *"¡Que viva Fidel!"*

When I stepped into the silent, sleepy streets of Miramar, I was momentarily disoriented by the stillness that surrounded me, the space. In the distance, I could hear the soft crash of the Caribbean, and I continued in that direction. I walked over to a pockmarked cement bench at the edge of the sea, where a handful of people waded in the brackish water, although most sat idly, star-ing out across the water.

A hot breeze swirled around me as I pulled my journal out of my back-pack, planning to jot down some of my thoughts. I got the date and location down and then the blue ink of my Cuban Solidarity pen, which had been scratchy from the start, dried up.

So I too turned my focus to the sea, and as I watched the waves retreat, my thoughts also drifted backward. I recalled my preconference conversation with Alfredo in which he had questioned my feelings about Cuba. In place of the defensiveness I had expressed in that moment, I now felt only a calm relief. It was as if just by posing his question, Alfredo had granted me a sort of permission—a permission, although I had forfeited it at the time, to say that I was irritated with the situation in Cuba. Alfredo's innocent question had opened a window in the wall of my discontent, and now, with no pen to record my feelings and no one around me to share them with, I chanted a silent song of longing to the sea.

I longed to leave the house without layers of oily sunscreen, to not have to walk one mile to find bread, a trash can, a store that sold soap (and that actually had it in stock). I longed to be free of drippy refrigerators and diesel exhaust, to wash my clothes in a functioning washing machine, to eat a burrito, to make a phone call without a neighbor picking up the extension every few minutes.

I felt embarrassed by my petty desires, which made me feel like the quintessential "Ugly American"—unappreciative of differences and wanting only what was easy. But then there was also my exhaustion over more substantial matters. I was tired of being sick so often, of being afraid of falling light fixtures and farmers market roofs, of running between balconies in summer and away from them in hurricane season. I was tired of the difficulty of finding email access so I could send my stories to editors in the U.S., and I was tired of this feeling that I was living my life, if not in slow motion, then more passively than I ever had before.

On my last visit to Hotel Nacional, the Internet had been working, and I had received an email from a former editor alerting me that she'd taken a job at a start-up magazine and was looking for a reporter. There was a notice from a writing contest that my story was now being considered in the final round of jurying. These two bits of news—neither of which offered any guarantee of future employment or publication—gave me the greatest sense of possibility that I'd had since my decision to try to stay on in Cuba, where new magazines didn't just start up and the few writing contests that existed were all sponsored by the state.

I thought about something else that Alfredo had said on that night when he'd called me on my complaining—his obvious comment about my not being Cuban. And I realized that, in the end, it all came down to *"Es Cuba"* and how Cubans used it to bracket their complaining, while I just complained, lacking the Cuban cultural context for rationalization, the national talent for accepting contradictions. When, I wondered, had *"Es Cuba"* gone from being comic to being a cop out?

I knew that Alfredo had been right when he'd told me that Cubans complained this way because it was their only recourse. My more frustrated complaining was a result of my foreign restlessness, although now I appeared as Cuban as the rest of them, staring out at the horizon like a hopeful *balsero* plotting the route for the inner tube that would take me away. I recalled the last time I'd looked out like this—a moment I had tried to push out of my mind ever since.

On my final day at Dinora's house, I had made one last ascent up to her *azotea* to retrieve the Trinidad coffee beans Alfredo and I had been drying in the sun. The view from the rooftop, like the view across the Caribbean now, had seemed endless. There had been people on every *azotea* just staring into the distance, reminding me of the exercises an eye doctor had suggested I do at twenty-minute intervals when using the computer. But I had known that none of these people had been using computers, and as I'd looked around me, I'd slowly realized that not only was I looking out at them as I always did, but they were looking out at me. They had looked at me as if I were one of them, caught in the same listless inertia, the lethargy and longing for something more. And it had scared me.

30

The Cuban Goodbye

When I returned home early and announced to Alfredo that I had decided to leave, a papaya he'd been slicing on the small stainless-steel kitchen counter slid onto the floor, its coral flesh splattering all over his bare feet.

"*¡Pinga, cojones!*" he cursed, stepping back from the offending fruit as he turned toward me, his face a mix of irritation and loss.

"Are you upset with me or your *fruta bomba*?" I joked.

"My *fruta bomba*," Alfredo said, his expression softening as he laughed. "I hadn't expected it to get away like that, but you, well, with you I already had my suspicions."

I stared at Alfredo, wrinkling my forehead in confusion. I had told him that I was leaving because, after the solidarity conference, I finally felt ready. Ready to return home and pursue my writing career there. Ready to acknowledge that my earlier decision to stay on in Cuba had been spurred both by the familiarity of our life here and by my fear of us failing as a couple in the U.S. Finally, after the frustrations of the past few weeks, I was ready to move beyond my fear and to risk testing out our relationship in my world.

But still, despite my clarity, I had expected Alfredo to appear a little shocked, to put up at least a small fuss over my premature departure. If nothing else, we had planned to spend New Year's Eve together in Cuba, and Alfredo had even told me that he had a surprise, a special place he would like to take me to celebrate.

"I felt bad after I asked if you liked Cuba, so I wasn't about to say anything else," Alfredo explained in response to my perplexed expression. "But I saw your frustration. I sensed that one day soon the life here was just going to be too much for you."

"Are you disappointed?" I asked.

"Of course," Alfredo said. "I was still holding out hope, but I knew it was a decision you had to come to on your own. And like you said before, you're not here just for me. You can't stay on just because I want you to. Especially," he added, casting me a knowing glance, "if staying on is going to make you not be nice to me."

"I've been nice to you," I said.

"Eeew!" Alfredo said in a high-pitched voice, pinching an imaginary towel between his thumb and index finger and holding it out to me. "You got the towel all wet when you dried off with it."

I burst out laughing, and soon we were both wiping tears off our faces.

"So what about the writing workshop?" Alfredo asked when he caught his breath, and I realized that with all my heightened focus on finding a job, I had nearly forgotten the reason why I'd decided to look for one in the first place.

"I guess I won't be going," I said.

"Okay, then we'll just have to go with our original plan," Alfredo said, exhaling slowly. "We'll wait to hear back about the fiancé visa, and in the meantime, we'll talk whenever we can. We managed to communicate okay before, right? And, *imagínate,* that was often without phone or email. And now our relationship is stronger than it was before, so things can only be easier this time around."

I stood momentarily stunned by the polished quality of Alfredo's pep talk.

"Have you been rehearsing that?" I asked.

"No," he said, smiling. "But I am right, aren't I?"

I nodded.

"So," Alfredo said, quickly averting his eyes. "You don't have to leave this week, do you?"

"No," I said. "But my visa does expire in a week. I'd have to leave by next Wednesday at the latest."

"Oh, that's perfect," Alfredo said. "Then I can take you to that special place I'd wanted to go on New Year's Eve."

"Will we need marriage papers?" I asked.

"No. No, it won't be anything like Trinidad," Alfredo said, laughing at my joke. "It'll be a Cuban vacation," he said and then, more seriously, "A Cuban goodbye."

Alfredo, who preferred small groups, surprised me by inviting every friend I'd ever made in Havana for our Cuban goodbye. He invited Liudmila, and—following through on his long-ago conversation with the Scandinavians about us all taking a trip together—he also asked Kajsa (who now lived in our bedroom at Dinora's), and Mielikki and the Danes, as well as the German guy and the Swiss woman who'd replaced them.

"Come join us on a Cuban vacation," Alfredo had entreated each of them, his voice so cheery he reminded me of those overly zealous telemarketers who left messages about free trips to Disney World, the beep of the answering machine always cutting off the catch.

Only the German guy and the Swiss woman were able to accompany us on our cryptic Cuban vacation, the whereabouts of which Alfredo insisted on keeping secret until we left. On the train ride over, he revealed that we were heading in the direction of Varadero. Rather than appease my curiosity, this news only made me want to know more, since Varadero was the beach Frank Delgado had sung of in his symphony concert, lamenting that this former Cuban vacation spot was now only for tourists.

"I thought you said Cubans didn't take vacations anymore, that there wasn't any place they could go," I questioned Alfredo shortly after our train had come to a screeching stop, the conductor ushering everyone into an empty field ringed by a forest of palms. Here he'd informed us that a bus would arrive in an hour for the second leg of our trip.

"Most Cubans don't go on vacations now because there are too many problems they have to resolve at home," Alfredo said. "But there are still a few places they're allowed to stay if they can get there. Does that make sense?"

"Sort of," I said. At the edge of the field, a cow emerged from the palms and swaggered across the grass, only mildly interested in the humans spread out over its grazing ground. "So where exactly is it that we're going?"

"We're going to a *campismo,*" Alfredo said. "Do you know what that is?" I shook my head.

"Aha," Alfredo said triumphantly as if I'd just given up on the last question of a guessing game. "I didn't think so. I doubt there's any information about *campismos* in your trusty guidebook. They're cabins that were built after the Revolution so Cubans could have affordable places to vacation in the country."

"I've been to this one at Peñas Blancas once, but not since I was very young," he continued. "I went there with my dad and sister right after my parents divorced. I can hardly recall what we did there anymore." Alfredo paused, searching his memory. "But what I do remember," he said dreamily, "is that it was just like paradise."

On the connecting bus to Peñas Blancas, when Niko and Petra tried to pay Alfredo for their bus tickets and cabins, which he'd paid for in advance, he waved his hand dismissively.

"I just got paid, and besides," he added proudly, "I invited you. In the city, foreigners invite Cubans out to dollar bars and clubs, but at the *campismos,* everything's still in pesos. Here, you are my guests."

When our bus descended a curvy road, revealing a grassy outcropping dotted with sky-blue shuttered cabins backed by a turquoise and, farther out, midnight-blue sea, I instantly understood Alfredo's pride and quickly forgave him his telemarketer sales pitch.

A pair of white horses raced each other along the beach, and on a sandy side street, Cuban couples strolled between the palm trees. As we stepped off the bus, Alfredo spread his arms, announcing, *"Bienvenidos a Peñas Blancas."*

"It's very beautiful," Petra said.

"Thank you," Alfredo responded, beaming as if he had created the landscape himself.

On our walk to the cabins, he filled us in on their history.

"They were constructed by the Soviets, but as you can see, they're smaller and more tasteful than the Russian buildings in Havana. The cabins I reserved are close to the beach but a little set apart from the others. Some cabins have a separate bathroom you have to walk to, and some have shared baths between them, but each of ours has a private bathroom. I got the fancy ones."

Yet when Alfredo unlocked the door to our cabin, a dingy sewer scent wafted through the dark cubicle, which, behind its soothing blue facade, was cinderblock gray. Alfredo flipped on the light switch, and a solitary naked bulb glared down from the center of the ceiling, illuminating an oblong brown stain on the sheetless, shapeless mattress that lay on the cement floor.

Save for a lopsided bunk-bed frame leaning against the wall, there was nothing else in the cabin, which filled me with a small sense of hope.

"Do you think we were assigned the wrong cabin? Maybe this is one that's undergoing repairs," I said to Alfredo. "I don't even see a bathroom."

"Me neither," he said, stepping inside to inspect while I stood tentatively on the front step.

"I guess it has been twenty years since I've been here," he said apologetically as he walked toward the back of the cabin.

A few moments later, I heard Alfredo call out, a disembodied voice, his figure concealed in a shadowy corner. "Oh, here's the bathroom. I can feel a doorknob."

There was a popping sound and then a flash of light, followed by a small gasp and the resounding echo of a door being slammed shut.

"What happened?" I asked from the safety of my step. "That wasn't the bathroom?"

"Oh, no, unfortunately it was," Alfredo said, walking into the light. When he reached me, he put his arm around my shoulders and said, "We're still going to have a good time, but I think maybe we should just plan to bathe in the sea."

We swam each morning of our three-day stay at Peñas Blancas, floating on our backs and trying to name the animals formed by the clouds above. In the afternoons, we took long walks by the sea, stepping over the *aguas malas*, neon-blue jellyfish scattered along the shoreline like deflated balloons. I wrote in my journal and read beneath a thick-trunked palm while Alfredo braved the bare backs of the near-wild horses I'd admired on our arrival.

In the late afternoon, we waited in line at a tiny food kiosk, which began serving chicken fried rice and mango popsicles at four, running out by five. There were no plates or napkins or utensils, so Alfredo and I ate directly from the oily plastic bags in which our meals were delivered. I chopped up some tomatoes we'd brought and dumped them in, using a fork we'd borrowed from the dentists to forage around for some chicken-free grains of rice.

Evenings, we joined Petra and Niko and our neighboring Cubans at a communal table outside the cabins. We drank rum out of the bottle, and by the faint light of the naked bulb shining through our open upstairs door, we played dominoes while the Caribbean crashed behind us.

At sunset on our last day, beneath a slowly rising crescent moon, Alfredo and I descended a jungly mountain that we had hiked up that afternoon, just in time to witness the eclipse of all the lights in Peñas Blancas. One moment there was a small, starlike flickering emanating from the cabin windows below, and the next, there was only darkness and a stunned silence, soon followed by defiant shouts of *"¡Coño!"* and *"¡Candela!"*

By the time we reached the cabins, guided by the light from a solitary pink streak in the sky, the outcry had died down and a shadowy stillness surrounded us.

I unlocked our door, and we entered the pitch-black cubicle, making our way to the mattress, where we sat without speaking, taking in the quiet. I'd become used to falling asleep to some salsa song I'd heard too many times blaring from our neighbors' boom boxes, my head resting on the narrow, fleshy underside of Alfredo's arm, which he silently offered me in place of a pillow. Tonight, I listened to the swift ripple of the wind against the cabin's corrugated aluminum roof, felt the unexpected touch of Alfredo's hand as he ran it gently along my body, searching for my hand.

"What are you thinking about?" he asked as he wove his fingers between mine.

"My return," I said, although this wasn't exactly true. Rather, I was thinking about how unimaginable my return was. How very surreal and sad it was to think that, in less than sixty hours, I would be on an airplane leaving Cuba, that in less than seventy, I'd be back home in California—a world away from where I was now, not knowing when Alfredo and I would see each other again.

"I've been thinking about your leaving too," Alfredo said softly. "I've been wanting to talk about it." He paused, and I wondered whether his eyes were open or whether, like me, he'd closed them, preferring the known dark to the mysterious murkiness of the *apagón*.

"What will you do if there's still no news about the fiancé visa when you get back?" Alfredo asked.

"Well, I know that one of the forms I filled out said not to call about its status," I said. "So I guess all we can do is start preparing as if it's going to be approved."

"I'll try to learn as much English as I can," Alfredo said. "Maybe I can take an extra class each week. And I'll get a letter of recommendation from my symphony director. Maybe he knows someone at the symphony in San Francisco, and maybe they'll need a lights technician."

Immediately, I recalled my old fear about destroying Alfredo's uncomplicated view of the world by introducing him to life in a capitalist country. I felt a rush of protectiveness, a desire to shield him from the inevitable, disillusioning challenges he'd face as an immigrant.

But also, something about Alfredo's eagerness to try out this new life made me realize that this fear of mine was not justification enough for prematurely abandoning the possibility of our having a future in the U.S. I understood now that to do so, to deny Alfredo the experience of living with me in the U.S. because I was afraid of how it might transform him, would be akin to Fidel's paternalistic dealings with his people, which so limited and frustrated them that any good intentions he might have had were now difficult to see.

"That's a good idea," I told Alfredo. "It might not be so easy to get a job at the symphony, but it's worth a try. And I'll ask around to see if any of my friends know of any under-the-table jobs."

"And what," Alfredo said hesitantly, "what if the fiancé visa doesn't come through?"

"Then we'll just have to find out whether we can apply again or appeal the decision," I said.

Instinctively, as if we were having a conversation in a place without *apagones*, where light from the street filtered in through a window at night, I opened my eyes, wanting to see the expression on Alfredo's face as I spoke. But the room was just as dark as before I'd closed my eyes, and Alfredo remained an auditory but unseen presence.

"Are your eyes open now?" I asked.

"*Sí, mi amor,*" he said. "They've been open all along."

The electricity came back soon after Alfredo and I drifted off, flooding our bed with light from the naked bulb above. For a moment, before I remembered that I'd bumped into the light switch when I was searching for my backpack in the dark, I was startled. But the rush of light brought with it something far more startling. Covering every free inch of the floor and writhing their way up the walls, an army of cockroaches advanced on our mattress.

Not usually squeamish around insects, I screamed, and Alfredo jumped to attention, shaking out the shoes next to the mattress before slipping them on and running from one corner of the room to the other, stomping his feet like a crazy man. The cockroaches scattered into their dark holes, where they hid during the day.

Although I insisted we sleep with the lights on, I continued to wake at regular intervals, imagining something slithering up my leg.

On my first morning back in Havana, my last full day in Cuba, Dinora called me at the dentists' house. I had bumped into her on Soledad Street before leaving for Peñas Blancas and, as a goodbye, we had made plans to see a movie playing at the European film festival this afternoon.

"Are you hungry?" Dinora asked me now, static rippling through her voice, even though she was less than ten blocks away. "I'm making a vegetarian lunch. Why don't you come over early? Abuela wanted to say goodbye too."

When I got to her house, Dinora handed me a leather clasp purse with a jagged mosaic print of autumn-colored triangles, which reminded me of stained glass.

"Thank you. It's beautiful," I said. I'd seen the purse before, passing by La Rampa's artisan market, where everything was sold in dollars.

"It's just a small present," Dinora said. "A token to remember me by."

Abuela joined us for lunch in the dining room, where I was relieved to discover that Dinora's and Luis's bed was gone.

"Is this real vegetarian?" I teased Dinora as she shuffled around the table, serving Abuela and me a soup that resembled a vegetarian minestrone but, given Dinora's history of hiding meat in food she prepared for me, could very well have been chicken-based.

"No, no meat at all. I swear, not even a bone for flavor," Dinora said. "Look," she handed me a spoon and had me stir it around to see that there was nothing hard for it to clink against.

"I had fun making it," Dinora said, adding airily, "Maybe someday I'll become a vegetarian too."

I smiled at her sentiment.

"Don't laugh," Dinora said. "It's possible. Before I met you, if someone had suggested such a thing, I would've said they were crazy, but now . . ." Dinora's voice trailed off.

"Lea, I've learned so much from you," she said, and I tried not to notice the gloss in her eyes. "Well," she continued, "we should have our soup before it gets cold."

~~~~~~

On our walk to Cine La Rampa, Dinora questioned me about my job search.

"So you couldn't find work?" she asked. "Is that why you decided to leave?"

I nodded to the first question, and before I could decide how to address the second, Dinora spoke again.

"Yes, it's difficult," she said. "Look at me. All my education, and I'm still a housewife."

I nodded again, although this seemed a strange thing to say when Dinora had left her job of her own will, going out of her way to pay her doctor for a diagnosis of mental illness. Whether she'd avoided returning because of her mother or because she was afraid of being in the place that had housed her youthful, idealistic dreams, I didn't really know. And maybe she didn't either.

I didn't voice my thoughts though, because by refraining from directly answering Dinora's second question, about why I decided to leave, I too was not telling the whole story. Saying I was leaving because I could not find work was the least messy, most dignified way of explaining my departure. But in truth—just as the fact that my room had been rented out was only part of the reason I'd left Dinora's house—I was now leaving her country partly because I couldn't get work, and partly because I no longer knew that I wanted it.

Perhaps neither of us really believed the other's stories, but we let it slide, content with our half-truths. When we got to the theater, we found it closed due to an *apagón*.

"*Si no es Juana, es su hermana,*" Dinora said, the Cuban equivalent of "If it's not one thing then it's the other."

I accompanied Dinora back to her house, and I told her about the *apagón* at Peñas Blancas, about the frightening bathroom, the menial food rations. She shook her head in disgust when I got to the part about the cockroaches.

"Maybe you made the right decision to go home," she said, laughing.

When we said our goodbyes on Animas Street, she told me, "I'm going to pretend you're coming back soon, and I'm going to try not to be too sad now. Write me whenever you know someone who can bring a letter to Cuba." She paused for a moment before adding, "And tell Alfredo not to be a stranger."

"I will," I said and, suddenly feeling bad for only having complained about my Cuban goodbye trip, I added, "The beach at Peñas Blancas was beautiful, and the weather too. We swam every day."

"Well, thank God for that," Dinora said, rolling her eyes. "What would this country do without its good weather?"

From Dinora's house, I headed for the sea, for my final walk along the Malecón. I stepped up onto the chalky white wall, intimately familiar with each of its crevices and cracks. I sauntered across this thick plank walk separating island from infinity, an invisible proximity to Miami. I stared out at the sapphire sea and walked all the way to Hotel Riviera in Vedado, stepping around schoolchildren and elderly women.

On the way back, when I jumped down near a twenty-something fisherman just feet from where I'd begun, caught up in the spell of the Malecón, I said, "*¿Qué día más lindo, no?*" The fisherman smiled at me, but it was a distant smile, both dreamy and disillusioned, which, even so, hardly prepared me for his response.

"Yeah, it's a beautiful day," he said, now a full-blown smirk on his face as he looked out past his line, past the Morro lighthouse to the open, empty sea, and added, in that quintessentially, contradictory Cuban way, "It's a beautiful day to escape."

At the dentists' house, I packed my duffel bag, biding my time until my next goodbye.

In an hour, Liudmila would be stopping by on her way home from the university, and I wanted to sort through my belongings to see what I might offer her, disguising it as something I couldn't fit in my duffel bag. Already, after Alfredo had commented on how well all the letters I wrote him from the U.S. would fit into the plastic briefcase from the solidarity conference, I'd set it aside for him.

My giveaway plan backfired with Liudmila, who, instead of accepting my unused bottle of shampoo and nearly new tube of toothpaste, rose to the challenge of fitting them into my duffel bag. Despite having never traveled anywhere, Liudmila was much better at packing than I was. To save space, she rolled my clothes rather than folding them, and she equally distributed my heavier items throughout the duffel bag.

"How did you learn this?" I asked her.

"A friend of my mother's showed me. He's a musician, so he's traveled a lot," Liudmila said. Alfredo, too, had been taught how to pack by a musician friend.

I imagined a Cuban welcome-back party where, instead of sharing photos or videos, returning travelers wheeled out their suitcases to demonstrate their packing prowess for their friends and family.

As Liudmila and I left the bedroom, my packing complete, I noticed her eyeing my solidarity conference T-shirt, which I'd laid out on the bed to wear on the airplane.

"Oh, what a pretty shirt," she said, admiring the silkscreen of different colored hands overlapping above the red, white, and blue of the Cuban flag. "We forgot to pack it. Or were you going to leave it here?"

Recognizing a glimmer of hope in Liudmila's voice, I quickly pulled the shirt off the bed.

"If we stuff anything else in that duffel bag, I'm afraid it'll explode," I said, handing her the shirt. "So please, give this to someone who'll use it."

When my alarm clock sounded at six-thirty on the morning of my flight, as much as I wanted to shut off its shrill ring, I felt incapable of movement, scared into stillness by the slowly dawning reality of my departure. Something about the timelessness of sleep and the disorientation of the early morning made it difficult to believe that this was it. My final morning of waking with bedbug bites and the bright November sun streaming in through an open window, with the sounds of salsa and the screechy *camello* brakes. With Alfredo.

My flight was to leave at ten, and although we'd reserved a taxi the day before for eight, by eight-thirty, it still hadn't arrived.

Alfredo called the dispatch every ten minutes, and every time they told him it was on its way. In between calls, he paced back and forth along the dentists' tiny street-side balcony.

"If it doesn't come in ten more minutes, maybe we should just bribe a *taxi particular* to take us to the airport," I suggested.

"*¡Cojones!*" Alfredo said, slamming his hand down on the balcony. For a moment I was afraid I'd offended him with my suggestion. But then I noticed the distant look in his eyes that I'd become familiar with by now, and I knew his anger originated within, from something he'd been thinking about well before I spoke.

"Socialism has a lot of good things," Alfredo said. "The health care, the education, the van that takes me to work for free each day . . . but look at this taxi. It makes you wonder, if under socialism everyone gets paid the same whether they do their job or not, who's going to be motivated to do a good job? Do you think we'll ever be able to get ahead like this, when there's no professionalism anywhere?"

Without waiting for an answer, Alfredo shook his head. "Sometimes I think this country has a curse on it," he said. "Sometimes I think someone said, 'You can have palm trees and sea and sun, but you'll have to suffer a leader who wants to control everything.'"

At the conclusion of Alfredo's rant, our taxi driver arrived.

"*Lo siento,*" he apologized as he called up to us, leaning across to the passenger window as he skidded to a stop beneath the balcony. "*No es fácil.*"

As he met us at the front door, holding out his hands for my luggage, he muttered something I couldn't completely understand about a flat tire and police harassment.

"*Lo siento,*" he repeated as he lifted my oversized suitcase into the back seat. "The trunk won't open."

I squeezed into the back, and Alfredo slid into the passenger seat. We drove in silence through the center of Havana, my hand on Alfredo's shoulder and his hand on top of mine.

At the airport, after I paid the *taxista,* he once again mumbled something I couldn't catch, but which made Alfredo laugh.

"She's the one leaving, *socio,*" Alfredo said, pointing to me. "I still need my sandals."

As we walked to the terminal, I examined the Timberland sandals I'd sent Alfredo with a Cuba courier. "What was that about?" I asked.

"He said he wouldn't charge us for the ride if I gave him my sandals," Alfredo said.

"How could he get away with that?"

"*Es Cuba,*" Alfredo said.

When we got to the check-in counter, Luis was standing there in his crisp, white-and-blue Cubana uniform, holding an airline barf bag, the edge of it rolled up tightly in his fist.

"I'm working your flight," Luis said, smiling as he walked over and shook hands with Alfredo. "Someone called in sick this morning, so here I am."

"Dinora was in a panic rushing to write you a goodbye note when she found out," he said. "I had to go before she could find a pen, but she made me promise to pick up a little present for you."

Luis extended the barf bag with a nervous laugh. "It's not much," he said. "But, well, it's all I could think of given the short notice."

I opened the bag to find a pack of peanuts and two Cristal beers.

"Don't be sad," Luis said. "Be drunk."

He gave me a quick kiss on the cheek, another handshake for Alfredo, and then he rushed off past check-in, past the airport tax counter, and past the thick white doors backing the immigration stand, beyond which only passengers and airline employees could enter.

"Wow, look at that," Alfredo said excitedly, more intrigued by Luis's exit than by his barf-bag present. "Did you see how he just walked through the immigration doors?"

"Well, he does work here."

"I know that," Alfredo said. "It's just, you're the only person I've known that I've ever seen go to the other side."

"What about your dad?" I asked. "When he left?"

"Oh, right," Alfredo said, animated again. "That's true. It was a different terminal, but he walked through a door just like this for his international flight." Alfredo said the last two words slowly, like he was rolling around marbles on his tongue. "Those aren't words I get to use very often," he said.

I nodded.

Alfredo accompanied me to pay my airport tax, and then we walked over to immigration, where several people were already in line. In a way, I'd hoped to be the only one—less time for goodbyes, but also less time to be sad.

I had made a pact with myself to not cry, but now, as Alfredo and I faced each other and he put his hands on my shoulders, looking me in the eye, I felt my heartbeat speed up, and I sensed the start of that nose burn that always preceded my tears. Determined not to go it alone, I looked Alfredo back in the eye and demanded to know why he wasn't crying. Immediately, as his red-tinged eyes welled up with water and his voice got scratchy, I felt sorry.

"Because I didn't want to," Alfredo said, openly sobbing now. "Because then I have to walk alone through the airport crying, and it . . ." he paused, gulping in his breath, "it just makes everything worse."

I too was crying now, fat, silent tears as the immigration woman called me up. I kissed Alfredo, and he held on to me so tightly, I could feel the imprints of his fingers when he let go.

The immigration woman tried to avoid my eyes as she asked for my passport, her voice trained and cool. After she copied down the information she needed and returned my passport, she told me to walk through the door. I turned to take one last look at Alfredo.

"I'll call you," I said, wiping away my tears. "At your grandmother's, nine o'clock your time tonight."

Alfredo nodded and motioned for me to come over.

"Un minuto," I told the immigration woman as I turned, but just as I stepped over the white line of tape toward Alfredo, the woman let out a shriek.

"No!" she yelled. "Not with your passport. *Dame tu pasaporte."*

I turned again, my heart beating so fast now that I wasn't sure I could speak.

"I'm sorry," I said, taking a big breath, trying to swallow my sobs. I handed her my passport. "Please, just one second. I think he wants to tell me something."

The woman nodded. "It's okay," she said, calmer now. "Just be quick."

I ran over to Alfredo.

"I just wanted to say," he said. "After you left last time, I went up there." Alfredo pointed to a staircase leading to the airport's second floor. "I saw you after you went through the doors. And I was thinking now, if you want, I can go upstairs and we can wave to each other as you walk away."

"No," I said immediately. "That's not a good idea. Someone might get suspicious, and besides, it's just too . . . sad. We just have to say goodbye now."

"Okay," Alfredo said, sounding somewhat relieved. "But just . . . just pay attention to the details. Lea, tell me . . ."

From her stand a few feet away, the immigration woman interrupted us, ordering me to come now or never. I ran back over the white line, retrieved my passport, put my hand on the heavy, knobless door, and pushed hard. Quickly, I turned to wave goodbye to Alfredo.

"Tell you what?" I called out, stepping behind the door, which slid past my hand, revealing only a sliver of Alfredo's tear-streaked face.

He waved back, calling out from behind the line, "Tell me what it's like on the other side."

Epilogue:
The Other Side

On September 22, 2001, ten months after our teary goodbye at the José Martí International Airport, two months after Alfredo's visa had been approved, and eleven days after the collapse of the World Trade Center, Alfredo arrived in the U.S.

It was not the best of times to be flying, especially for someone who had never been higher than the top floor of Havana's thirty-five-story Focsa building. Even then, Alfredo had felt queasy looking out the window at his hometown.

It wasn't an ideal time to be meeting someone at the airport either. The week before Alfredo's trip, the weekly Havana-to-Los Angeles flight—for Cubans bearing fiancé and musician visas or *bombo* lottery passes and other special government permission—had been canceled. It wasn't until the day before Alfredo was to arrive that I knew for sure that he was coming.

Pulling into the LAX parking lot, after six hours of Interstate 5–induced monotony and self-supplied nervousness (ranging from specific and immediate worries about Alfredo's flight to more vague and distant concerns about how he would adapt to life in my world), I suddenly realized I hadn't stopped to pee.

The desire to do so only grew greater as I followed a sign that redirected me to the long-term parking lot, and then, counting the minutes until I'd be in a bathroom, I boarded a shuttle to what I assumed would be the international pickup terminal. Once aboard, though, I learned that only passengers were being allowed inside the airport. Everyone else had to wait in a centralized parking lot, where the passengers would be bused after they'd made it through the heightened customs and immigration security searches—which, according to our driver, could take upward of an hour.

Alfredo's flight was scheduled to arrive at 8 PM and, to allow time for traffic, I'd gotten to the airport at seven. I'd brought a book and some snacks, but under the enormous tents where hundreds of people huddled like refugees, rushing each passenger bus as it stopped and shouting out in a mismatch of different languages, there was neither the quiet to read nor the room to eat. And nowhere, as far as I could see across this darkening encampment, was there a porta-potty.

All my earlier worries about Alfredo and me in the U.S. were now eclipsed by a dual fear of peeing on myself and missing his arrival. I stood as close to the edge of the roped-in waiting area as possible, only moving back when a security guard across the way shot me a wayward glance.

As the air cooled, I rubbed my shivering legs together, regretting my decision to wear a dress. Without a watch or anyone nearby with whom I shared a language and could commiserate with about the situation, the time passed in a vacuum, forty-five minutes indecipherable from seventy-five, two hours an infinity.

To keep myself busy, I counted buses, trying to guess the nationality of their occupants. Bus 4 had Asians, bus 7 was full of French-speakers, and bus 9 contained several Italians, an elderly Russian couple and, at the very end of the passenger parade, one bewildered Cuban.

Alfredo's eyes anxiously scanned the crowd until he saw me, and then he immediately readjusted the medium-size duffel bag slung over his shoulder and came running toward me.

"How was the flight?" I asked him as we hugged.

"*Me encantó,*" Alfredo said, beaming. "*Qué grande es el mundo, qué lindo.*" The world is so big, so beautiful.

"So you weren't scared at all?" I asked.

"No," Alfredo said, solemnly shaking his head. "I think I was born to fly."

He kissed me on my lips and on my forehead, and then his forehead tilted up to the Los Angeles sky, which remained eerily light, a hazy blue-gray even so many hours past sunset.

"Where are all the stars?" Alfredo asked, and I remembered how he had stared up at them in Havana before our first kiss.

"They're there," I said, wishing he could have flown directly into San Francisco. "They're just difficult to see because Los Angeles is so polluted."

Alfredo raised his eyebrows in disbelief, his eyes widening as he looked behind me, past the parking lot to the bumper-to-bumper traffic merging onto the freeway.

"Is that the street?" he asked. "Are those all cars?"

"It's like a different world, isn't it?" I asked.

"*Like,*" he said, laughing. "It *is* a different world."

Alfredo and I spent his first week in the U.S. traveling up the coast of California, visiting friends of mine in Los Angeles, camping in Big Sur, and stopping in Santa Cruz to see another friend. Then we cut inland to the I-5 and drove north to the chilly peak of Mt. Shasta, where Alfredo had me photograph him holding his first snowball.

I had more planned, too—a backpacking trip in Point Reyes, a stay in a cabin above Stinson Beach—but I could also see that, as much as Alfredo was enjoying my real-life show-and-tell, he was also more than a little overwhelmed by all he'd seen and experienced in the past week. He was jetlagged and culture-shocked and, in seemingly unrelated moments that caught me off-guard with both their timing and their poignancy, homesick. At a campsite beneath Mt. Shasta, as we were staring, mesmerized into the red-blue flames of our bonfire, Alfredo suddenly announced, "I miss my *abuela.*"

On the ride south through Marin County, with each business or storefront we passed, Alfredo asked, as he'd done numerous times on the ride north, "*¿Del gobierno o particular?*"

When I replied that most of these businesses were owned by individuals or private corporations rather than the government, Alfredo once again widened his eyes in amazement and then launched into a new round of questions.

"What about the roads?" he inquired. "And the airports? And the banks?"

"And the water, who owns all this water?" he asked in Sausalito, looking out at the Richardson Bay as we walked down the dock to the houseboat studio that would be our new home.

I had moved in just a few days before I'd left for Los Angeles and, as much as I'd tried to organize my many belongings in the small space, multiple boxes had remained unpacked when I'd left. My mother had offered to bring some plants over while I was away, and my father, who in his own quiet way had eventually come around to the idea of Alfredo's arrival, had offered to construct a closet for him under our loft bed. Now I held my breath as we approached the front door.

"It's tiny," I said. "But really, I think it'll be comfortable once everything's in order."

I opened the sliding glass door and pulled up the shade as the September sun spilled over a futon sofa with a crisp white sheet cover. A fern hung from a hook in the redwood ceiling, its feathery fronds swaying in the slight breeze created by our entrance. The stereo had been installed, its speakers no longer cluttering the floor but now attached to the top of the wall. There was a bouquet of sunflowers on the coffee table where we would eat our meals, and the sooty wood stove had been cleaned out.

"It's beautiful," Alfredo declared, dropping to the floor pushup style and, like a sailor reaching land, planting a kiss on the white berber rug.

"Well, I'm glad it has your blessing," I said, laughing with relief.

"Yes, I can see us being very happy here," Alfredo said, standing up. He spun around to take in the full view of the studio, his eyes settling on the sleeping loft, which, with its packed bookshelves jutting out over a good quarter of the queen-sized futon, looked more like a reading nook than a bedroom.

Alfredo turned toward the side window, where an outdoor staircase led to our landlord's apartment, which ran the length of our studio and a neighboring one.

"So," he said, smiling expectantly. "Are you going to give me the upstairs tour? Is that where our bedroom is?"

Slowly, we settled into a shared life in our cramped sleeping compartment (Alfredo was always colliding with the bookshelves in his sleep). Our bathroom was barely big enough for one person to turn around in.

Unlike when I'd returned to Cuba, our adjustment in the U.S. was more than a matter of merely catching up on what had happened while we'd been apart. Now, in addition to getting used to being with each other again, Alfredo and I had to get used to the new world we were inhabiting together.

In this landscape, so physically and politically foreign from the one we'd met in, I often felt like we were recreating our relationship down to the very rhythm of how we talked to each other.

Alfredo was so excited about the English classes I had signed him up for, so eager to learn the language being spoken around him, that he instructed me to address him only in English. He covered his ears when I slipped into Spanish.

With other changes, though, Alfredo was not so quick to adjust. He acquiesced to using a washing machine but was afraid of dryers, preferring instead to erect a clothesline across our studio. He was scared of spicy foods, which had not crossed the Caribbean from Mexico to Cuba, and broke out into a sweat while eating his first burrito, ordered with mild salsa. He was horrified by hot tubs, looking at me as if I planned to cook him alive when I took him to one as a surprise for his twenty-eighth birthday. And whereas I had often been terrified of the toilets in Cuba, Alfredo was now traumatized by the telephones in the U.S., which often rang more in a day than they did in a week in Cuba.

When he answered the phone while I was out, Alfredo couldn't understand most of the messages my callers gave him. After one caller, who must have assumed she had reached the wrong number, hung up on him, Alfredo discovered the answering machine. Once he realized that the machine would essentially pick up the phone for him, Alfredo abandoned answering it altogether.

This inventory of fears was matched only by the multitude of services and gadgets and natural phenomena that fascinated Alfredo. He was so taken by our mailbox that he checked it several times each day, including Sundays and holidays, on the off chance that a letter for him had been misplaced in a neighbor's mailbox and was now being returned. He was amazed by my backpacking stove, declaring it *una maravilla* the first time he witnessed it boil a pot of water. But by far the most exciting discovery for Alfredo was static electricity, something that hadn't existed in his hot, humid homeland.

"*Mira,* Lea," he'd say, motioning for me to look as he pulled a polyester hiking shirt I'd given him on and off. "*Escucha,*" he'd add, tapping his ear and putting his index finger to his mouth to hush me so we wouldn't miss the quick, sharp zapping sound of the static. And then, as he did each time the car door shocked him, Alfredo would break into a smile.

Just as I didn't know how to predict or react to Alfredo's widely varying responses to life in the U.S., he sometimes seemed equally unsure of which emotion to commit to.

While clear on his dislike of the national health care system and my country's custom of segregated neighborhoods, Alfredo was alternately enthralled and appalled by all the goods—from cashmere sweaters to functioning computers—that our neighbors discarded daily in a communal grab box by our dumpster.

"Can you imagine what people in Cuba could do with just half of this stuff?" he'd ask, shaking his head dejectedly.

Yet despite this initial despair or perhaps because of it, Alfredo set about salvaging everything he could. He filled the small closet beneath our sleeping loft with sunglasses for his friends, an answering machine for his mother, an unopened package of butterfly-shaped candles for his grandmother, a pair of child's Nikes (which he called "Neeks") for his nephew, and several skirts for his sister.

Underlying the question of how Alfredo would be able to transport his burgeoning collection to Cuba was the greater question of when, and whether, he would be returning—which, in turn, was inextricably linked with the as-of-yet-undetermined future of our relationship.

Essentially, for a cost of fifteen hundred dollars (including plane fare, paper processing, and Alfredo's physical exit exam), our fiancé visa had bought us three months to decide whether we could make a life together in the U.S.

Our time limitation made me recall the night in Cuba when Alfredo had invited me out for a drink, but we'd gotten a late start and all the peso bars had turned into *fula* bars for the evening tourist crowd.

Now in the U.S., with each passing day, I was reminded that if we didn't make a decision soon and act on it quickly, Alfredo would have to return to Cuba with no possibility of coming back to the U.S. Just like that, the curtains would drop on us midscene. Our movie would be over, our coach a pumpkin once more. I didn't even attempt to share my Cinderella metaphor with Alfredo this time.

For Alfredo, the decision was obvious and easy. Just as he'd responded, "Whenever you're ready," when, after finding our houseboat studio, I had called him to ask when he thought he could come out, Alfredo was now ready to get married whenever I was. Although he wasn't sure how he felt about the U.S., he knew he was in love with me, and from there, he believed everything else would fall into place.

Unfortunately, my love for Alfredo didn't alleviate my worries about our future. Often, it actually seemed to exacerbate them, my mind working double time to counter each quality I admired in Alfredo with a corresponding concern.

Alfredo had arrived in the U.S. with just three dollars, of an original hundred dollars I'd sent him for exit expenses. He was unable to work legally with his fiancé visa. So, just as Alfredo had introduced me to the underground economy in Cuba, I did the same for him in the U.S., finding him work painting houses and doing construction with friends and friends of friends. But since Alfredo barely earned enough from these temporary jobs to help out with groceries, he decided to save money the only way he could—by not spending it.

One day he put his bike on the bus for the ten-mile ride to his early morning English classes in San Francisco. And then, to save fare on the way back, he pedaled through the city until he found his way to the mountain trails leading up and over the Golden Gate Bridge and down the steep bayfront hill to Sausalito.

As I admired both Alfredo's creative way of cutting costs and his navigational skills, having gotten lost the first time I'd attempted a solo ride over the Golden Gate, I also worried about being poor.

If we got married, Alfredo would receive work papers, but I worried about how many months, or possibly years, it would take for him to be able to support himself. Right now, paying all of our rent, both of our health insurances, and most of our groceries meant I needed to work more than forty hours each week. This left little time for writing, and I knew that if I had to give up this one dream I'd had since childhood, I would not be happy with myself, not to mention with Alfredo.

I loved how Alfredo encouraged me to write during the little free time I had, how he'd sneak up behind me, call out my name and, when I turned around, snap a photo of me, declaring, "For when you become a famous writer."

And then I wondered how long it would be before Alfredo could read my writings and get the cultural commentary or the humor or the flow or, at times, the choppiness of my sentences. Before Alfredo, I had always dated writers, and now I felt a sense of longing in not being able to share this part of my personality with him.

I looked forward to Alfredo's evening reenactments of the new phrases he'd learned in English class, such as when he asked, "Can I call you a health food nut?" while I was cooking a pot of beans without salt or oil.

Alfredo's transformations of difficult-to-pronounce words were also amusing—he called the photographer Robert Mapplethorpe "Robert Maple Syrup", and pronounced "Zinfandel" as "*sin Fidel*," without Fidel.

Yet throughout all of Alfredo's word games, which I admired for their wit, I continued to miss that easy communion and intellectual rapport that comes from a shared culture and educational background. Sometimes I felt exhausted by the futility of attempting to answer all of Alfredo's questions. They ran the gamut, from the meaning of "yuppie," an alien life form for someone who grew up under communism, to questions about the U.S.

system of recycling, which was equally perplexing for someone raised in a culture where cooking oil was reused while it was common to throw plastic bottle tops into the street.

Basically I was scared, because as much as I sensed that all this would change with time, I generally tried to avoid situations that in the present didn't match what I wanted them to be in the future. "Wait and see" had always seemed a bad policy to me, but now I had few other options.

I could say we shouldn't get married because, at the start of this new chapter in our life together, everything was not yet perfect. Or, like returning to Cuba despite my fear that both the country and Alfredo might not live up to my expectations, I could take a risk here. I could grant myself permission to be vulnerable, allow Alfredo time to adjust, give our relationship a chance to grow, for the first time in its nearly two-year history, with no deadlines imposed by anyone but ourselves.

On November 23, 2001, we married atop Mt. Tamalpais in Mill Valley, with no witnesses but my parents and the San Francisco Bay, silent and glimmering behind us.

Afterword

When I began writing this book, I did so as a way to keep at bay my Cuba memories, which followed me everywhere, preventing me from starting up my life again in the U.S. Now, three long years later, I write to remember.

It has been a strange experience, almost as surreal as Cuba itself, to live in the present and, on a daily basis, be rewriting and reanalyzing the not-so-distant past. Up until this point, I could sketch out the story of Alfredo and me in the U.S. as a line running parallel to the chapters of my book. As I completed the chapter about Guelmis, the young girl I met at the pizza stand in Miramar who had warned me, on my way to see Alfredo, that *"Los cubanos son candela,"* I was again preparing to meet Alfredo, although this time it was to take him to the DMV for his driving test, which he passed with flying colors. As I described my first day at Dinora's, I was wishing Alfredo good luck on his first day of work at the health food store, where he is now a full-time, benefited employee. As I write this afterword, I am helping Alfredo with a paper on civil disobedience for his English class at the local community college where he has been studying for the past two years. He plans to apply to a four-year university in another year, and is considering majoring in environmental science or geography.

As a couple, Alfredo and I have been able to communicate in ways I previously feared language and culture would make impossible. As Alfredo's vocabulary has grown, we've been able to watch and talk about American films, from political pieces like *Fahrenheit 9/11* to cult comedies like *Fargo.* Two summers ago we read our first book together—*Next Year in Cuba*, the memoir of a Cuban American coming of age in the U.S. Alfredo read the English edition, and I read the Spanish one, each of us peering over the other's shoulder in bed during difficult passages.

As has become the pattern with so many of our conversations, afterward we discussed the book in our own version of Spanglish. It's a mishmash of our separate languages and our connected personal references—people we've met and places we've been together, from Cuba to California and beyond to Canada (where we went backpacking near a glacier-fed lake north of

Vancouver) and Florida (where we visited Calle Ocho in Miami and agreed that it was nothing like Havana) and, most recently, Oregon (where we frequented Powell's bookstore and the coffee shops of Portland). The sum of all these experiences, I now realize, is the shared culture I'd been seeking.

Despite my worries about finances and not being able to pursue my writing career, I did manage to write the majority of this book with Alfredo here. And we still paid the rent and, thanks to his discount at the health food store, he kept the refrigerator stocked.

Writing this book with Alfredo here has been both affirming and redeeming for our relationship. During those days when every decision, from whether to answer the phone to how to dry the wash, seemed to involve a tug-of-war of cultures, the act of retelling our romance has reminded me of why it was I fell in love with Alfredo in the first place. It has given me memories of a simpler, easier existence to hold onto during the most difficult times.

Mixed in with the beauty of finally being able to share my world with Alfredo, there have been many hardships, few of which I could have predicted during our allotted ninety-day trial period, when everything was still new and thus all collisions—both cultural and personal—seemed temporary.

Trying to determine whether our problems are personal or cultural has often felt like attempting to answer the age-old nature-or-nurture question. Am I content traveling alone and, in my own home, sitting silently by myself because I come from a culture that values independence and privacy? And does Alfredo feel lonely when driving in the car by himself and uncomfortable in a room without music or overheard street conversation because he comes from a culture that values community? Isn't it also possible that, had Alfredo been born in the U.S. and I in Cuba, we would still be as we are?

Recently, I bumped into an acquaintance, a wise woman whom I hadn't seen since soon after Alfredo's arrival, when I was full of worries about whether or not we should marry. At the time, she'd empathized with my situation, shaking her head at the politics that forced us to make such a major decision in such a short time.

"Well," said my acquaintance, who was divorced, "there's never really any way of knowing for sure, even when you are from the same culture and you speak the same language. Ultimately, you just have to go with your gut feeling in the moment."

Now, when I gave my acquaintance the brief update on what had happened since we'd last spoken, she smiled, looking relieved and said, "Oh, I'm so glad it's all worked out."

I nodded, thinking about the nature of storytelling. Through the details we choose to leave out (whether because of time and space limitations or pride we can't part with), we rewrite our life's narratives as we tell them.

But then, before I could say anything, my friend edited herself. "Or really," she added, "probably, you're still working it out."

Because Alfredo wants to save up a certain amount of money to help his family, and because I've been waiting to finish this book, we have not returned to Cuba. And as much as I miss my friends and many of the moments of my life there, on another level, I haven't minded waiting.

With time, the intensity and immediacy of Cuba has faded, making it easier to accept an indefinite return date. And from the perspective of an exhausted writer, it's simply tidier and more concise and—at the risk of sounding lazy—easier to end the story here.

As is my tendency, I also worry. I worry about Alfredo returning and feeling so comforted by being in his own culture, by being instantly and intimately understood, that he won't want to come back to the U.S. Conversely, I worry that after so much time in the U.S., Alfredo might feel like an outsider in Cuba. I worry about him seeing, with stranger's eyes, a life that was once his own—like seeing a photo of yourself from a long time ago, taken without your knowledge, and no longer recognizing who you were.

When I told Alfredo I was writing an afterword and explained that it would, in part, be an update on what's happened in Cuba, he looked perplexed.

"I don't know, Lea," he said. "Things change in other places, but not in Cuba."

On the surface, Cuba's situation with the U.S. is much as it was when I left. Despite Jimmy Carter's 2002 visit (the first by any U.S. president since the Revolution) and the Senate and House's fall of 2003 votes to ease the travel embargo (the language for which was stripped from their bill before it could go to a vote by the President), Cuba remains an illegal island. Ironically, unlike other immigrants, Cubans themselves are never illegal once they reach U.S. soil—even if, as happened in March of 2003, they hijack a plane to do so. As long as the action was undertaken in protest of Fidel Castro's regime, they are welcome in the U.S. The rest of the eleven million Cubans who remain on the island are, according to George W. Bush's "Axis of Evil" list, the true terrorists.

As a result of this reclassification of Cuba as a terrorist country, Cuban artists and musicians scheduled for U.S. tours have not been allowed into the country, and the majority of U.S.–Cuban exchange programs (including the one I originally participated in) have had their licenses revoked. Although we live in a country that, according to our president, is attacked by others who are jealous of our freedom, Americans once again are not free to visit Cuba.

In June of 2004, President Bush passed a new law that restricts the ability of Cuban Americans to visit their homeland. Whereas before they could travel to Cuba for up to thirty days each year, bringing with them as much as three thousand dollars to help their families, they are now only allowed to visit for fifteen days every three years and can only take three hundred dollars.

I have, sadly, lost touch with several of my Cuban friends, perhaps because of the distance, which is increased by the impossibly expensive phone calls (that is, when the lines are working), the difficulty of getting email access on the island, and the current dearth of Cuba couriers.

In her last letter, in February of 2002, Dinora wrote me that Abuela had passed away, and despite her constant complaining about having to take care of her, she cried every day. Dinora's other big news was that she had become a vegetarian, perhaps the first in the history of Cuba.

"I was inspired by you," she wrote. "I feel healthier and I have fewer headaches now, but still *no es fácil* trying to come up with creative combinations for vegetables. Please, send me recipes!"

Occasionally I receive an email from Liudmila, who has completed her

Japanese and accountant studies and is now taking French classes and partic-ipating in a training program to work on a cruise ship. Like her country, this most *fidelista* of my friends continues to reinvent herself in order to stay afloat.

The friends I am most in touch with are those who have left Cuba—one for Toronto and one for Berlin. Alfredo's friend Gerardo, who went to Bel-gium on a tourist visa, is reported to now be residing somewhere in Spain, and Mamito, Alfredo's best friend at the symphony, recently fled to Miami.

Alfredo's nephew, born two months before my last visit to Cuba, is now four years old and talking. On the telephone, Alfredo's sister, who speaks fluent English, gives Bruno verbal cues, and he speaks to Alfredo in gurgled English.

Unfortunately for Alfredo's sister, not being able to live with her hus-band took its toll on her relationship, and she is now divorced.

Alfredo's maternal grandfather, who told me that there are "other types of wealth," passed away in November of 2004. Fortunately, the rest of his family is fine, and whenever Alfredo calls, perhaps feeding his belief in the stagnation of Cuba, they tell him that nothing has changed.

A few months ago, a friend who found one of the few organizations still offering legal travel to Cuba returned from the island with photos of Alfre-do's family and a minimovie she'd made on her digital camera. She emailed us the movie, which showed Alfredo's nephew and sister playing catch with an inflatable red ball in the living room and Alfredo's grandmother sitting in her rocking chair wearing her favorite piece of clothing—a brown, orange, yellow, and white carnival-striped sundress. Her hair was pulled neatly back with a flowered silk scarf wrapped around her head and cascading over her shoulder and down her arm. She looked beautiful and ethereal and, despite her virtual proximity on the computer screen, very far away.

"*Dile algo,*" Say something, someone in the background called out, and then, rocking slowly back and forth in her chair, Alfredo's grandmother spoke.

"My grandson," she said. "I love you. I miss you very much. I hope you visit soon." She paused for a moment, and then, again, a muffled demand came from offstage.

"Well, things here . . ." his grandmother continued. "We're getting along fine. Sometimes it's difficult, but, well, you know. . . ." And then, as abruptly as it had begun, the movie ended.

But I knew what Alfredo's grandmother had started to say, what she had either abandoned saying or had been cut off in the middle of. It was the chant that, despite whatever else may change, seems to always remain the same: *"Es Cuba."*

Acknowledgments

First, for encouraging me early on in my writing career, thanks to Bill Jones, my creative writing teacher at Dulaney High School in Timonium, Maryland.

I am thankful for the existence of libraries, specifically the Mill Valley Public Library and the Sausalito Public Library—my home offices away from home, where most of this book was written.

Thanks to Michelle Hamilton, Michelle Snider Luna, Mija Riedel, Amra Stafford, and Tara Weaver for your careful readings and detailed comments on the first half of *Es Cuba*. *Muchas, muchas gracias* to Bridgett Novak for not just saying you wanted to, but actually reading the whole six hundred and seventy pages of my preedited book and then sitting down with me for five hours that Sunday soon after it sold to help me cut. Thanks to Jean Paik Schoenberg, Dana Sachs, and Brad Newsham for writerly support. Thanks to Deborah Fleischer for in-country research on ice cream flavors and airline outfits. Thanks to Olivia Boler for all of our writer commiseration sessions. Thanks to Mark Baker for your friendship and for making all the students in your travel writing class at UC Santa Cruz read the *Travelers' Tales Cuba* excerpt of my book each year. And thanks to Larry Habegger and Tom Miller for publishing the excerpt and thus encouraging me to continue with the story.

Thank you to my dad, Bernie Aschkenas, for encouraging me to call Travelers' Tales and ask if I could submit, even though I'd missed the deadline. Thank you for always telling me after our conversations, "You have to write that down." And thank you for being who you are—a good friend and listener and a voice of reason and calm in a world that often appears to be anything but.

Thanks to my mom, Sherry Gooltz, for holding my head up for my first passport photo when I was barely a month old, for reading to me from the O. Henry Prize Stories books at bedtime in elementary school, for encouraging me to learn Spanish at an early age. Thank you for your ongoing, unconditional enthusiasm.

Thanks to my grandmother, Ruth Gooltz, for all your support.

Thanks to Brooke Warner, my editor, for never wavering about my book. Thanks also to the rest of the Seal Press editing crew—managing editor Marisa Solís and my amazing copy editor Wendy Taylor.

Thanks to Alfredo for asking me, "When are you going to write something about me?" the first week I met you, and for everything that came after.

Finally, I am grateful to all my Cuban friends for sharing their lives and stories with me. I am grateful for the existence of Cuba itself, a brave sovereign country struggling to stay afloat and preserve its social system against great odds.

Lea Aschkenas has written about travel, literature, and life at large for the *Washington Post,* the *San Francisco Chronicle,* the *Los Angeles Times,* and Salon  .com. She has also contributed stories to the books *Travelers' Tales Central America, Travelers' Tales Cuba, The Unsavvy Traveler,* and *Two in the Wild.* A graduate of Pomona College, she works at a public library and teaches with the California Poets in the Schools program in Northern California, where she lives with her husband, Alfredo.

Selected Titles from Seal Press

For more than twenty-five years, Seal Press has published groundbreaking books. By women. For women. Visit our website at www.sealpress.com.

Atlas of the Human Heart by Ariel Gore. $14.95, 1-58005-088-3. Ariel Gore spins the spirited story of a vulnerable drifter who takes refuge in the fate and the shadowy recesses of a string of glittering, broken relationships.

Waking up American: Coming of Age Biculturally edited by Angela Jane Fountas. $15.95, 1-58005-136-7. This collection includes twenty-two original essays by first-generation women—Filipino, German, Mexican, Iranian, and Nicaraguan, among others—caught between two worlds.

Italy, A Love Story: Women Write about the Italian Experience edited by Camille Cusumano. $15.95, 1-58005-143-X. Two dozen women describe the country they love and why they fell under its spell.

Reckless: The Outrageous Lives of Nine Kick-Ass Women by Gloria Mattioni. $14.95, 1-58005-148-0. This inspiring book documents the lives of nine women who took unconventional paths to achieve extraordinary results.

Colonize This!: Young Women of Color on Today's Feminism edited by Daisy Hernández and Bushra Rehman. $16.95, 1-58005-067-0. This diverse collection of some of today's brightest new voices takes on identity, family, class, and the notion that feminism is one cohesive movement.

Tales from the Expat Harem: Foreign Women in Modern Turkey edited by Anastasia M. Ashman and Jennifer Eaton Gökmen. $15.95, 1-58005-155-3. In this illuminating anthology, female expatriates from several countries describe how the Turkish landscape, psyche, people, and customs transformed their lives.